CW00673563

Mysteries in the Music:

Other Books by Jim Berkenstadt

THE BEATLE WHO VANISHED
Amazon Bestseller - Soon to be a Major Motion Picture
By Jim Berkenstadt

NEVERMIND NIRVANA
By Jim Berkenstadt and Charles R. Cross

BLACK MARKET BEATLES: THE STORY BEHIND THEIR LOST RECORDINGS
By Jim Berkenstadt and Belmo

THE BEATLES DIGEST
By J.G. Schuberk (aka Jim Berkenstadt) and others

JOHN, PAUL & ME BEFORE THE BEATLES
By Len Garry
Edited by Jim Berkenstadt

Mysteries in the Music:

Jim Berkenstadt

Foreword by Butch Vig

Los Angeles, California USA

Editor: Leya Booth
Copy Editor: Gary Schumacher

Published by:
Genius Music Books, an Imprint of Genius Book Publishing
31858 Castaic Road, #154
Castaic, California 91384 USA
https://geniusbookpublishing.com
+1.818.585.9945 (USA)

Library of Congress Cataloging-in-Publication Data is available upon request
Library of Congress Control Number: 2022932385

ISBN: 978-1-947521-79-7

Mysteries in the Music: Case Closed / Jim Berkenstadt—First Edition

220207

Table of Contents

Dedication

This book is dedicated to Holly, Becca, and Brad

Acknowledgements

First of all, I would like to thank my family: Holly, Becca, and Brad Berkenstadt, Kyle Dillman, Gene and Laurie Berkenstadt, Joy and Jack Charney, Bonnie Laviron, Scott Cremer and Ellen Whitman, and all the rest for their love and support. Thanks so much to my late, great parents, Dr. Edward and Lois Berkenstadt.

Thank you to the many friends and colleagues, whose friendship and advice have been so valuable: Gary Schumacher, Butch Vig, Duke Erikson, Taylor Hawkins, Gregg Jakobson, Jann Wenner, Ally Lewis, Rolling Stone, Marshall Terrill, Ray Kelley, Chas Newby, Rod Davis, The Quarrymen, Klaus and Christina Voormann, Jim and Cynthia Keltner, Alex Orbison, Roy Orbison Jr., Ashley Hamilton, Chuck Fleckenstein, the late Neil Aspinall, Charles Cross, ZINA, Scott and Lynne Faulkner, Jane Metzler, Nicole Michael, Jude Southerland-Kessler, Lanea Stagg, Ken Womack, Tom Frangione, Chuck Gunderson, David Bedford, Casey Fox, Bill Harry, Mark Lewisohn, Mark and Carol Lapidos, Wayne Rogers, Ivor Davis, Andres J. Washington, Jon Elliott, Nick Newton, Jay Olsen, Victoria Busch, Holly Bayless, Jeff Barry, Olivia Keast, Leanne Kohlbeck, Kaleem Caire, James "Pie" Cowan, Kristy Genna, Dave Benton, Ken Dorsch, Billy Bush, Garbage (Shirley, Butch, Duke, and Steve), Elana Cattledge (guitar logo design), Michael Frondelli, Frank Caiazzo, Ken LaBarre, Blair Foster, Laura Gross, Roy and Stephanie Elkins, David Spero, the late Alan Rogan, Dinah Gretsch, Lynn Aspinwall, Darcy Deadman,

"Rad" Robin Bougie, Jackie Thomas, Alan H. Fraser, Brian & Nicole Bell, J.G. Schuberk, Steve Christian, Paul Barrosse, Gary Kroeger, Rush Pearson, Julia Louis-Dreyfuss, Brad Hall, Mike Spound, Mike Regan, Jim Joyce, Nancy and Tommy Turman, Linda Chorney, Scott Fadynich, Matt Hurwitz, Simon Weitzman, Roger Steffens, Stu Levitan, Tom Salva, Joseph Palumbo, Roger Epperson, Andrew Doe, Stevie Riks, the Fiji's, The Hack 'N Slash gang, Genna's, The Sunset Ridge gang, The Practical Theater Company, Riffmaster & The Rockme Foundation, KIAB, and CLAW.

Interviews: I cannot thank these people enough for sharing their eyewitness accounts, memories, and expertise. Without their assistance, these mysteries would still be mysteries: Gregg Jakobson, Jann Wenner, Bobby Whitlock, Glyn Johns, Butch Vig, Rod Davis, Al Cooper, the late Hal Blaine, Jim Keltner, David Gold, Stephen Desper, Nick Grillo, the late Jerry Dennon, Jack Ely, David Leland, Alex Orbison, Roy Orbison, Jr., Julia Baird, the late Derek Taylor, Klaus Voormann, the late Scotty Moore, Dinah Gretsch, Colonel Oliver North, Phil Kaufman, John Tefteller, Bernard MacMahon, Alex van der Tuuk, U.S. District Court Judge James Peterson, Keidi Obi Awadu, Candy Leonard, Larry Wassgren, Brandi Carlson, Jeff Walker, "Joey" (ex-CIA), and Roger Steffens.

Thanks to my Teams!
Publishing Team: Steven Booth, Leya Booth, & Sabrina Lee
Management Team: Barry Krost/BK Management
Social Media Team: Becca Berkenstadt, Worldly Strategies, Brad Berkenstadt
Medical Team: Dr. Jeremy Smith, Dr. John Wilson, Dr. Thomas Zedeblick
Legal Team: Henry Root, Andrew Clarkowski, Michael Westcott, Dan Hardy

Finally, I would like to thank my Editor Leya Booth and Copy Editor Gary Schumacher, who both gave me unbelievable assistance and support in making this book more articulate, fun, and readable. Gary and I have been partners in crime for 50 years. Thanks also to Katherine "Kato" Anderson for her editorial suggestions.

Foreword

by Butch Vig

As a teenager growing up in Viroqua, Wisconsin in the '60s, AM radio was our only lifeline to a daily dose of the music that played such a significant role in our lives. Nothing beat saving up a few dollars for a trip to the record store to pick up copies of our favorite new 45s and LPs. The "big bang" moment for many of us was watching The Beatles for the first time on the Ed Sullivan Show in 1964. They launched a British Invasion that could be heard around the world. That pivotal moment grew into a love for all things Rock and Roll. After seeing The Who's Keith Moon destroy his drum kit on The Smothers Brothers Show at age 12, I inherited a set of "Ringo" Ludwig drums from my cousin Carl and dove in, playing relentlessly. I was 16 and, at that moment, I knew Rock and Roll was my destiny.

Laying in bed late one night, I heard strange sounds on the radio. I felt like I had entered a secret door into an alternate music universe. These were songs that were far removed from the pop music on Top Forty Radio, like Black Sabbath, King Crimson, The Allman Brothers, Neil Young, and Led Zeppelin. I became obsessed with how the music sounded, what the lyrics meant, the killer drum grooves, and the searing guitar solos. *I wanted to make music that sounded like that.*

In the '80s in Madison, Wisconsin, I joined forces with Spooner. We considered ourselves a New Wave band and developed a hardcore fan base. We wrote and recorded our own songs and put out several albums. I found myself fascinated with the recording process, the engineering and production side of making records. *How do I get that snare drum to sound more explosive?*

In the late '80s, I opened Smart Studios with my buddy and Spooner's roadie, Steve Marker, now my bandmate in Garbage. I never had any formal recording instruction. My education was all DIY. But bands like Tar Babies, Mecht Mensch, and Killdozer didn't care. They thought everything sounded fantastic. Mostly through trial and error, I got better as an engineer and producer. One of the albums I produced for Killdozer was *12 Point Buck*, a god-awful and glorious sledgehammer of sound. It didn't sell that well. But Nirvana heard it. So did Smashing Pumpkins. And I moved from the underground rock scene to the chart-topping world of Alternative Rock.

Music drives me. I've always been obsessed with the sound: the hooks, the noise, the groove and energy, the X factor that makes a killer song. And I still am.

Walking along his own parallel path was author Jim Berkenstadt, who was just as infected with the passion and love of Rock and Roll as I was. But Jim is not a musician. He is an uber fan, a collector, an archivist, and a world-renowned historian. I first met Jim when he worked with my brother at a mail order company as the head of legal affairs. Over beers at a local pub, he casually said, "You should come and check out my record collection." And oh my God, what a collection it is! As he built this mighty rock and roll archive, he became obsessed with documenting and preserving pop music's most intriguing moments. Jim has written books about The Beatles' lost recordings and the inside story of *Nevermind*, the album I produced with Nirvana. His best-selling book about drummer Jimmie Nicol, *The Beatle Who Vanished*, is a fascinating and mysterious must-read for hardcore Beatles fans and anyone else who wants to understand their meteoric rise to pop stardom and the subsequent crash landing. It is headed to the silver screen soon. Jim has also served as historian to our band Garbage since the release of our debut album.

While most kids leave their albums to collect dust in a box as they enter adulthood, Jim never lost the passion he felt for pop music. He has been asked many times to use his extensive knowledge of rock music to get the facts straight. Director Martin Scorsese tapped Jim to serve as his historical consultant in the HBO Emmy winning film, *George Harrison: Living in the Material World*. I also engaged Jim to serve in the same role for me in our documentary, *The Smart Studios Story*.

Growing up, the music we listened to reflected the changes in the world around us. We learned many of our lifelong values from the lyrics contained in our generation's songs. However, it was not just the music that drew us in. We also wanted to know more about our favorite rockers. *How did they live their lives? What was their "day in the life" like?*

Occasionally, we would hear a rumor about dirty lyrics passed around in school. *Did they really sing that?* Or we would read a Rolling Stone article about an album recorded by a secret supergroup made up of The Beatles, The Rolling Stones, and Bob Dylan. *Really? Where can we buy that?* And there were also darker stories, the conspiracy theory about the CIA trying to assassinate Bob Marley. *Did that really happen?* After Charles Manson was arrested for his horrific killing spree, he claimed that it was The Beatles' fault! And then he alleged that the Beach Boys had stolen his music. *What role did The Beatles play with Manson? Did the Beach Boys really become musically involved with him?* What was the real story and what was merely a hoax?

Now Jim Berkenstadt has written the definitive book to, once and for all, clear up some of pop music's greatest mysteries, conspiracies, hoaxes, and wildly inexplicable events. As a former trial attorney, he digs into each story, locating key witnesses, lost photos and recordings, top secret government documents, and other original research to solve these mysteries. Jim, the Rock And Roll Detective, uncovers the unknown details and colorful characters in these music mystery accounts.

So sit back and enjoy these compelling stories of Rock and Roll lore, as Jim sifts through the clues to bring you *Mysteries in the Music: Case Closed*.

Butch Vig
Summer 2020

Introduction

Mysteries in the Music: Case Closed examines the secrets, myths, legends, hoaxes, conspiracies, and the wildly inexplicable events that are such an intriguing part of rock and roll history. As the Rock And Roll Detective®, I have spent decades researching the mysteries hidden within the music and the people who *made* the music. This collection of popular music's most intriguing stories investigates original evidence and primary source materials in order to challenge some of rock's most enduring legends. In many cases, original stories were hastily prepared or even fabricated by PR flacks or the media, and just as often these legends became frozen in time, mired in hasty or flawed conclusions. Blogs, podcasts, and social media conspiracies have further fueled and perpetuated inaccurate stories, in order to create more click-bait for online readers.

Many mysteries still exist in rock and roll for the simple reason that many of the surviving participants and eyewitnesses have never spoken out or have never been asked the tough questions… *until now*. Additionally, no one has taken the time to dig through the primary source documentary evidence left behind… *until now*.

Travel back with me to the 1950s to uncover "Who Really Discovered Elvis Presley?" Revisit a time in the 1960s when a famous folk troubadour tried to form a supergroup with members of The Beatles and The Rolling Stones. Go behind the scenes of CIA intrigue in Jamaica 1976 to discover whether the Spy Agency tried to influence an election and arrange for the assassination of reggae superstar Bob Marley. Learn the origin behind big name artists using pseudonyms to mask their true identities. Uncover the secrets in the making of Nirvana's *Nevermind* album, considered by many to be the most influential rock album of the 1990s. Finally, discover whether The Beach Boys actually *stole* a song and copyrights from psychotic cult murderer Charles Manson, and kept all of the royalties.

I approached every case in this book with an open mind. I had no preconceptions or advance agenda whatsoever, and I let the facts speak for themselves. Each chapter unfolds like a detective story. I dug into the oral histories of eyewitnesses and carefully examined artifacts left behind in photographs, videos, interviews, press accounts, top secret government documents, sworn court testimony, music, liner notes, bootlegs, and more—all in an attempt to reconstruct a mosaic of history that reveals what really happened *all those years ago*.

After many decades, the back stories of pop and rock music lore are finally unearthed and the truth is revealed. If classic rock was the soundtrack of your youth, or if you wish you had lived through these moments in time, or if you are just plain curious about rumored events you have heard about over the years… then this book is for you! Let me take you down, cause we're going to… *Mysteries in the Music: Case Closed*.

Jim Berkenstadt, January 1, 2022

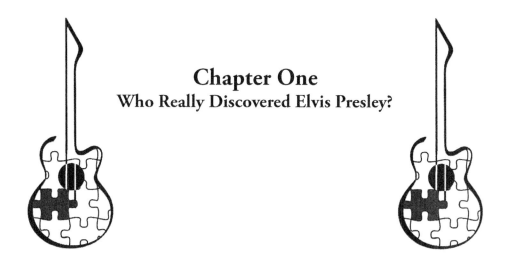

Chapter One
Who Really Discovered Elvis Presley?

All it took was the relatively small investment of $3.98 for Elvis Presley to set in motion a sequence of events that would ultimately launch his singular and unique brand of rock and roll upon the world. It was perhaps the best investment anyone has ever made, and it was this investment that first brought the teenager to the attention of Sam Phillips' assistant, when Presley walked off of Union Avenue and through the doors of Memphis Recording Service on a steamy July 18, 1953.

Rock and roll history has consistently credited one—*and only one*—individual for the discovery of ground-breaking singer and recording artist Elvis Presley, the late producer Sam Phillips. Indeed, the venerable BBC News still credits Phillips as "the one who... will go down in rock 'n' roll history as the man who discovered Elvis." As the years rolled on, Phillips reinforced this claim at every opportunity. During a 1986 *Rolling Stone* interview, when asked if he knew Elvis was the person he had been looking for, Phillips replied, "I sure did. I wouldn't have called him back and back and back again. I knew he had the fundamentals of what I wanted. He was the first one I had seen who had that potential."

It is certainly fair to give Phillips credit for his development of Elvis' talents. However, it would be short-sighted to give *sole* credit to one man for perhaps the greatest musical discovery of the 1950s—an unearthing of talent that lit the fire of a new all-American phenomenon soon to be christened "rock and roll music." But was Phillips solely responsible for launching Elvis Presley? If we peer below the surface of the "one man" discovery theory, there is compelling evidence to support the conclusion that three other people also deserve credit for helping Elvis get his start. The Rock And Roll Detective decided to dig into the likelihood that more than one person deserved credit for discovering Elvis Presley.

Who are these unsung heroes that made it possible for Elvis to quit driving a truck and become the biggest entertainment superstar of his era? Stepping back through the misty memories of time, the Rock And Roll Detective sought to revisit the sequence of events and testimony of key witnesses that led to Elvis' first recorded single and record deal, and to definitively explore the "one man" discovery narrative that has pervaded pop culture legend for more than sixty years.

Unfortunately, all five of the principal players in our investigation have passed on. But guitarist Scotty Moore, the last to survive, was kind enough to revisit this moment in rock and roll history with this author. In addition, first-hand interviews, historical artifacts, session recordings, documents, photos, and records do survive—all of which point to an expanded view of the individuals and circumstances surrounding Elvis' discovery.

Sam Phillips—"I've got to have this little laboratory"

Sam Phillips was born on a farm near Florence, Alabama in 1923. His parents were poor tenant farmers, and he worked in the fields as a child alongside many black laborers who sang while they worked. Their singing and work ethic served as an early inspiration for him.

Shortly after high school, Phillips was hired to do his own radio show on WMSD which later morphed into WLAY in Sheffield, Alabama, the "Center of the Shoals." Jimmy Connolly, the station's general manager, gave him his first chance in radio but it was more than just an opportunity. It was an education in business, audio engineering, preparation, presentation and, most of all, music.

Connolly inspired Phillips to think about music for everyone when the General Manager launched a new radio show called the "Atomic Boogie Hour," an hour-long show of "race records" directed mainly at the black population. Phillips, however, who had grown up listening to black music in the cotton fields as a kid, believed that this music could and would appeal to all races. Years later, this belief inspired his "musical color blindness" when it came time to record and sign young artists upon opening his own recording studio.

In his early 20s, Phillips and his young family moved from Alabama to Memphis, Tennessee. The move served as a musical awakening. Memphis was a place where black men played in clubs and bars and sang about their hard-life experiences. At the age of 25, Phillips was on the air at WREC in Memphis, recording live radio feeds of big bands at

The Skyway Ballroom. Unlike other engineers of his day, he realized the need to closely mic the rhythm sections to bring out a stronger sound that propelled the music along. His microphone placement techniques were highly innovative for their time.

For Phillips, hearing more "race music" on the airwaves only made him restless for something new in his life. It may have taken him time to figure out exactly what it was, but he was thinking about it constantly. He recalled, "My conviction was that the world was missing out on not having heard what I had heard as a child." Yet in Memphis, citizens were exposed constantly to the rich, original rhythm and blues musical culture, both on the air and in the streets. "I mean, going out and hearing a black man pick a guitar and pat his foot and put a wood box under his foot to pat as he sings. These were elements that I knew were not going away," said Phillips. Although he was busy raising his young family, appearing on the air multiple times per day, and recording evening concerts, Phillips could not shake the feeling that something important was missing in his life.

Then the epiphany came. "I've just got to open me a little recording studio, where I can at least experiment with [some of] this overlooked humanity… I've got to have this little laboratory." Phillips wanted a place where musicians could come and feel relaxed enough to play their own style of music. In the words of historian Peter Guralnick, noted Presley and Phillips biographer, "Sam envisioned a music that would conquer the race prejudice. He envisioned an African American music that eventually would be called rock and roll."

On January 3, 1950, Phillips embarked on his dream while still holding down a full time radio job and supporting his family. Originally named the "Memphis Recording Service," the studio (later named "Sun Studio") opened at 706 Union Avenue in Memphis, Tennessee. The studio would also eventually serve as the home of the Sun Records label.

Memphis Recording Service was housed in a simple two-story brick building. The studio shared the building with Taylor's Restaurant when it first opened. Memphis Recording Service was quite sparse by today's standards. A simple entry area served as the assistant's office, and a large open area (approximately 18' x 33') was used for the studio and control room which featured a large picture window.

Phillips' motto at the Memphis Recording Service was "We Record Anything, Anywhere, Anytime." And he was not kidding! No events were turned away, including weddings, meetings, private demos, conventions, and more. Rather, all were memorably preserved on disc by the Memphis Recording Service.

In the early 1950s, Phillips began recording a number of black artists, including Junior Parker, Howlin' Wolf, and Ike Turner. In March 1951, he recorded a pivotal rhythm and blues song called "Rocket 88" by Jackie Brenston (Ike Turner's sax player) and his Delta Cats who were, in fact, part of Ike Turner's Kings of Rhythm band. The record caught fire on radio and eventually reached No. 1 on the Billboard R&B charts. Many historians

Memphis Recording Service

acknowledge the significance of "Rocket 88" in the development of rock and roll music, and some consider it the first-ever rock and roll record.

Clearly this was Phillips' first big success. But the producer yearned for something more, something different, a distinct sound that could cross the boundaries of country, R&B, and the blues—as well as racial barriers—and break through across the entire country. At the same time, young teenage Baby Boomers were looking for a new style of music they could call their own. They were tired of their parents' big band music and wanted something different. Phillips was keenly aware of this, and he wanted to be the first to capture this magical new sound on record. In his quest for a new musical genre, Phillips enlisted the aid of a fellow DJ who would help him to realize his dream.

Marion Keisker—A Woman's Intuition

When she was a young girl, Marion Keisker began her career in 1929 working on a Memphis children's radio show called "Wynken, Blynken and Nod." As a young woman, Keisker was truly an unsung pioneer in the male-dominated world of media. From the 1940s onward, in her first major role in Memphis radio, she had an interview show under the name of "Kitty Kelly" at WREC where she came into her own as an excellent radio announcer.

One of the many shows Keisker was involved with was called "Treasury Bandstand." This patriotic show featured an orchestra playing music and making an appeal to listeners to invest in U.S. Savings Bonds. It is serendipitous that the man who cut (recorded) the transcription records of the show (which were later sent to New York for network broadcast) was none other than Sam Phillips. Before long, the two grew close professionally. Phillips shared his dream with Keisker, of starting up a little studio in Memphis where he could experiment with his goal of recording black artists playing their own style of music. Keisker was immediately taken with Phillips and his dream, and signed on to be his "Girl Friday" at the Memphis Recording Service.

Yet Keisker was much more than a secretary at the recording company. "I scrubbed the floors, did the publicity, the works," she recalled. "I was office manager, assistant engineer and general Jane of all trades." She organized the company and the records, acted as its administrator, and stepped in to engineer sessions. Keisker also operated the studio's direct to disk lathe and ran the mono recorder.

Most importantly, she was truly another set of critical ears, providing feedback to Phillips and keeping contemporaneous notes on artists that had future potential. As Phillips began to record black artists such as B.B. King, Junior Parker, Howlin' Wolf, and Ike Turner, he began to wonder out loud to her regarding his idea of a white singer who could sound "black" on record. Keisker filed this idea away in her head as she listened to the parade of vocal aspirants that entered their little studio on a daily basis. One singer would eventually catch her ear.

Elvis Presley

Born in Tupelo, Mississippi on January 8, 1935, young Elvis Presley was exposed to a melting pot of musical genres that included New Orleans jazz, gospel, R&B, blues, and lots of hillbilly music thrown in for good measure. It would be impossible for young Elvis to resist the rich musical heritage of his native South as he grew up. From singing with his local church choir to listening to Grand Ole Opry radio broadcasts, he was exposed to a wide range of musical styles and genres.

Presley began to sing at a young age. "Old Shep" was an early favorite. At age 11, Elvis received his first guitar for his birthday. In 1946, the Presley family moved into a black neighborhood in Tupelo where Elvis became immersed in the music of black churches, juke joints, and local culture. By 1948, Elvis' family had settled in Memphis where he immediately discovered a new world of diverse musical styles on the radio. He listened to the Dewey Phillips radio show which featured R&B music. Bob Neal's radio show provided a steady and healthy dose of hillbilly music. Young Elvis continued to strum his guitar and occasionally sing at school. According to Presley's father, Vernon, "At the time, he was more interested in gospel singing, the quartet singing. So, he tried for two or three of the different young groups to get in with them." Unfortunately, at the time, there were no vacancies.

Elvis began to wonder what a life of singing on the radio and recording might be like. He wondered what *he* would sound like on record and on the radio. As an attentive music fan, Elvis had noticed the Memphis Recording Service in town, and he likely had heard about producer Sam Phillips and the professional studio's early success. Apparently, Presley decided to save up his money and summon the courage to walk into the professional recording studio for a session.

Elvis Presley's First Demo Session

Was it Keisker or Phillips who stood in the doorway to welcome a young Elvis into the office of Memphis Recording Service on this fateful day? This is a question with enormous implications that has been debated for decades. In fact, Keisker and Phillips have each claimed to be the first to record young Elvis.

According to Keisker, who occupied the alcove, Phillips was not around at the time. He was in a meeting. "It was a busy Saturday afternoon. The office was full of people wanting to make personal records," she recalled. "My recollection is that it was a Saturday. The reason, I think it was a Saturday is because I was there [at the studio] and not rushing off to do my daily radio program at WREC. He [Elvis] came in, said he wanted to make a record. I told him he'd have to wait and he said, 'OK.' He sat down." Keisker could not help noticing that Elvis had unusually long sideburns, a trait that distinguished him at the time from other teenagers. His hands were very tense around his guitar. She clearly recalled her conversation with the young man on his first visit:

> Elvis: You know anyone that needs a singer?
> Keisker: What kind of singer are you?
> Elvis: Well, I sing all kinds.
> Keisker: Who do you sound like?
> Elvis: I don't sound like nobody.
> Keisker: [Thinking to herself: "Oh dear, Yes. Well, all right," and rolling her eyes.]

While Keisker was setting up to record Presley, Sam Phillips, Jim Bulleit (Sam's partner), and Jud Phillips (Sam's brother) came out of the back of the studio where they had been having a conference. Jud Phillips corroborated Keisker's account of what happened next. "And I remember turning to Sam and say[ing], 'Do you want to do [record] this?' And he said very abruptly, having his mind on other things; 'Can't you see I'm busy?' The three men headed next door to Ms. Taylor's for more coffee and conversation. Finally, I decided that I would go ahead and make the record myself," said Keisker.

Eventually, Elvis took his turn in the studio. He had his material ready, and he was prepared to sing and play. He later stated publicly that the record was to be a gift for his mother's birthday. However, given that Gladys Presley's birthday was not until April 25 of the following year, this was likely a cover story for Presley simply wanting to hear what his own voice sounded like on record. One can infer his true motivations for making a demo juxtaposed with his question to Keisker inquiring if she knew "anyone that needs a singer."

Elvis had picked out two songs: "My Happiness" and "That's When Your Heartache Begins." Accompanied by his acoustic guitar, he led off with the plaintive ballad, "My Happiness." The original recordings from this private acetate session still exist, allowing us into the studio on the very first day leading up to Elvis' amazing career. In listening to this musical artifact, one hears a slightly timid, well-rehearsed young man with a pleasant sound, strumming simple chords. He measures every phrase somewhat mechanically and adds a bit of dramatic vocal crescendo as the song moves toward its conclusion, always perfectly on key.

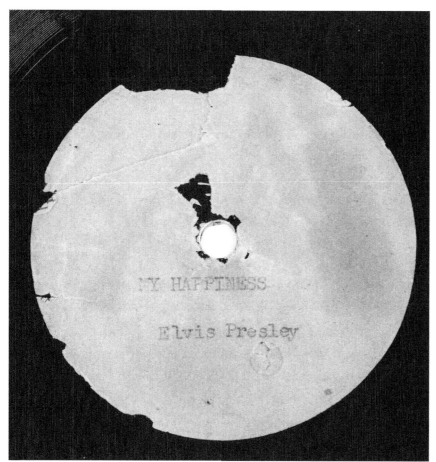

Elvis Presley's first recording "My Happiness" 78 rpm (Record Store Day facsimile)

With one song "in the can," Elvis stepped up to the mic again to record "That's When Your Heartache Begins." His performance was vocalized with a sophistication and experience well beyond his tender age of 17. The song is about a friend who steals the singer's girlfriend away. For added dramatic effect, Elvis ended the song with a spoken recitation of the lyrics, warning the listener not to let a friend meddle in your love affair, or you might lose your girl. With that final caution the song came to an abrupt conclusion. The sad ballad pulled on the listener's heartstrings, but gave no foreshadowing of the rock and roll voice that Elvis would soon develop. His guitar playing demonstrated only a fundamental ability to strum a few chords on each song.

According to music historian Nick Toches, author of *Country: The Twisted Roots of Rock 'N' Roll*, Keisker recognized something of interest in Elvis' voice and recorded a portion of "My Happiness" and all of "That's When Your Heartaches Begin" on a piece of discarded audio tape. She later explained to Elvis' biographer Jerry Hopkins, "The reason I taped Elvis was this: over and over, I remember Sam saying, 'If I could only find a white man who had the Negro feel, I could make a million dollars.' This is what I heard in Elvis, this… what I guess they now call 'soul,' this Negro sound. I wanted Sam to know." Keisker did not realize the importance of making her own copy of Elvis until she heard him singing partway through the first song. She told the BBC in a documentary, "I looked around wildly somewhere and there was an old tape that was lying there, while I was still making the record, I reached out with one hand and kicked up the tape and put it on and turned it on so that it would record simultaneously." Elvis was taking home the demo record, so Keisker would have had to make a separate recording on tape. A recording that still exists today.

We may never know whether Elvis was pleased with his performance and the sound of his voice on disc that day. However, Keisker was inspired to document his name and contact information. "So, I wrote down on a little strip of paper, 'Elvis Presley, good ballad singer' and a telephone number where I could reach him and wrote 'save' on it. And I put it under my desk blotter." Just in case Phillips ever told her he needed a good singer for a certain song.

Keisker's recollection of being the first to record Presley is so specific in nature, she even remembered a woman who was at the studio that day waiting for her son, a sailor and a songwriter, stationed at Millington, who listened in while Presley recorded "My Happiness." "While Elvis was making his record, this lady got up and she came over. And she was listening to him. She said, 'Who is that?' So, I told her what his name was, and she said, 'Ooohh! He just makes goose pimples on me!'" (Marion laughed). Keisker responded, "'Really?' This was a middle-aged lady."

Keisker subsequently told Phillips about Elvis, "the kid with the sideburns," and played him the tape she had made. Phillips was not initially that impressed, but said, "He, he, you know, he has potential, but we're too busy," recalled Keisker. Over the next several months, Elvis came back to the studio to talk—*not* with Phillips, but again with Keisker. He was hoping that someone needed a singer and that his persistence in visiting with her might somehow pay off. Eventually, Elvis rehearsed another couple of songs and saved up the money to record another personal demo.

Elvis Presley Demo Session #2

On January 4, 1954, roughly six months after his first demo session, Presley returned to the Memphis Recording Service to record and pay for demos of two more songs. He was likely hoping to attract the attention of Sam Phillips and make a positive impression, while maintaining Keisker's interest. The songs he recorded that day were "I'll Never Stand in Your Way" and "It Wouldn't Be the Same without You."

Most historians agree that Phillips did in fact record this *second* Elvis session. The Rock And Roll Detective found written archival documentation of this recording session that itemizes the service charge to "Elvis Presley," dated January 6, 1954. It likely took two days after the session to prepare the acetate and paperwork. The document indicates that Elvis paid $8.25 for this acetate master for two songs. The Memphis Recording Service document lists Elvis, his home address, and is marked "paid and signed" by Phillips himself.

At the conclusion of the session, Keisker returned to the studio following her Monday radio show. She recalled, "And I came in from doing my show and Sam was there and there was a note stuck on the [desk] spindle and it said, 'Elvis Presley,' had a telephone number, 'good ballad singer save.' I said, is that the kid with the sideburns, come in here again? And he said, 'Well, um yeah.' Even at this time, he [Phillips] didn't seem to have any recollection of the earlier incident [referring to the first time Keisker recorded Elvis Presley], which now he has said really didn't happen. Well, even at that time [in 1954] he didn't remember." While Phillips now had a firsthand experience hearing Elvis sing in the studio, the session was apparently not yet impressive enough to move him to action beyond making a note of his name.

Presley Rehearsal Session—June 26, 1954

Roughly six months after Elvis' second demo session at the Memphis Recording Service, Sam Phillips heard a demo of a song called "Without You" by an unidentified black singer from Nashville. He wanted to find this unknown singer and professionally record the song for possible release; however, he was unable to learn the identity of the artist. Instead, Phillips decided to find a local Memphis singer to record the song, at which point Keisker suggested to Phillips, "What about the kid with the sideburns?" She was, of course, referring to Elvis. According to Keisker, Sam said, "Oh, I have forgotten his name.

I don't think I know how to get in touch with him." Once again Keisker pulled out her original note and called Elvis. This time, Phillips agreed with Keisker's idea. There is little doubt that it was Keisker who had continuously kept Elvis' name in the forefront.

On June 26, 1954, Keisker called Elvis to come in and record the song "Without You," with Phillips producing behind the control board. Phillips played the Nashville demo for Elvis and tried to record a decent demo of Presley singing the same tune, but he was not satisfied with the results. Elvis also tried another Phillips' song suggestion, "Rag Mop," which was also a washout. Elvis may have been nervous or needed more time to familiarize himself with the material, but his performance was suitably unremarkable. Phillips eventually asked Elvis to sing *any songs* he was familiar with, calculating he might as well make use of the studio time they had scheduled that day. Elvis proceeded to sing a number of songs from various genres—including country, R&B, and gospel—but no recordings appear to have been made or survived from this session, and Elvis was sent home with no scheduled follow-up plans for the future. However, unbeknownst to Elvis, he was about to meet his future bandmates.

Scotty Moore and Bill Black

In the spring of 1954, a young and ambitious guitarist started hanging around the Memphis Recording Service. Scotty Moore was a musician who had served four years in the Navy, including ample time spent playing guitar with his buddies. He was currently working long days at his brother's dry-cleaning business, removing spots and dirt from hats, as well as playing around town in different bands.

Moore told the Rock And Roll Detective, "The hat department was independent. The man had just more or less rented a space upstairs at the cleaning plant and he would go out and pick up hats from different places—other cleaners—and bring 'em in, block 'em, clean 'em, and then deliver them back the next day. And Carney, my oldest brother, asked me, 'Do you think you'd like to do that?' And I said, 'Well, it don't look too hard,' you know, so I took that over, and in two weeks I was a full-blown hatter. The unfortunate thing was, just about the time I had learned everything, well, the hats started goin' out of style." The hat cleaning industry's loss would be pop music's gain.

Moore was singularly focused on making a career out of playing guitar. His first band was a country and western outfit named "Doug Poindexter & the Starlite Wranglers." As their manager, he had secured them a 15-minute show on local radio to play a few tunes and announce where they would be performing next. The band included Moore's good friend and talented bass player, Bill Black.

Black was born in Memphis, Tennessee into a large family. Growing up, his father entertained the family by playing banjo and fiddle. When he was 14, Black learned to play music on a homemade "guitar" fashioned by his father out of an old cigar box with a board nailed to it and strings attached. During World War II, he served in the U.S. Army where he continued to play his homemade guitar and met his future wife Evelyn (also a guitarist). In 1946, he left the military, got married, and returned to Memphis where he was hired to work in the local Firestone tire plant.

Black switched over to the upright bass in his free time and developed a style of clowning around on stage while plucking the bass, calling attention to his good-time playing style. He sought to entertain and bring a smile to the faces of his audience. In 1952, Black joined forces with Moore and other musicians to perform country tunes in the Starlite Wranglers band. The group appeared in local clubs, honkytonks, and on radio shows.

Moore recalled trying to think of new ways to attract more interest in the Starlite Wranglers. "I thought that if I could get a record or a single made," he reasoned, "and get it on the radio, then that would lead to more live jobs for my band." He had heard about Sam Phillips, the radio announcer who had started his own little studio, so Moore went to see Phillips and asked him if he would give the Wranglers an audition. Phillips readily agreed.

In the spring of 1954, Moore took his band over to the Memphis Recording Service for an audition with Phillips. He recalled, "We just went in and played like we'd go out and play a dance or anything else." Phillips liked what he heard from the Starlite Wranglers that day, but inquired whether the group had any original material. The band did not. To date, they had only played cover songs. So Phillips told Moore, "If you get some original material, come back and see me. Let me hear it and I'll give you another shot."

With the incentive of recording two sides of new material, the Wranglers (specifically Poindexter, Moore, and Moore's brother Carney) set about writing two original songs, "My Kind Of Carrying On" and "Now She Cares No More for Me." When they brought the tunes to Phillips, he liked the songs well enough to take a chance. He recorded both songs in the studio with The Starlite Wranglers on April 12 and 15, 1954.

Phillips released the single on his Sun Records label to record stores, jukeboxes, and local radio. After that, said Moore, "I had a reason to see Sam almost daily… I bugged the hell out of him in other words. My biggest goal was, if that Starlite Wranglers record didn't do it, we'd get to do another one." Although the record sold "maybe twelve copies," according to Moore, and never made any money, it did give the opportunistic Moore a chance to go next door to Ms. Taylor's restaurant and try to talk Phillips into recording his band again, perhaps with a new lead singer. Moore was not altogether thrilled with their lead vocalist, Doug Poindexter.

"The story of my first meeting with Elvis starts with Marion Keisker," said Moore. "Marion had good ears. She recognized Elvis' talent." Moore described the circumstances that led to his first encounter with Elvis. "Sam and I were just discussing the business and 'have you heard so-and-so' just in general. Marion was having coffee with us. And she asked Sam, 'Did you ever listen to that boy [Elvis] that was in here?'" Moore specifically recalled Sam's answer, "And he said, 'No I haven't.'" Moore picked up on Keisker's comment and he too inquired every so often about using this unknown kid as a vocalist.

One day, Phillips finally responded to Moore's persistence. Moore recalled, "That's when he turned to Marion and told her, 'Go get that boy's telephone number for me if you would.' So, she went over and got it, came back, and she gave the paper to Sam. Then he gave the paper to me with the name 'Elvis Presley' on it. I looked at Sam and said, 'What kind of damn name is Elvis Presley?' Sam replied, 'Scotty, call this guy and see if he'll come over to your house and you listen to him and see what you think about him.' I never heard his name 'til he handed me that piece of paper. This was July 3, 1954."

For the seasoned guitarist Moore, this was intended as an audition for his group, The Starlite Wranglers. "When we did that audition with Elvis," revealed Moore, "… in the back of my mind I was thinking about, well, maybe here could be another singer for my group, a younger voice. If he did pretty good, well that was my first thought, to make him a Wrangler."

Scotty Moore and Bill Black—Private Audition of Elvis Presley, July 4, 1954

When Moore returned home from Taylor's Restaurant, he called and left a message for Elvis. "It was 5 or 6 o'clock in the evening I guess, when he returned my call," said Moore. "I asked if he'd come over to my house the next day, that I was workin' with Sam Phillips and Sam was looking for new artists. I asked if he would be interested. He said, 'Well sure.'" Moore's good friend and bass player, Bill Black, lived about three or four houses down the street. He told Black that Elvis was coming over and that he wanted his opinion too, so Black joined the session. None of these three men could have realized at this point that history was about to intervene and their lives would be intertwined forevermore.

"I lived in a place at 983 Belz Avenue, which is no longer there, in North Memphis," said Moore. "The neighborhood was just like the day after the war ended; all the houses looked alike. It was just rows and rows of duplexes. I really lived there 'cause Bill [Black] lived there. He was working at the Firestone plant, which was just real close. One of the apartments opened up and I moved over there so he didn't have to carry his big bass around for the Wranglers' gigs."

The day Elvis came over for his audition was a hot day in Memphis. "It was a scalder," recalled Moore in his unique way. The temperature that afternoon had reached a high of 100 degrees with 93% humidity. "The best I remember, I was in the back room when he came to the door. My wife came back there and just said, 'The guy you called is at the door.'"

"When I first met Elvis, on that Sunday afternoon, he had on a pink shirt, pink pants with white stripes down the legs, and white shoes! I thought my wife was gonna run out the back door! I think she was shocked because people weren't wearing that kind of flashy clothes at the time," affirmed Moore. "Elvis had long sideburns and a ducktails hairdo; just a whole load of hair."

As they got started, Moore was both pleased and surprised by Presley's wide-ranging knowledge of music. "My first impression of Elvis was, number one, it seemed like he knew every darned song out there. And he'd play along with things that he could sing and when he didn't know the chords, well, he'd just quit playin' and he'd keep singing 'til he comes back to where he could play it again. I don't think I plugged in my guitar because we were just sitting there in the living room." Moore did not want to drown out Elvis' voice with his electric guitar because the primary reason for the audition was to judge the quality of his singing.

None of the songs Elvis auditioned that day were upbeat or rocking. Moore recalled, "He knew all the words and melodies, but they were all medium to slow tempo songs. We're talking Ink Spots and classics by Bing Crosby and that sort of thing. He sang some Marty Robbins, Hank Snow, and Roy Hamilton songs, and some of the current R&B hits at the time; a little bit of everything really. If I could think of a song, it seemed like he knew it. Songs like 'Because of You,' and 'I Love You Because.'"

Moore recognized that Elvis had a youthful-sounding voice. He was, after all, still a teenager. He observed, "Elvis was singing all these old ballads and poor Doug Poindexter sang mainly country type things. Doug had a nasal voice. He was a real Hank Williams fan, and if he did a pop song, he *still* sounded like Hank Williams singing." First and foremost, Moore was hoping he could use Elvis in the Starlite Wranglers. "Really, all this was in the back of my head, you know, thinking of having a different vocal singer in my band." Moore and Black shared the same impression of Elvis that day. After the teen left the house, Moore asked Black for his opinion, "Well, what do you think?" Black replied, "Well, he sings good. He didn't really knock me out, you know." This was essentially Moore's opinion as well, but he later revealed his full thoughts at the time, "If we got the right song, with good music backing, and recorded it the right way, we could really do something. He was a young voice and he knew all these songs. Now, see, I'd already had this thing with Sam asking, 'You guys got any new material? Bring that in'; so that was my first thought. I told Bill if Elvis could find a good song to sing, we might get to record something with him." Moore did not reveal his motives to Elvis on the day of the home tryout.

When Black left, Moore called Phillips and reviewed the Elvis audition with him. "I told him Bill had been down and we'd listened to Elvis and we liked him." By this time, Phillips respected Moore's opinion on musical issues. Moore recounted, "That's when Sam said to me, 'Well, let me call him [Elvis] and I'll ask him to come in tomorrow night and you and Bill come.' He said, 'I don't need the whole [Starlite Wranglers] band. Just you and Bill come in so I'll have a little music behind him.'" Moore continued, "It didn't matter to me that Sam didn't want all of the Starlite Wranglers. He wasn't auditioning me or Bill. I could have played 'Who Caught John' on that one and it wouldn't have mattered to him. *He wanted to listen to Elvis' voice.* He just wanted to hear some kind of musical thing going on behind him. That day led us to our first Elvis demo recording session with Sam Phillips."

The Studio Audition—Elvis, Scotty, and Bill, July 5, 1954

Elvis Presley's first studio session with Scotty Moore and Bill Black, produced by Sam Phillips, was intended only as a recorded audition to hopefully create a demo of a couple of songs. It was meant to test Presley's vocals in combination with two proficient musicians backing him in a professional studio setting.

Moore took us back to the tryout: "That first session with Elvis, Bill, and me was a demo. I want to stress that 'cause that's what it was, a *demo*; an audition. Sam did not isolate us on the first record; it wasn't so separated, so it had that beautiful blend, right? Nobody thought about baffling things and all that kind of stuff back in those days, you know."

The microphone Phillips used was a long black mic, tapered down at the end and omni-directional. Moore explained, "It was a real hot mic and it picked up—and I'm sure that's the reason Sam used it. The mic just picked up the voice and the guitar and Elvis didn't even have a separate mic on his guitar. If it had been a real session, he would have had each one of them mic'd separately."

Moore modestly downplayed his guitar playing on the session: "Bill and I only went into the studio with Elvis to have just some kind of meager accompaniment behind him, so he wouldn't be standing alone in the studio, you know. The first songs I think we put down were 'Harbor Lights' and 'I Love You Because.'" Fortunately, the tapes from this first session have miraculously survived, more than sixty years after they were first recorded. The listener feels like a fly on the wall at this historic recording session that first featured Elvis, Moore, and Black. The sounds reveal the deep creative process achieved on that historic evening.

The first song attempted that night was "Harbor Lights," a lightweight Hawaiian-styled pop song that had been a hit for Sammy Kaye and covered by Bing Crosby. After some false starts by Moore (who, like Black, was learning the song by ear), Elvis finally got to sing on Take 3. Presley whistled a solo in unison with Moore's lead guitar in the middle of the track. Take 5 featured a slightly more confident Elvis as Moore ran a chromatic scale on his guitar, searching for just the right feel for his lead part. The result was that his guitar playing sounds too "busy" for the song. By Take 6, Phillips aborted attempting to give Elvis advice on vocalizing the tune. The final Take 8 sounded like an edit piece for the solo; however, it abruptly terminated as Moore's guitar hit the mike stand, causing a noise. Moore chastised himself in frustration, yelling, "Dawg Gone It!" Undeterred, the foursome decided it was time to move on to another tune.

"I Love You Because" was the next song attempted that night. It was yet another slow, syrupy ballad that Elvis loved. Over the course of five somewhat shaky takes, we are treated to Elvis singing, whistling, and even speaking his love for a fictional girl. Once again, Moore searched for a lead part to wake up this dreary tune, while Black sleepily plunked away at the bass chords. The song was so maudlin that they all dropped it. In fact, it is at the complete opposite end of the spectrum from the eruption of rhythm and passion that would accidentally spill forth later in the session.

Reflecting on the first two aborted tracks of that fateful evening, Moore recalled, "Those were all just audition things. Those two or three songs came out much later—Sam cut those songs on tape and kept 'em. I don't know why. Maybe he just stuck 'em back there and forgot about 'em."

The session dragged on into the evening as the three musicians tried to find a song they all knew, one that would impress Phillips' ears. "We went through several different songs and, again, it was a problem trying to get him [Elvis] to sing something that we knew because Bill and I both played by ear. It was getting late and Bill and I had to work the next morning," said Moore. Everyone involved grew tired, and none of the earlier songs had yielded anything worthwhile. Around 10:00 p.m., the group decided to take a recess, a pause in playing that many later asserted launched rock and roll!

"We were more or less taking a break, having a coffee or a Coca-Cola," said Moore, casually describing the historical moment as if he was talking about mowing his lawn. His narrative gathered momentum as he described the happy accident that would reveal success. "Elvis just picked up his guitar and started playing and singing 'That's Alright' and clowning around the studio, dancing, just cuttin' up in general, and Bill picked up his bass and started slapping it and clowning around also." Moore joined in on his electric guitar, just fiddling with a song that neither musician had ever heard before. "Apparently Elvis owned the 78-rpm record by Arthur Crudup. It was some R&B song," said Moore. "And then I joined in and just played what I thought sounded good with the song."

"Sam was in the control room with the door open, and he suddenly came out and asked, 'What are y'all doing? That sounds pretty good!' We answered, 'We don't know.' He said, 'Well, see if you can do it again the same way and let's put it on tape, see what it sounds like; sounded pretty good through the door.' So, we kind of looked around at each other and said, 'Well, what was we doin'?" The trio practiced the song a while, jamming to get on the same page, and then Phillips suggested to Moore that he simplify his guitar flourishes. "We backtracked and tried to do it again and I think we did it twice," said Moore. "Once for Sam to get a balance and then we put it on tape and that was it."

From the session tape archives, it appears that there were four takes in all. Take 1 broke down at :08 seconds after an out-of-sync, raggedy instrumental intro. Take 2 began with

Moore playing in the wrong key as Elvis started to sing, "Well, That's Alright, Mama..." Take 3 was complete, but not perfect. It was likely the one Phillips used to obtain a proper balance, and it also provided Moore a chance to change keys and to work out his now-famous lead guitar solo. Finally, Take 4 was the keeper, as all three musicians were synced together with Presley's spirited singing and Black's amazing bass and drum-like sound.

Elvis' singing was passionate, loose, and carefree, yet it was unlike anything he had ever sung before. "I never sang like that in my life until I made that first record," said Presley. "I remembered that song because I heard Arthur [Crudup] sing it, and I thought I would like to try it." He had freed himself at last from maudlin ballads and love songs on this fateful night, leading the world into a new genre of music that blended R&B and country into a rock and roll minestrone, a new style of music that would ultimately carry him to the top of the entertainment world in just a few short years. Presley later reminisced, "We more or less landed upon it accidentally. Nobody knew what they were doin' until we had already done it. We just had a ball and it kind of... it surprised me 'cause it went over very well."

Once the song was completed, Phillips invited Presley, Moore, and Black into the control booth to listen to the playback. Moore related, "When we first recorded 'That's Alright,' that night we heard it on playback and our reaction was 'This is interesting.' The whole thing about it was the rhythm. The rhythm was good, and that was it. It was driving, whereas Elvis had been standing up there doing these slow ballads all evening. 'That's Alright' was interesting." And *interesting* was what Phillips was always looking for—something fresh and different.

Black also played a crucial role in shaping "That's Alright" besides clowning around with Elvis and egging him on during a Coca-Cola break. "You could hear a rhythm sound in 'That's Alright' that almost had a drum feel to it," explained Moore. "That was Bill slapping his bass. I tell bass players now and they're just amazed. See, what Bill did, he only used three strings to play on. The bass string, he tuned down completely till it made nearly no sound at all. He would hit that string with the palm of his hand as he plucked the other strings and it would pop against the neck." Most people listening to the master recording thought the session featured a drummer hitting the rim of his snare drum, but no drummer was used. Black not only carried the bass part, but also added a unique drum-like, rhythmic sound to the recording.

"Did we know it was a hit?" recalled Moore. "Of course not; all we knew was that it was different. But I had to wait, and I guess Bill did too, for Elvis to sing something that Sam liked, that he thought would sell. But he was still just singing and playing old songs." This up-tempo R&B/country style has led more than a few music historians to declare "That's Alright" as rock and roll's launch point. Whether Presley, Moore, and Black knew they had created a seminal moment in music is unlikely. However, Phillips *knew* he had forever captured a life-changing moment on tape that night, so much so, in fact, that he woke up his wife around midnight to tell her. Becky Phillips recalled, "He was excited, he was happy… and felt that nothing would ever be quite the same again." And he was right.

On the Radio

The very next day, Phillips called his friend and popular Memphis DJ Dewey Phillips (no relation) to excitedly describe his amazing new recording. Later in the day, he rushed over a couple of acetate discs of "That's Alright" to the station. The record had not been commercially released and did not yet have a B-side. No management deal, artist agreement with a record label, or publishing deals were yet in place for Presley at this point.

Dewey was equally fascinated hearing the song for the first time. When he played it that night on his radio show, WHBQ's "Red, Hot and Blue," the phone lines lit up with scores of listeners asking to hear the song again! Eventually, the response was so rabid that Dewey (with help from Elvis' parents) brought Elvis down to the station to introduce the 19-year-old teenager to his audience on the air. This moment clearly cemented Sam Phillips' vision of finding a white artist who could generate the same exciting feeling as the black R&B records he had previously produced.

Blue Moon of Kentucky

Once he realized he had a special song everyone liked, and one that was receiving steady airplay around Memphis, Phillips called Presley, Moore, and Black back into the studio for an encore to record a B-side, in order to release a 7-inch, vinyl single by this newly-formed group on his Sun Records label. "So, we went back into the studio," recounted Moore. "We already had 'That's Alright' in the can, but we really didn't know what we had. We knew it was different. So now the problem was to get something in the same vein for the other side."

According to Moore, the threesome walked into the Memphis Recording Service with nothing prepared musically. They rehearsed "a number of different songs during this next session" that were not quite ready for recording. Once more, it took a Coca-Cola refresher to bring out the best in this new musical trio. "Again, during a break," recalled Moore, "Bill Black was sitting on his bass and started singing 'Blue Moon of Kentucky' in a high falsetto voice a la Bill Monroe. Elvis joined in and started singing it with him. I think we all knew immediately when this happened that this might be what we was lookin' for. So, we figured out where to start and stop and put it on tape and that was it. There were no drums on those songs, just the three of us."

Moore credits Black with coming up with a significant change to the traditional country tune that immediately created a different sound dynamic for the song. Explaining the key ingredient in "Blue Moon of Kentucky," Moore said, "Bill had just changed the tempo of this country waltz to a 4/4 tempo that was more upbeat." An understatement if there ever was one! This pivotal change to the tempo freed Elvis up again to sing in a more rocked-up fashion, as he had done when recording "That's Alright."

Only one rehearsal outtake survives from the "Blue Moon of Kentucky" sessions that allow the listener to hear a primitive version of the song. In this minute-long snippet, a confident Elvis is heard performing a guide vocal to help Moore and Black work out their instrumental parts. Moore's lead solo had yet to take shape. The song was mostly a guitar playing rhythm at this point. At the end of the take, Phillips peered out of the control room at Elvis and Company. Moore witnessed, "On one of the early takes of 'Blue Moon of Kentucky,' Sam Phillips can be heard at the end of the take. I remember that. He came out of the control room to comment after we had just tried a run-through of the song." Phillips can be heard on tape, enthusiastically stating, "That's fine man. Hell, that's different. That's a pop song now, just about!"

Commenting on the rehearsal, Scotty recounted, "That outtake is a little slower than the version that was finally released. I guess that's when he [Sam] finally decided, 'Let's just stay with that upbeat one.' Yeah, once we locked on to any of 'em, I don't think there were over five cuts [takes] on anything we did, really. It was just a matter of getting Elvis to either lean in on the mic or back up or something like that, you know. It turned out that 'Blue Moon of Kentucky' and 'That's Alright' had a very similar feel."

When the master take of "Blue Moon of Kentucky" was finished, Phillips added some of his now-famous slap-back echo to Elvis' vocals, and the finished song was played and sung at a more frenetic pace, including a beautiful and simple lead guitar part from Moore.

Once more, the trio of musicians had hit upon the winning formula of transforming a slower song into a more upbeat style which in turn created a new and different sound for its day. Within two weeks, the finished single was released: "That's Alright" backed with "Blue Moon of Kentucky" (Sun Records Single No. 209, credited to "Elvis Presley, Scotty and Bill"). The single quickly sold 4,000 copies in its first week. Both songs appealed to a wide new audience because they crossed the lines of pop, hillbilly (country), and R&B. However, it took the hard work and determination of Sam Phillips, traveling the countryside and investing every dollar and measure of sweat into promoting the record to DJs and record distributors, to ensure its success.

Promotional photo of Elvis Presley, Scotty and Bill record, "That's All Right."

Back at the studio, Marion Keisker was busy setting up interviews for Elvis, filling record orders, and sending out promo copies of the record to DJs. "We were back-ordered more than five thousand records… before we could even get our mastering done and get some pressings done out here at Plastic Products. So, it was that immediate," she recalled. She sent out one thousand records of the first Presley single to disc jockeys around the country. When DJs called her about this new and different sound with skepticism, Keisker replied, "All I did was say, 'Play it once. Just play it once.'" Her simple advice worked.

"That's Alright Mama" 78 RPM record.

While Phillips was plugging the record to the industry, Marion Keisker was also pushing the record—and Elvis, Moore, and Black—to any newspaper editor who would listen to her. It was a team effort of great magnitude. The first published record of Keisker's promotion of Elvis comes shortly after the record was completed. One interview with Elvis Presley and Marion Keisker appeared on the pages of the Memphis Press-Scimitar on July 28th, 1954. In the article entitled "In A Spin," Keisker is quoted as saying, "The odd thing about it, is that both sides seem to be equally popular on popular, fold and race records programs. This boy has something that seems to appeal to everybody." Continuing, Keisker describes large sales orders from big cities across the country such as Dallas and Atlanta. She concludes by telling readers, "So there's a good chance of a big national sale." Her words were prophetic.

"Blue Moon of Kentucky" 45 RPM single.

To date, the single continues to please modern-day ears. It has sold well over a half-million copies and has been awarded a Gold Record by the Recording Industry Association of America (RIAA).

Elvis Presley's First Manager

As Presley, Moore, and Black began to play their two new songs live around town, Moore again made all of the arrangements. With fame and fortune just around the corner, agents began sniffing around, trying to sign Elvis, who had no manager but was now signed to the Sun Records label with a hit song. Moore related how Elvis handled the early pressures of business: "Elvis had a great mind on him, and he was constantly asking me about places I'd been, serving in the Navy, and that type of thing. I was still the leader of the group, only there were just three of us." Eventually, the new trio would dub themselves "Elvis Presley and the Blue Moon Boys." Moore continued, "It went from five with the Starlight Wranglers to just Elvis, Bill and me. That's how it all evolved when the issue of a manager came up because I was the leader."

A short time later, the three musicians were back in the studio when Elvis said that two or three people around town had called him, trying to get him to sign up with them. According to Moore, "When these folks would call, he [Elvis would] tell them, '… well I don't know anything about it, I'll get somebody else to talk to you.' Phillips was the one that said to Elvis, 'Hey, tell you what. Why don't you just sign a contract with Scotty [Moore] for a year and give us time to find somebody that we all like and that way you won't be lying. You just tell 'em you've already signed up.'" In short, this is how Moore came to serve as Elvis Presley's first manager for his accelerating career. Moore recalled, "I mean, it turned out to be a little more work, but it was okay. It was just for a year. I did everything—booking shows, getting him into the studio, transportation, arrangements to stay overnight, and negotiating fees for a show. Anything you can think of that a manager does; I did." In the process, Moore often consulted with Phillips about details until Bob Neil later took over as manager, at which time Moore continued his work as road manager and lead guitarist.

PERSONAL MANAGEMENT CONTRACT ENTERED
INTO BETWEEN W. S. MOORE III AND
ELVIS PRESLEY

WHEREAS, W. S. Moore, III, is a band leader and a booking agent, and Elvis Presley, a minor, age 19 years, is a singer of reputation and renown, and possesses bright promises of large success, it is the desire of both parties to enter into this personal management contract for the best interests of both parties.

This contract is joined in and approved by the Father and Mother of Elvis Presley, *Vernon Presley* and *Mrs. Vernon Presley* Presley.

IT IS AGREED that W. S. Moore, III, will take over the complete management of the professional affairs of the said Elvis Presley, book him professionally for all appearances that can be secured for him, and to promote him, generally, in his professional endeavors. The said W. S. Moore, III, is to receive, as his compensation for his services, ten (10%) percent of all earnings from engagements, appearances, and bookings made by him for Elvis Presley.

IT IS UNDERSTOOD AND AGREED that this is an exclusive contract and the said Elvis Presley agrees not to sign another contract pertaining to his professional work nor make any appearances at any time for any other person or manager or booking agent, for a period of one (1) year.

Now we *Vernon Presley* and *Mrs. Vernon Presley*, father and mother of Elvis Presley, join in this contract for and in his behalf, confirm and approve all of its terms and his execution of same and our signatures are affixed thereto.

The said W. S. Moore, III, agrees to give his best efforts to the promotion and success of the said Elvis Presley professionally.

SIGNED AND EXECUTED on this *12th* day of *July* 1954.

Scotty Moore - Elvis Presley first management contract.

Who Really Discovered Elvis? Who Deserves the Credit?

Elvis Presley went on to a remarkable career that earned him 18 Number One records; 31 films; more than 140 Gold, Platinum, and Multi-Platinum RIAA record awards; and amazing fame and fortune. Over the years, Sam Phillips chose, for reasons known only to him, not to share the "discovery" credit of Elvis with his other collaborators. The facts, however, point to four people who should rightly share the credit for discovering Elvis, if we define "discovery" in this case as the detection, support, and early career development of Elvis and his latent talent.

The case for Marion Keisker is clear and compelling. However, Phillips has gone so far as to deny his trusted assistant any credit at all. When specifically asked by *Rolling Stone* if it was Keisker, in fact, who first recorded Elvis Presley, Phillips tried diplomatically to spin the story:

Well, I would love to say Marion did it. She did an awful lot for me, man. I mean we painted floors together. I wouldn't take anything away from Marion Keisker. And I think she made the statement inadvertently. I don't want to make Marion look bad on the thing. I wish you'd just drop it, 'cause I don't care who it was. But it was simply me. That's all.

Rolling Stone's interviewer continued to dig further into the discovery phase of Elvis' career and asked Phillips directly, "There are many stories about how Elvis came to Sun in 1954. I'd like to hear your version of it**.**" And Phillips replied tersely:

He [Elvis] was working for Crown Electric. I'd seen the truck go back and forth outside, and I thought, "They sure are doing a hell of a lot of business around here." But I never saw it stop anywhere. So, Elvis had… he had *cased the joint* a long time before he stopped the truck and got out. And there's no telling how many days and nights behind that wheel he was figuring out some way to come in and make a record without saying, "Mr. Phillips, would you audition me?"

Once again, in seeking to take full credit for discovery and the first Elvis recording, Phillips calls his own credibility into question in describing Elvis' "casing out" his studio as a truck driver for Crown Electric. Although his comments made for a nice revisionist history, they fail to fit the chronology of factual events as they actually occurred, and therefore bring into question Phillips' credibility as a witness to these events.

It is well established that Elvis began work at Crown Electric for $1.00 per hour on April 20, 1954. His trade involved delivering electrical supplies to job sites. However, his first demo session, which Keisker recorded at Memphis Recording Service, occurred on or around July 18, 1953 ("My Happiness" and "That's When Your Heartaches Begin"). So Phillips' claim that Elvis "cased the joint" in his Crown Electric truck before coming in to have Phillips first record an audition or demo is impossible, because Elvis did not have the Crown Electric job or drive that truck until some nine months *after* his first recorded demo session!

A detailed examination of the facts yields support for Keisker's invaluable contributions to the discovery and launch of Elvis' career. She was the first to write down Elvis' name and number when he made his first private demo record. She recalled the actual conversation with Elvis when he first sat in the outer office of the studio, a story she repeated *early* and *often* in his career, when she visited newspapers with him promoting his first record. In contrast, Phillips did not recall any dialogue from his alleged first encounter at the private demo session performed by Elvis. We must also bear in mind that it was Keisker who had the foresight to record and save a brief tape of Elvis singing at the first demo session so that Phillips could hear it later. Why would she have done so if Phillips (as he claimed) had recorded this session? And why would Phillips fail to mention this detail in his account?

Moreover, it was Keisker who continued to believe Elvis had potential, periodically reminding Phillips about "the kid with the sideburns." Beneath Elvis' timid voice, Keisker heard potential that inspired her to repeatedly suggest that Phillips use him when new song demos came into Sun Records. Scotty Moore also credits Keisker for bringing up Elvis' name when he was pestering Phillips about finding a new singer.

While most of Sam Phillips' recollections occurred decades after the fact, the events reflected Marion Keisker's detailed, corroborated account of both the big and small moments attached to the Presley discovery. Many of Keisker's accounts come from contemporaneous statements close to the time of the event. Our memory has no guarantees. There is a degree of fallibility of human memory that changes over time, particularly where a dispute over facts exists. Memories are often subconsciously overlaid by perceptions and self-interest. It is for this reason that courts of law often place additional weight or credibility on contemporaneous statements or records. Greater weight is often given to evidence captured in the immediate aftermath of an event. In this case, the bulk of facts sourced and presented here seem to favor Keisker's account.

Unfortunately, no photographs, spoken word recordings, or session notes prove definitively whether Keisker or Phillips recorded Elvis the first time. We only have the recordings themselves, which offer no clues, and the witness assertions and credibility of Keisker's and Phillips' respective statements. Keisker's version of events—of being the first to record Elvis and to recognize and champion his value as a singer—began long before Elvis was ever famous. It also began long before the time Elvis might have been driving his truck by the recording studio and "casing it out" (if you believe Phillip's inaccurate version). Keisker insisted she first recorded him and said, "… I had reason to remember for many, many years afterwards, having gone through it [the story] with every editor that I tried to talk to during the time that I was promoting him for Sun." Regardless of which person helped Elvis record his first private demo, Keisker's continued reminders and lobbying to Phillips, her belief in the young man's singing abilities, and her relentless promotion of his records are unquestioned, even by the King himself.

Perhaps the best evidence for Keisker earning a credit for discovering Elvis came from Elvis Presley himself. In 1957, she had left the Memphis Recording Service to join the

Sam Phillips, Elvis Presley and Marion Keisker.

U.S. Air Force, reuniting with an already-enlisted Elvis. The two had not seen each other in a few years when, on March 1, 1960 at a Presley press conference in Germany, their paths crossed again. Upon seeing Captain Keisker, Elvis exclaimed, "I don't know whether to kiss you or salute!" Her response was, "In that order!" In describing Keisker to the press corps attending, Elvis stated, "We wouldn't be having a press conference [today] if it weren't for this lady."

Marion Keisker and Elvis Presley Press Conference in Germany.

Years later in January 1971, Presley spotted Keisker again at a Memphis luncheon honoring the U.S. Jaycees' Ten Most Outstanding Young Men of America. On this occasion, Elvis grabbed her arm and brought her over to meet his wife, Priscilla, and his buddies, declaring in front of all of them, "*She's* the one who made it all possible. Without her, I wouldn't even be here!" It is hard to receive a better endorsement for Keisker's contributions in discovering Elvis than these two documented endorsements by Presley himself.

In later years, when Keisker heard Phillips taking *sole* credit for his discovery of Elvis, she decided to defend herself and her role in Elvis' career, writing a letter to Elvis biographer Jerry Hopkins, complaining about Phillips' version of events. In the letter she stated, "I can only say this ain't the way I remember the first visit of EP [Elvis Presley] to our small shop. Perhaps he [Sam] is actually recalling a later visit. Elvis did come by several times in the months between his first record and the time Sam actually started to work with him."

In short, it was Keisker's musical instincts, ear for good sounds, assessment of Elvis' vocal potential, ability to see the big picture, perseverance, aggressive PR promotion, and a desire to help Phillips reach his goal of finding a crossover singer that benefited Elvis. Clearly, Marion Keisker deserves a "discovery" credit—especially given the eyewitness support by Scotty Moore and Elvis Presley himself.

It is equally convincing that Scotty Moore and Bill Black should also receive credit for discovering and developing Elvis Presley. As one of the most modest guitar slingers of all time, Moore never did take personal credit for the "discovery," yet it was his persistence in badgering Phillips for a singer (who he hoped would outshine Doug Poindexter in The Starlite Wranglers) that led Phillips to ask Keisker for Elvis' phone number. In addition, it was Moore who invited Elvis over to his house for an extended private audition, along with Bill Black, to assess the singer on his own. In modern recording industry parlance, Moore and Black served as Artist and Repertoire (A&R) men assessing the potential talent of a prospective recording artist.

This is especially significant when one recalls that Phillips himself had tried—without success—to nudge something special out of Elvis on June 26, 1954. He sent the young man home with no promise of future work. However, when Moore and Black conducted their private audition of Elvis on July 4 that same year, and then suggested to Phillips that they position Elvis in the studio with musical backing, this paved the way to successfully recording the hits "That's Alright" and "Blue Moon of Kentucky" over the next few days.

ELVIS PRESLEY, SCOTTY and BILL.

Elvis Presley with Scotty and Bill, The Blue Moon Boys promotional photo.

Perhaps not surprisingly, in the same *Rolling Stone* interview in which Phillips hijacked the credit from Keisker, he also downplayed Moore's and Black's contributions to Elvis' career. The Rock And Roll Detective, however, believes Phillips entangled himself once more in the web of his own "spin." During this interview, Phillips related, "The two of them [Scotty and Bill], they'd been around the studio... Scotty had been playing with different bands, although *he hadn't ever done a session for me...*"

Once again, Phillips engaged in revisionist history by marginalizing two major contributors to the launch of Elvis' career. Scotty Moore and Bill Black, along with The Starlite Wranglers, *had* indeed recorded a session with Phillips that yielded a single and a B-side for Sun Records. The Wranglers' single ("My Kind Of Carrying On" and "Now She Cares No More For Me") was recorded by Sam Phillips on April 12 and 15, 1954, *before* the first formal Elvis Presley recording session. And it was this single, in fact, that inspired Moore to hang around the studio to see if the single was selling and, more importantly, to pester Phillips about finding another lead vocalist to replace Doug Poindexter. Moore's persistence led directly to obtaining Elvis' contact information in order for Moore to privately audition him; and it was Moore, the natural group leader, who became Elvis' trusted first manager.

The ever-modest Scotty Moore pointed to his buddy Bill Black as the inspiration for launching Elvis' career as a singer: "Number one, if it hadn't been for Bill in the very beginning," asserted Moore, "Elvis would've never happened, at least not the way he happened. Elvis had the talent and everything and he would've come to the forefront in some way, but there's no tellin' how. He thought everything had to be ballads at the time." Black's upbeat playing between takes clearly created an atmosphere for Elvis to let down his guard and create a new vocal dynamic on their early recordings. Black's change of rhythm on "Blue Moon of Kentucky," from a slow waltz to a quick 4/4 rocker, was ultimately the key to creating a popular hit recording. This creative change did not originate from Phillips' control booth, but rather from a fellow musician working side by side with Elvis that day.

Moore continued his argument for Black's contribution by discussing how his unique bass playing spurred Elvis on: "If you're talking about Bill's playing—see, I think it came about because there weren't many drummers around town right around that time, or in that era. 'Blue Moon' was originally a country tune… country music didn't really recognize drums at the time. So Bill turned his bass string down again, hit the fourth string, which was tuned down, and it would smack against the neck and you'd get that pop! And that's where he got that beat for 'Blue Moon of Kentucky' and so many others. Bill's part was just as important as Elvis' was as far as I'm concerned, because he absolutely provided the beat in the early days."

Moore also credits Bill Black for warming up audiences who had never heard of Elvis Presley when they first started out. "If it hadn't been for Bill, we would have bombed so many times in the early days. What you don't realize is that some of the crowds had not seen Elvis. They'd heard the records, but they had not seen him. They're sitting there like, 'What is he?' And Bill would start riding the bass and clowning, and get the crowd loosened up. Once he'd done that, then Elvis would have them in the palm of his hand. He was winding them up for us."

Lastly, we cannot forget that Black was also present at Moore's private, and now legendary, Fourth of July audition of Elvis back in 1954. After this session, Black also believed that Elvis was a good enough singer to merit an audition session at the Memphis Recording Service. Common sense inferences drawn from these contributions lead a reasonable person to believe that Bill Black clearly deserves a credit for Elvis' discovery.

When Keith Richards, lead guitarist for The Rolling Stones, was asked about his biggest influence, he shared a similar sentiment. "All I wanted to do in the world was to play and sound like that. Everyone else wanted to be Elvis—I wanted to be Scotty." One would be hard-pressed to find greater endorsements for Moore's contributions to Presley's music than from this rock and roll legend.

Many writers and fans have described the studio where Elvis got his start in lofty, romantic, almost-Biblical terms. According to the Memphis Travel website, "If music was a religion, then Memphis would be Jerusalem and Sun Studios its most holy shrine." Certainly, the studio served as the birthplace for some of the greatest American music ever made by B.B. King, Elvis Presley, Roy Orbison, Johnny Cash, Carl Perkins, Jerry Lee Lewis, and many others. Without question, the vision, determination, and perseverance of Sam Phillips made this possible by creating the incubator for the new phenomenon of rock and roll music. However, the facts also clearly support the argument that four integral players—not just one key individual—had significant roles in the discovery and eventual success of Elvis Presley. The essential contributions of Marion Keisker, Scotty Moore, and Bill Black, with Sam Phillips, are significant and undeniable as the *foursome* who discovered Elvis Presley.

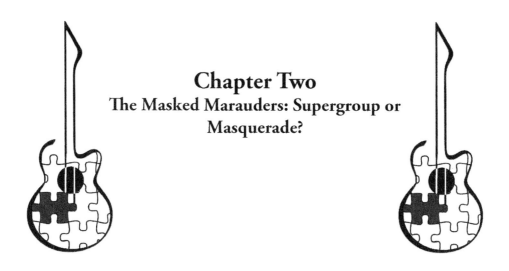

Chapter Two
The Masked Marauders: Supergroup or Masquerade?

It was mid-July, 1969. The weather in New York City was sweltering and humid, averaging in the lower 90s. Record producer Glyn Johns had just arrived back in New York at LaGuardia Airport. Johns and *Rolling Stone's* Editor, Jann Wenner, had flown to Georgia to check out an up-and-coming band, The Allman Brothers, to determine if Johns wanted to produce them. Neither Johns nor Wenner realized that this trip would lead them down the rabbit hole of a new supergroup made up of the biggest names in rock and roll.

By 1969 Glyn Johns was perhaps the most in-demand producer/engineer in the world, having worked with The Rolling Stones, The Beatles, Steve Miller, Led Zeppelin, and Traffic, to name just a few. So it was no surprise that Johns was being asked to take a look at The Allman Brothers. But his return flight to New York would lead him to a chance meeting with a much bigger rock legend and a new opportunity.

The producer recalled his flight back from Georgia to New York with Wenner. "During the flight, he [Wenner] was editing an interview he had recently done with Bob Dylan. It was something of a coup, as Dylan had not been interviewed for several years." Wenner and Johns disembarked their flight in New York City. Amazingly, within a few minutes of walking into the gate area, there was a *simple twist of fate* as the two men suddenly crossed paths with Bob Dylan! He was leaning up against the wall silently watching people pass by, perhaps seeking inspiration for his next song. Wenner, who had recently interviewed Dylan, introduced him to Johns. "He asked me about The Beatles album I had just finished and was very complimentary about my work with The Stones over the years," said Johns. Johns returned his sincere admiration for Dylan's work.

Bob Dylan

Then the bomb dropped, directly in front of Jann Wenner and Glyn Johns. Bob Dylan shared an astonishing new idea: he wanted to make a record in collaboration with The Beatles *and* The Rolling Stones! He inquired of Johns if he would ask the two biggest bands in the world if they might be interested in forming a supergroup. Johns recalled, "I was completely bowled over. Can you imagine? The three greatest influences on popular music in the previous decade making an album together!" Imagine indeed. Glyn's mind was already working overtime figuring out how he would select the best material from each of the three sets of songwriters (George Harrison & Bob Dylan/Mick Jagger & Keith Richards/Paul McCartney & John Lennon); then he would select the appropriate rhythm sections from each band to fit the songs. At this point, the conceptual supergroup did not have a name.

Once he returned to England, Johns reached for his office phone to call each of the members of The Rolling Stones and The Beatles to gauge their interest in and agreement to participating in the greatest popular musical collaboration of the century.

Mick Jagger and Glyn Johns in the studio

The End of an Era: 1969

The twilight of the sixties was an intriguing and chaotic time in a decade that had already experienced Kennedy's "Camelot," the Civil Rights movement, Cold War with the U.S.S.R., the Space Race, the Vietnam War and anti-war demonstrations, the Summer of Love, and the assassinations of John F. Kennedy, Martin Luther King Jr., and Robert F. Kennedy. Whew! The decade was anxiously lurching toward a close, but not before many more strange events would take place—events that were coupled to music and pop culture. Perhaps more than any other decade in the 20th century, the sixties were encapsulated by the music and musicians whose art mirrored the turbulent times.

In the fall of 1969, word of an astonishing rock and roll summit had spread like wildfire. It was dispersed by underground radio DJs and by word-of-mouth through America's high schools and college campuses. It was to be the end-all, be-all of rock and roll collaborations. No one had yet heard any of the music, nor had they seen a copy of the album; but the divinity of rock royalty had apparently blessed the Baby Boomers with the greatest *come together* of all time. Was it possible that John Lennon, Paul McCartney, and George Harrison of The Beatles had combined with Bob Dylan and The Rolling Stones' Mick Jagger (along with an unknown drummer rumored to be Ginger Baker of Blind Faith) to record the most mind-blowing album of all time?

And why not? They were all friends and had *obviously* jammed together. Fans all knew The Stones were name-checked on the cover of The Beatles' *Sgt. Pepper's Lonely Hearts*

Club Band album, which also featured Bob Dylan's face on the top row. And of course, The Rolling Stones had returned the favor, hiding each of The Beatles' faces on the 3D lenticular cover of *Their Satanic Majesties Request* album. Additionally, Mick Jagger and Keith Richards had sung background vocals on The Beatles' "All You Need Is Love"; and John Lennon and Paul McCartney had returned the favor on The Rolling Stones' song "We Love You."

Midway through 1969, The Beatles were working on what no one knew would be their final album, *Abbey Road*. Later that year, Paul McCartney would retreat to the countryside and "drop out." This act and the ensuing "clues" (postulated first by the Drake University student newspaper and spread further by DJ Russ Gibb at Detroit's WKNR-FM radio station) led the U.S., and ultimately the world, to suddenly wonder if "Paul is Dead" and had been replaced by a sound-alike/look-alike, singer/songwriter, left-handed bassist. As fans searched for clues on album covers and in between LP grooves, the story spread quickly from college newspapers and FM radio to schoolyards and ultimately the nightly news.

Meanwhile, The Rolling Stones suffered the first of two tragedies that year. In July, founding member and guitarist Brian Jones—an excellent swimmer—was found dead in his swimming pool, a victim of "misadventure." Nothing was black and white anymore. The mystery of Jones' death and how it happened remains a murky tale. While the Woodstock Music and Art Fair created positive vibrations in August, it also served as an ominous bookend to the December free concert organized by The Rolling Stones at Altamont Speedway outside San Francisco. Altamont turned ugly and deadly when The Stones' live set was disrupted by violence from the Hell's Angels (serving as security). Singer Marty Balin of Jefferson Airplane was knocked unconscious, and one concert-goer was stabbed to death right in front of the stage during The Rolling Stones' performance.

Bob Dylan's legend had grown to mythical proportions throughout the decade. His poetic songs of protest mirrored the disenchantment of the young and rebellious Baby Boom generation. There was an almost insatiable appetite for new music from Dylan by his devoted followers. His lyrics often served as a newspaper editorial of underground insights on society's foibles at a time when there was little electronic media—and certainly no social media—to spread what was happening.

New Dylan music finally arrived on a humid summer day in Los Angeles. The only problem is, neither Bob Dylan nor his record company had released the music! The simply packaged, two-record set containing 26 tracks had a blank white cover, except for a stamp, that announced the title: *Great White Wonder*. The album contained tracks that Bob Dylan had indeed recorded, yet never released. Many heralded this new-style, underground record as the first rock and roll "bootleg" album.

The first set of 9 recordings on the LP, dubbed the "Basement Tapes," had been recorded in upstate New York approximately eighteen months earlier. The "Basement Tapes" were notable for the presence of Dylan's backup band which would later become known as The Band. Another 16 songs were sourced to a Minneapolis hotel room recording featuring Dylan playing solo with his acoustic guitar and harmonica, circa December 1961. These songs had been recorded even before Dylan had signed a record deal with Columbia.

Radio stations jumped on the bandwagon airing these forbidden tracks. During the fall of 1969, newly minted bootleggers copied the record and released their own versions to keep up with the healthy demand of fans flocking to record stores. Finally, on December 16, 1970, Dylan's label Columbia won a temporary restraining order in the Los Angeles Federal District Court against one "Mr. Dub," two other men, and a California pressing plant. The success of *Great White Wonder* was unparalleled for its day. Sales of this bootleg were estimated to have reached a range of 75,000-150,000 copies, although there was no way to reliably track or gauge underground sales accurately. The impact of the record spurred a new cottage industry of bootleggers that specialized in previously unreleased recordings of Dylan, The Beatles, and The Rolling Stones. Unreleased concerts, demos, rehearsals, studio outtakes, alternates, and radio and TV appearances were all now fair game for bootleggers.

The summer of '69 grew even more bizarre. After his release from prison in 1967, ex-con Charles Manson began to socialize with rock stars and producers such as Dennis Wilson (The Beach Boys' drummer), Neil Young, Byrds' producer Terry Melcher, and others. Manson was trying to get signed as a singer-songwriter to a record deal. (For more on this, see Chapter Eight.) However, Manson and his "Family" tragically veered off-course and killed Sharon Tate and other innocent Hollywood elites in a bizarre series of ritualistic, bloody murders intended to cause "Helter Skelter," or in Manson's mind, a race war.

Supergroups Give Birth

Despite all of the weird vibes swirling around at the close of the decade, 1969 was also a signature year for rock and roll musical heroes to collaborate or jam together in new combinations. The term "supergroup" came into the hip vernacular around May and gave birth to folk-rockers Crosby, Stills and Nash (CSN). Each member had broken off from their respective bands to work together on a completely new sound, featuring incredible multi-part harmonies. Crosby left the Byrds, Stills exited Buffalo Springfield, and Nash removed his harmonies from the Hollies to parlay them with CSN.

Another supergroup rose to prominence in August of that year with the release of an album by a new British band, Blind Faith. Blind Faith was a blues-rock band composed of guitar virtuoso Eric Clapton, Ginger Baker, Steve Winwood and Ric Grech. One of the early supergroups, their style took equal parts from their most recent bands—in the case of Winwood from Traffic, and Clapton and Baker from Cream.

Long before The Beatles had formally broken up, John Lennon formed a one-off supergroup late in 1968 named "The Dirty Mac" to perform in The Rolling Stones' film "Rock And Roll Circus." Beatle Lennon was accompanied by Eric Clapton, Rolling Stone's Keith Richards, and Jimi Hendrix drummer Mitch Mitchell. Unfortunately for fans, the film and soundtrack from this project lay dormant on the shelf, unseen and unheard for decades.

Unofficial super sessions surfaced with jams that featured, for example, Jimi Hendrix with Traffic. George Harrison provided a secret guest spot (credited as *L'Angelo Misterioso*) on the song "Badge" for Cream's album *Goodbye*, and he jammed with Bob Dylan in the United States. John Lennon formed the interchangeable Plastic Ono Band, made up of Eric Clapton, Yoko Ono, Klaus Voormann, and future Yes drummer Alan White, to play the Toronto Rock And Roll Revival (aka "Toronto Peace Festival") in 1969. Suddenly, we had a musical epidemic of artists who were enthralled with collaboration and cross-pollination. The only question left to fans was, what amazing supergroup would be created next?

Many newly-minted rock journalists of the day became jaded by the supergroup concept, despite the insatiable appetite of music fans that made up their readership. In particular, writer Greil Marcus was annoyed with the supergroup concept as he stated, "We were talking about the ridiculous 'super-session' albums that were coming out, particularly the Mike Bloomfield, Al Kooper, Stephen Stills 'Super Session' record, but also the Joe Cocker album with all kinds of famous people on it, and Eric Clapton popping up on everybody's record…" Marcus likened the trend to "covering records with endorsements rather than music." To use the pop underground vernacular of the day, the supergroups were accused of "selling out."

To fans, the supergroups, jam sessions, and collaborations of their rock heroes were remarkable and a gift from the gods. They wanted their favorite rock stars to stretch out more musically, be it on a bootleg or via the assemblage of a new official group. Fans imagined that late night jams of loose chords and improvised solos by their idols were occurring with regularity. No matter how strangely the year 1969 had twisted and turned for the rock music scene, fans were anxious for, and almost willing into existence, the most amazing collaboration ever to take place.

The Masked Marauders

On a hot August day in 1969, their collective wish came true when the story surfaced in a warehouse located at 746 Brannon Street. This was home to *Rolling Stone* magazine, situated in the old Printer's District in San Francisco, California. A rock critic with the pseudonym of "T.M. Christian" entered the office and submitted a record review for an album simply called *The Masked Marauders*. He handed his review of the group's debut album to *Rolling Stone's* founding Publisher and Editor, Jann Wenner, and the review was accepted for publication.

The startling narrative hit magazine racks in September (with a publication date of October 18, 1969) where it would ironically appear alongside a review of Bob Dylan's *Great White Wonder* bootleg album, along with a review of another "super session" album by the band Merryweather (a group that included Neil Merryweather, with help from Dave Mason, Steve Miller, Charlie Musselwhite, and other heavies).

The breathless review of *The Masked Marauders* explained how "they began months ago, the rumors of an event that first seemed hardly believable but which in the end seemed accepted as all but inevitable." Christian described the album's inevitability, given all of the other super sessions and groups forming that year. The review exclaimed:

> ... lobe of the ear recognition in some, or cries of "No, No, it can't be true" in others. But yes, yes it is—a treasured, oft-Xeroxed sheet of credits (which for obvious contractual reasons, will not be reproduced on the album), and the unmistakable vocals on the album make it clear that this is indeed what it appears to be: John Lennon, Mick Jagger, Paul McCartney, and Bob Dylan, backed by George Harrison and a drummer as yet unnamed—the "Masked Marauders."

One could envision scores of *Rolling Stone* readers, like thousands of lemmings, skipping the rest of the review and running to their local record stores to find this vinyl Holy Grail. *Rolling Stone* was the reliable bible of underground music news in the United States—the pre-Internet, pre-email, pre-cell phone, pre-texting, pre-Facebook, and pre-Twitter source of information for a generation of die-hard music fans who had woven music into the fabric of their life experience. This generation believed rock and roll could change society for the better. Young readers likely re-read the first paragraph to confirm they had not imagined (or hallucinated) the amazing copy before moving on to learn more about this yet-to-be-released album on the appropriately named Deity label.

According to the review, Al Kooper had been tapped to produce this super-recording session over three brief days, secretly holed up in a small town near the site of the original Hudson Bay Colony in Canada. Kooper was well known to fans of the day for having played the signature Hammond organ riff on Dylan's classic "Like A Rolling Stone," forming Blood Sweat & Tears, and playing sessions for The Rolling Stones, Jimi Hendrix, The Who, B.B. King, and Cream, and producing the 1968 *Super-Session* album with Stephen Stills and Mike Bloomfield. He was the obvious choice for such a momentous recording gig. The secluded Canada "Deity" sessions were alleged to have taken place in late April 1969, according to *Rolling Stone*.

Christian certainly had listened to the entire two-album set, as he described the songs in great detail. In gushing prose, he related, "After the listener has recovered from this string of masterpieces, Side Four opens with a special treat, two songs written especially for this session: Dylan's 'Cow Pie'… and Mick Jagger's new instant classic, 'I Can't Get No Nookie.'" Christian added insider details to this amazing album review, telling us about the difficulties of the band secretly forming a new label, scheduling charter flights, and even some of the ego clashes one might expect. However, he closed with the most astonishing statement about The Masked Marauders' amazing collaboration: "It can truly be said that this album is more than a way of life; it *is* life." Anyone reading this review was ready to get in line at their local record store and buy two copies—one to keep mint in original shrink film and the other to play until the grooves wore off!

Within days, the reaction to the *Rolling Stone* review of *The Masked Marauders* was off the charts. Fans, radio stations, record store retailers, and distributors began to flood *Rolling Stone* with letters and phone calls. They all wanted to know the same thing: "How can I get my hands on this record?" The siege of inquiries didn't stop there. It escalated. In came a phone call from The Beatles' manager Allen Klein asking for a copy of the album and more details. Klein was aware of the *Great White Wonder* bootleg issue and had not authorized this release with his artists, not unless he was going to get a cut of the action. Ironically, Klein could have merely asked any of The Beatles for more details, but called *Rolling Stone* magazine instead. Similarly, Bob Dylan's manager, Albert Grossman, inquired of *Rolling Stone* about the mysterious super session album. *Circus* magazine, an underground music fanzine, called for details. Even regional newspapers began to dig into the story.

One writer at *Rolling Stone* recalled the upheaval caused by *The Masked Marauders*: "Almost immediately the tremendous uproar broke out. There were people calling their record stores all over the country demanding to know when this record would be available. There was one store, *at least one*, [that] called *Rolling Stone* and said that they'd simply told their customers that the record would be in the next week, and *would it be?* And how did *Rolling Stone* get it?"

Adding further fuel to the fire, one New York reporter tracked down Al Kooper, the man who had "produced" *The Masked Marauders* up in Canada. When cornered about the "super-est" of super-sessions, Kooper coolly replied, "No comment." This statement, of course, poured more gasoline onto the flames of the story as it raged unabated. His response was assumed to mean, *of course he did it, but he can't reveal anything.* The "no comment" did more to blow up the story than a simple denial or admission could ever accomplish.

From a Review to a Real Vinyl Record
Of course, by now, we have all deduced that no such super-album existed when the review came out in *Rolling Stone*! It was, in fact, one completely fictitious and clever

piece of music-fantasy penmanship. One of the first clues, which should have tipped off readers, was the fictional name of reviewer T.M. Christian, who was in fact *Rolling Stone* Record Reviews Editor, Greil Marcus. The *nom de plume* was a reference to Terry Southern's then-popular novel (about a satirical prankster) and forthcoming film, "The Magic (*TM*) Christian," starring Peter Sellers and Ringo Starr. If no one could decipher that reference, then surely one had to laugh at the concept of Bob Dylan singing an 18-minute cover version of "Season of the Witch" in tribute to Donovan, whom everyone considered at the time to be a Dylan imitator. (Also, of note, Al Kooper had produced a jam version of this same song on his *Super Sessions* album the previous year.) Or, if that wasn't convincing enough, how about "an amazing jam between bass and piano, *both* played by Paul McCartney." Perhaps the funniest giveaway was the new song sung by Mick Jagger, "I Can't Get No Nookie," by the one man in rock and roll who got more "nookie" than anyone!

According to Marcus, after hanging out with a friend one evening discussing the current super-session craze, he said to himself, "I think I am going to see if I can write this. And I decided to run it. I figured it was so ridiculous that everybody could see through it, but I sort of hoped not everyone would." Publisher Jann Wenner loved the idea. He told the Rock And Roll Detective, "I thought it was an interesting parody," he said. "If it went well, we could try it again."

With record companies, radio stations, and music fans still clamoring for the actual album from the review, the parody had taken on a life of its own, so Marcus decided "… maybe we could push this a little farther." Marcus and fellow *Rolling Stone* writer and musician Langdon Winner rounded up their musician friends, The Cleanliness and Godliness Skiffle Band, and a few others to record the songs from the fictional review. The Masked Marauders lineup for the "costumed" recordings was created by the following musicians:

Anna Rizzo –Drums
Vic Smith—Bass
Allen Chance—Vocals
Langdon Winner—Piano and Backing Vocals
Mark "The Fox" Voorheis—Drums and Vocals
Gary Salzman—Lap Steel Guitar
Phil Marsh—Guitar and Vocals
Annie "Dynamite" Johnston—Vocals and Percussion
Brian Voorheis—Harmonica, Guitar, and Vocals

Marsh took the band to a 4-track studio in South Berkeley, California called Guerrage Productions, which was owned by Reg Paradis. You could not make up a better owner's name (*Paradis*), for the *parodies* they were about to record. "We just decided that we'd try to do three songs, and would pretend like we were other people," said guitarist Phil Marsh. Not just any "other people," but John, Paul, George, Mick, and Bob. "It was kind of a wish fulfillment recording."

The group began work on Greil Marcus' composition of "I Can't Get No Nookie." Winner helped out by creating a Rolling Stone-esque arrangement that he borrowed from that group's instrumental track, "2120 South Michigan Avenue." It was one of the "original compositions" from the faux album review. Musically and vocally, the song sounded quite convincing.

Next was an attempt to create the song "Cow Pie," another "original" from the *Rolling Stone* review. The track was a country tune, reminiscent of Dylan's style on his recent release *Nashville Skyline*. The song's title bore a close resemblance to an authentic *Nashville Skyline* track, similarly named "Country Pie." The song cleverly inserts some studio chatter at the end—"Is it rolling Al?"—in order to validate the point from the review that Al Kooper had indeed "produced" these super-sessions. The track was completed as an instrumental when the vocalist felt the Marcus-penned lyrics were inappropriate.

The third track was a group vocal by The Masked Marauders performing a cover of "Duke of Earl," which turned out to be more difficult than imagined when Marcus wrote the review. "We always thought those songs were very simple," said Marsh, "but the vocal parts are very complicated, very hard."

Once the tracks were in the can, it was time to test them on unsuspecting radio listeners, so Marcus dropped in on two San Francisco area radio shows and announced the virgin spins of the amazing supergroup The Masked Marauders. Within days, some of the underground radio stations in Los Angeles had obtained tapes of the songs and were adding them to their playlists.

Spilling the Beans

On October 8, 1969, *San Francisco Chronicle* writer and co-founding *Rolling Stone* Editor Ralph J. Gleason spilled the beans in his column. He summed up the super-session masquerade ball as follows: "All in all it's a delightful bit of instant mythology. There were so many give-away lines in the *Rolling Stone* review that it is simply incredible ANYONE believed it." Even *Rolling Stone's* "Letters to the Editor" section admitted, "If it is not obvious by now, *The Masked Marauders* review was just a laugh; in other words, a fabrication, a hoax, a jest, an indulgence, or—in the word of the trade—a shuck."

However, this was 1969 and there was no Internet and no 24/7/365 news cycle. The reach of the *San Francisco Chronicle* was localized to northern California. As for *Rolling Stone's* "Letter to the Editor" section, it was usually ignored by readers more interested in delving into the latest rock and roll news. As a result, the revelation of the hoax did not reach nearly as many people as those who had first read and believed the initial review of *The Masked Marauders* album.

Amazingly, the hoax continued to have legs. Once the initial record review and reports of actual recordings came out, people did not notice or care that the truth had been clarified. But why did so many people buy into this story? According to sociologist Candy Leonard, "It is interesting to note that The Masked Marauders went viral in a pre-viral age. The story gave fans something to talk about. Baby Boomers loved these guys [Dylan, The Beatles, and The Stones] so much. They were the focal point of our generation. So, the fun of sharing the story with friends and looking around for *The Masked Marauders* album after the review came out helped spread the original story far and wide."

In an astonishing turn of events, record labels actually started bidding on the right to release a full album. Allegedly, Motown was prepared to offer $100,000 to sign the mystery band. (Note: This is the equivalent of $675,619 in present day dollars). Warner Brothers' Reprise label finally signed the deal with The Masked Marauders for $15,000. Warner even permitted the creation of the faux boutique label, "Deity," to match the *Rolling Stone* review. Almost immediately, a single was released: "Cow Pie" on the A-side and "I Can't Get No Nookie" as the B-side. Located under the Deity logo on the single was the Latin phrase "Deus Est Vivus" ("God is Alive"). The gods of rock and roll were indeed alive, though in parody form on a living breathing 7" vinyl 45-rpm record. With viral word of mouth, publicity, and radio airplay, the only Deity single ever released reached the low 100s on the *Billboard* Bubbling Under Hot 100 chart in November 1969.

At this point, Marcus bowed out in order to avoid any conflict of interest in profiting from creation of the fictional LP in *Rolling Stone's* pages. Jann Wenner and *Rolling Stone* took no part in the making of the album. Langdon Winner and the other musicians continued on in another recording session and created the rest of the album. Press releases covered up the fact that *The Masked Marauders* album did not exactly match the song titles in the review. But no one cared! They just wanted the supergroup—or parody or hoax or whatever it was—in their hands. The press release from Warner Brothers said that the album "had been recorded at one of the annual meetings where The Beatles, The Rolling Stones and Dylan would gather to plan pop music trends for the next year," recalls Marcus. "I thought it was a hilariously fascist notion."

Although the songs mentioned in the original *Rolling Stone* review did not match up with the songs on the finished *The Masked Marauders*, we can see the album comparison of the two works:

Rolling Stone review	WB/Reprise/Deity LP
The Masked Marauders	**The Masked Marauders**
Track Listing (2LP)	**Track Listing (1LP)**
Season Of The Witch	I Can't Get No Nookie
With A Little Help From My Friends	Duke Of Earl
In The Midnight Hour	Cow Pie
Masters Of War	I Am The Japanese Sandman
Prisoner Of Love	(Rang Tang Ding Dong)
Duke Of Earl	The Book Of Love
The Book Of Love	Later
I'm The Japanese Sandman	More Or Less Hudson's Bay Again
Mammy	Season Of The Witch
Cow Pie	Saturday Night At The Cow Palace
I Can't Get No Nookie	
Kick Out The Jams	
Oh Happy Day	

The album cover design featured a female model reminiscent of the late actress Sharon Tate with a mysterious man's hand lurking near her right breast. The record contained no production or artist credit information to reveal *who* The Masked Marauders actually were. The cryptic liner notes stated, "When Gods meet and pool their talents… the result is certain to be a monument to creativity itself." Reprise even ran an ironic ad for the forthcoming record… **"Coming Soon: The Masked Marauders—AN ALBUM OF COMPELLING HONESTY."**

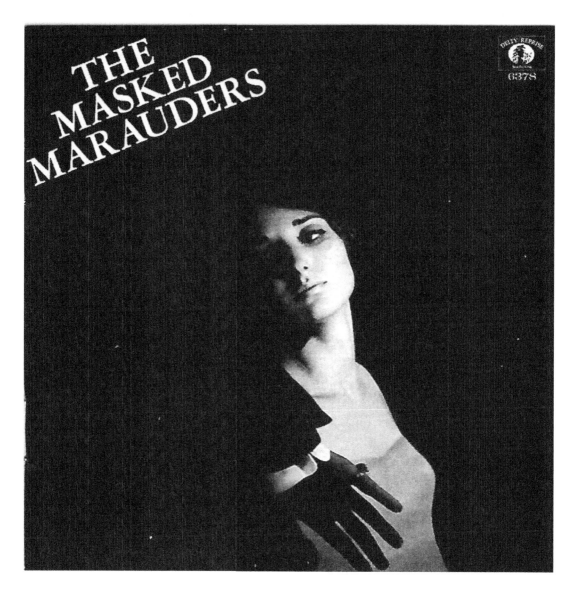

Cash Box magazine selected the album to be a four star Pick Hit. *Variety* ran a story on the album. Finally, record distributors and retailers had something to sell. After poking fun at the record industry, *Rolling Stone* was once again having the last laugh as record buyers lapped up the fictional album. On December 20, 1969 the album entered the *Cash*

Box LP charts, peaking at #89 three weeks later. On January 3, 1970 the album peaked at No. 114 on the *Billboard* LP charts and ultimately pushed more than 100,000 copies out the door of record stores. Summed up best by Winner on the *Marauders'* liner notes, he spoofed, "In a world of sham, The Masked Marauders, bless their hearts, are the genuine article."

In the end, when all of the facts were revealed about this faux record review that had invented a fictional super-session and a nonexistent supergroup album, what did it all really mean? Robert Christgau, the "Dean of American Rock Critics," chose to call it simply the "Album of the Year." Christgau complimented critic Greil Marcus for not just producing some rock group on a major label. Rather, the "Dean" stated, "… Marcus, has proven himself more resolute—instead of stooping to such mundane experiments he has caused an album to happen with one godlike act of unsullied critical will, and he has done it with a concept that epitomizes Rock '69. There is no other choice. *The Masked Marauders* is album of the year…" For Christgau, "artistic concept" triumphed over great musicianship. Marcus is congratulated for the illusory review and the fact that he masterfully took it one step further by creating an actual group to match the review.

The Story Behind the Story

Like most conspiracy theories and hoaxes, there will always be believers convinced that the grooves of Diety's album actually *do* contain the voices and instruments of John, Paul, George, Mick, and Bob. They will always believe *The Masked Marauders* review was the real deal. After all, the album's liner notes even supports their beliefs. "From their flimsy tin thrones of journalistic cynicism, they [critics] will continue to exclaim, 'It's all a shuck'… But truly devout rock listeners will not be swayed by such bitterness. They know a super session when they hear one." Sociologist Leonard explains the phenomenon, "Once the original version of a story is out, it sticks with people. It is easier to keep believing your position than to consider new evidence." In fact, one study from Winchester University in the UK suggests there is a good reason for the longevity of supposed plots and conspiracy theories—about everything from UFOs to the death of Princess Diana. People find them so romantic and interesting that they ignore the holes or contradictory facts in their arguments.

Music culture writer Bob Lefsetz opined on The Masked Marauders phenomenon. "It's hard to explain to the younger generation," he said, "that's something from the Sixties…. The greatest goal was not to score bread [money], but to put one over on those so busy running the gauntlet of life that they'd left their sensibilities behind, they were not only unable to take a joke, they couldn't see it." It seems people become fascinated by a particular media story and suspend belief when an alternative explanation may appeal to them for some cultural or political reason. There have been a number of examples that have captured the imagination of many generations. For example: "the Sandy Hook Elementary School murders were an elaborate hoax by the government to promote gun control.."

The Rock And Roll Detective wanted to discover the details behind The Masked Marauders hoax and delve further into the "making" of this piece of convincing rock and roll fiction. Believing that Al Kooper would be a good starting point, the Rock And Roll Detective interviewed the alleged Marauders' producer and inquired if his "no comment" to the media after the *Rolling Stone* review was due to his hiding the fact of the real super-session, helping the magazine with its put-on, or some other reason. Kooper was forthcoming during the interrogation. "I thought that whole episode was obviously a joke," he said. "And I was a little dismayed when people took it seriously. I treated it like the waste of time it actually was." Clearly, Kooper had no involvement in perpetrating the hoax and was annoyed at being name-checked in the story.

Next, the Rock And Roll Detective interviewed *Rolling Stone* founding Publisher and Editor Jann Wenner to see if he was surprised by the massive reaction of fans, readers, retailers, DJs, and others to the faux record review. "I *was* a little surprised," said Wenner. "It was such a blatant parody, and for this type of thing to be taken so seriously was funny." Wenner also confirmed that there was no connection between The Masked Marauders and the "Paul is Dead" hoax which both began to buzz in September 1969. However, Dr. Candy Leonard believes the perception of this supergroup album was clearly within the realm of probability and possibility given the established friendship of the respective artists. "These guys hung out, were friends and some jammed together, so why not believe in the possibility of doing an album together," she argued. "The Rolling Stones' 1968 *Rock And Roll Circus* film project made it even more plausible. The concept as represented in the record review was very compelling at the time, despite the little ironies and jokes that are easy for us to see in hindsight years later."

Not wanting to leave any (*rolling*) stone unturned, the Rock And Roll Detective decided to check the actual schedules of each alleged Masked Marauders participant to determine if they all could have actually met up in Hudson Bay Colony, Canada for the late April 1969 recording sessions, utilizing the as yet to be invented "80-track tape machine" as mentioned in the review. (Note: Only 16-track machines were in use by the end of 1969, and that was merely limited use.)

The Rolling Stones held some live rehearsals at their London warehouse in mid-April 1969. Prior to that, in early April, Mick Jagger and Keith Richards were seen on holiday in Positano, Italy. From April 17-30, 1969 The Rolling Stones resumed recording with Glyn Johns at Olympic Sound Studios in London, England, working on the songs "Monkey Man" and "Downtown Suzie." Also, during this period, while waiting for Keith Richards to arrive for an April 23 session, Mick Jagger, Charlie Watts, and Bill Wyman joined in a recorded jam session with keyboard player Nicky Hopkins and guitarist Ry Cooder. This was a genuine supergroup and super-session that resulted in an authentic studio release called *Jamming with Edward*, produced by Glyn Johns at Olympic Studio in London. Clearly The Rolling Stones were too busy to attend the alleged Masked Marauders sessions.

What were The Beatles doing in April 1969? The answer is similar to The Rolling Stones' itinerary. According to official EMI recording documents compiled by Mark Lewisohn in his book, *The Beatles Recording Sessions: The Official Abbey Road Studio Session Notes 1962-1970*, The Beatles could not have made it to Hudson Bay for any April 1969 sessions because their "dance card" was indeed quite full that month.

The Beatles' April 1969 London schedule included the following:

9 April—The Beatles are at an all-day photo session around the city

14 April—Lennon and McCartney work on "The Ballad of John and Yoko." Ringo Starr is filming "The Magic Christian" in London. George Harrison is at home in Henley

18 April—The Beatles finish recording "Old Brown Shoe"

20 April—The Beatles record parts of "I Want You" and "Oh! Darling"

22 April—John and Yoko record their heartbeats for the duo's *The Wedding Album*. Also, that day, The Beatles posed for one of their final photo shoots as a group

23 April—The Beatles worked on recordings of "Oh! Darling" and "Come Together"

26 April—Paul overdubs a lead vocal onto "Oh! Darling" and The Beatles work on recording "Octopus's Garden"

27 April—John and Yoko record another take of their heartbeats

30 April—The Beatles work on a lead guitar part for "Let It Be" and revive the recording of "You Know My Name (Look Up The Number)"

Meanwhile, Bob Dylan was busy with two different albums. On or about April 19, 1969, Dylan released his first album in over a year, *Nashville Skyline*. He would spend the next couple of weeks being interviewed in New York City by *Newsweek*, *Rolling Stone*, *New York Times*, *The Guardian*, *The Village Voice*, and others to promote the album. And by the last week of April, Bob Dylan found himself back in Nashville, Tennessee, at Columbia Studio A, working on sessions for his next album, *Self Portrait*.

In summation, it is elementary to conclude that The Beatles, The Stones, and Bob Dylan were quite busy with their own respective projects in late April 1969, and were witnessed, photographed, documented and/or recorded in England and America, but *not* in Hudson Bay, Canada.

Mythology Based in Reality
The concept of a faux record review that created the ultimate super-collaboration, while at the same time poking fun at such sessions, was a creative writing gem. But is there more

to the story? Could there have been some basis in fact for the selection of The Beatles, The Stones, and Dylan to form the "legendary" Masked Marauders? The Rock And Roll Detective dug beyond the headlines to discover the reality behind the myth.

Remember the aforementioned chance meeting at the airport in New York between Jann Wenner, Glyn Johns, and Bob Dylan? Once Johns returned to England, he jumped on the telephone to each of the members of The Rolling Stones and The Beatles, to gauge their interest—and hopefully agreement—with Dylan's supergroup idea. He tallied the votes as follows: "Keith [Richards] and George [Harrison] both thought it was fantastic, but then they would since they were both huge Dylan fans. Ringo [Starr], Charlie [Watts], and Bill [Wyman] were amicable to the idea as long as everyone else was interested. John Lennon didn't give a flat 'no,' but he wasn't that interested. Paul [McCartney] and Mick [Jagger] both said absolutely not." And with a mere two "no" votes, the idea died. But only weeks later, *Rolling Stone*'s Greil Marcus would suddenly give mythological life to Bob Dylan's supergroup concept. Was this a coincidence, or did the idea come from Jan Wenner being privy to Dylan's conversation with Glyn Johns?

Wenner discussed *why* Dylan likely proposed the idea. "It was the era for super groups," he said. "There was already Blind Faith, CSN and the Bloomfield, Kooper and Stills *Super Sessions* albums." When pressed on whether *he* had created the idea for The Masked Marauders hoax, Wenner clearly recalls it was Marcus' concept. However, when asked if Wenner had told Marcus about Dylan's proposed super-group collaboration with The Beatles and The Stones, Wenner admitted, "I might have mentioned it to him at the time." Clearly this "mention" likely influenced Marcus (even subconsciously) in his selection of the musicians listed in *The Masked Marauders* record review. Marcus did not reply to this author's request for an interview.

When asked if he learned anything about the success of the faux record review from a journalistic standpoint, Wenner chuckled and said simply, "Not a thing. It was just to have a laugh." Perhaps the most interesting fact about The Masked Marauders case was learning from Glyn Johns, as he revealed for the first time to the Rock And Roll Detective, "I was not ever aware of *Rolling Stone's* [*The Masked Marauders*] record review. I never heard of the review." In fact, Johns never even called Jann Wenner back to tell him that The Beatles and The Stones had turned down Bob Dylan's idea. Johns further stated, "I never attempted to revisit the idea of a supergroup to The Beatles, The Rolling Stones and/or Bob Dylan after that summer in July, 1969."

The timing for such a momentous collaboration would have to wait. As George Harrison recalled, "… it was a thing that went on in the late '60s and '70s, the big craze of super-groups and super-jams and everything was super-duper. Just getting some famous people together doesn't guarantee success." He cautioned, "More often than not, it's a clash of personalities and a big ego detour."

Although Bob Dylan never got the chance to merge his creative talents into a band with The Beatles and The Stones in 1969, he found another way. Some 19 years later, his concept was revived by a friend of his, albeit with a slightly different lineup. That group would be formed by Nelson Wilbury, Otis Wilbury, Lefty Wilbury, Charlie T. Wilbury Jr, and Lucky Wilbury... collectively, The Traveling Wilburys. And by the way, it turned out their real names were George Harrison, Jeff Lynne, Roy Orbison, Tom Petty, and Bob Dylan. Jan Wenner observed, "It is interesting that Dylan finally did get to be in a supergroup with the Traveling Wilburys." Candy Leonard adds, "The Traveling Wilburys is as close as we get to The Masked Marauders." In the opinion of the Rock And Roll Detective, the Traveling Wilburys' collaboration was indeed a great consolation for music fans.

Chapter Three
Did the CIA *Kill* Bob Marley?

The sweet smell of Jamaican ganja floated through the rehearsal space as Bob Marley and The Wailers began a live run-through of "I Shot The Sheriff." The group had already polished off rehearsals of "Baby We've Got A Date," "Trenchtown Rock," "Midnight Ravers," and "Rastaman Chant." Marley was playing his Gibson Les Paul Special guitar and singing a laid-back guide-vocal of the song in order to save his voice for the upcoming Smile Jamaica concert they would headline in two days on December 5, 1976. The irony of playing this particular song at this moment in time would not become immediately apparent as Marley sang one particular lyric: "Aiming to shoot me down…."

It was a typical hot and humid night in Jamaica. Marley and his Wailers were encamped at the Tuff Gong House, an old tropical mansion at 56 Hope Road in Kingston. The house had been transferred to Marley by his Island Records label boss, Chris Blackwell. Now it served as a home, rehearsal space, and all-around Rastafarian headquarters for soccer, "reasoning" sessions, and smoking ganja.

Once Marley was satisfied that he and the band were well-rehearsed on the song, it was time for the horn players to practice their part with the Wailers. But first, Marley decided to take a break. According to Wailers' keyboard player Tyrone Downie, "Bob had stepped out, cause the horns weren't on that record and the horn players wanted to play on it [at the concert]. So, we were working all the horn parts, and Bob got bored from hearing 'da-da-da.' He came out of the rehearsal room and went into the kitchen to get a grapefruit or something."

Marley began to peel a grapefruit as his manager, Don Taylor, returning from a meeting, entered the kitchen from outside. As Taylor approached Marley, chatting about business, the quiet tropical night was suddenly shattered by rapid staccato noises. Taylor recalled, "I heard a sound like firecrackers. It was Christmas in Jamaica. Firecrackers at this time of year are a common background noise. I paid little attention. Bob, however, looked startled and asked, 'Who the blood claat [Jamaican slang for 'Who the fuck?'] a bus [set off a] firecracker in my yard?'" Instantly, gunmen burst into the home firing wildly everywhere. In the rehearsal room, the Wailers scattered, with several members hiding in the bathroom. Bursts of *Pop, Pop, Pop, Pop* were randomly sprayed throughout the Wailers' rehearsal room as the musicians dove for cover. Back in the tiny kitchen, a single gunman stuck his gun into the partially open door from the outside and began to fire bullets blindly. Taylor took five bullets in the back of his body, but Marley stood his ground; he did not try to run, hide, or cower. He was an easy stationary target for any type of gun at close range in this narrow kitchen, but amazingly, Bob Marley was shot only once with a bullet that grazed his chest and lodged in his left arm. The firepower in the rehearsal room was immense with bullet holes everywhere, yet the Wailers all miraculously survived intact. As quickly as it had started, the shower of bullets abruptly ceased, and the gunmen sped away in their cars.

Marley vividly recalled a premonition of the actual assault: "Well, it was about 9:00 at night. What happened is that, about three nights before that… I had a vision, a dream that I was in a barrage of gunshots, ya know what I mean? The vision showed the mother [of my children, Rita,] got shot in the head. And that vision said, 'Don't run, stand up.' So, when the gunshot started, the first thing that came to my head was that vision. It said, 'Don't run.' So, I stand up ya know."

At the time of the incident, Bob's wife, Rita Marley, was in a car in the front yard. As she started up her car to leave the compound, she heard the shooters begin "firing wildly." She recalled, "The sound of the motor distracted one guy, who half turned around as he got off a shot toward where I knew Bob was speaking with Don Taylor." Immediately, bullets began to fly at her through the car. "I bent as low as I dared over the steering wheel and kept driving," she said, "until I felt a warm thing coming down my neck and I thought, shit, I'm dead! I'm dead, because a bullet hit my head." She played dead until the shooters left.

As soon as the coast was clear, Rita ran into the house to see if Marley was okay. She was in a state of shock and clearly more concerned with the condition of others than with her own injury. Fairly quickly, the police arrived and Marley, his wife, and Taylor were transported to the hospital, and the other Wailers all scattered back to their homes or other places to hide out. Incredibly, no one died that night, but Taylor was critically injured during the attack. He required surgery and a trauma flight to Miami, but he would survive. Bob Marley was treated and chose to leave the bullet in his elbow because surgery to remove it might have jeopardized his ability to ever play guitar again.

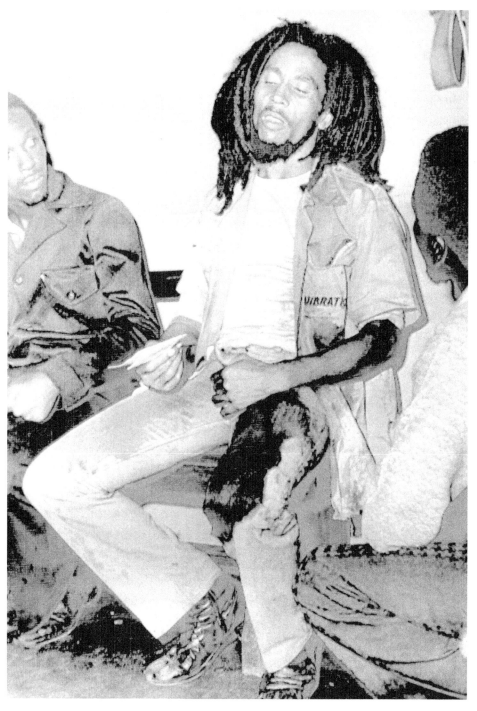

Bob Marley in the hospital with a bullet wound

What had just happened? Questions and conspiracy theories spread like wildfire by the time Marley, his wife, and his manager reached the hospital. Why would anyone want to kill Bob Marley, a worldwide superstar and the first to come from Jamaica? Was he even the intended target? Questions quickly emerged regarding the possible motive for this shocking assault. Was it gang-related? Was it possible, as some have suggested, that one of Marley's associates—Don Taylor or Alan "Skill" Cole—may have been involved in sketchy activities gone bad? Or, as some allege, was it a secret plot by the United States Central Intelligence Agency (CIA), fearful that Bob Marley's impending concert would sway votes to the Democratic Socialist leader Michael Manley in the upcoming national election? Did the CIA attempt to assassinate Bob Marley, and if so, would they try again? Questions and conspiracy theories began to spread like wildfire. Speculation centered on the source of the shooting, but also a second alleged attempt on Marley's life one day later.

"Get Up Stand Up/Stand Up For Your Rights"

Before one can begin to investigate the credibility of conspiracy theories that developed around Bob Marley's eventual death, it is crucial to understand the historical and political context from which they emerged. The attempted shooting of Bob Marley in December 1976 culminated a tumultuous year of increased political violence and gun deaths in Jamaica, along with allegations that the CIA was attempting to destabilize the country. The Rock And Roll Detective probed the genesis of political changes that had begun almost a year earlier involving Jamaican Prime Minister (PM) Michael Manley; Jamaica Labor Party (JLP) political opponent, Edward Seaga; U.S. Secretary of State, Henry Kissinger; and the CIA. In simple terms, it all boiled down to two factors: Cuba's Fidel Castro and a mineral called bauxite.

Michael Manley was born in Jamaica in 1924. His father, Norman Manley, led the country to its national independence in 1962. After serving in World War II, Michael Manley studied at the London School of Economics and Political Science. He returned to Jamaica in the 1950s and worked in journalism while entering the political arena. In 1962, Manley was elected the First Vice President of the Caribbean Bauxite and Mineworkers Union where he gained an understanding of the economic impact of bauxite on both Jamaica and U.S. multinational corporations, which were extracting and exporting it back to the U.S. for the manufacture of aluminum. Manley was later elected President of the People's National Party (PNP), and after leading his party to victory in the 1972 Jamaican general election became Prime Minister of Jamaica.

Bauxite is an aluminum ore, the world's main and essential source for the production of aluminum. In the 1970s, sixty percent of the U.S. supply of bauxite came from mining in the Caribbean, with the majority coming from Jamaica. Prior to Manley's assuming power in Jamaica, powerful U.S. multinational corporations such as Alcoa, Reynolds,

Michael Manley, Prime Minister of Jamaica

Kaiser, and Revere Copper and Brass had negotiated a very profitable deal with Jamaica. These companies were permitted to buy up roughly eleven percent of the land on the tiny island, which they subsequently mined and processed for aluminum manufacture in the United States. They also paid a meager amount in taxes to Jamaica in exchange, raking in huge profits in return. When Manley came into power in 1972, he decided he needed to negotiate a better deal for Jamaica by asserting greater control and ownership over the country's most valuable natural resource.

Manley's first salvo—to assert dominance over the multinational corporations—was to obtain their acquiescence to sell a fifty-one percent share in the mining and bauxite processing facilities to the Jamaican government. He followed up this bold move by discussing a plan for Jamaica to build its own processing plants, which meant Jamaica could then set the price of its own bauxite and sell to other countries as well. In essence, Manley was nationalizing the bauxite industry. Not surprisingly, this move struck fear in the hearts and wallets of the huge U.S. corporations which had extensive investments ($700 million) in mining and refining centers in the country, investments that were now vulnerable to Jamaica's demands.

Manley's actions caused the U.S. corporations to lobby Washington to "save" their businesses from ruin. Bauxite was a significant commodity that could slip out of the United States' control, and it was also a signal to U.S. Secretary of State Henry Kissinger that another small but politically significant country was beginning to move left towards socialism or communism. According to the North American Congress on Latin America (NACLA), the biggest U.S. fear was that "… demands for a bigger share of the capitalist pie introduced a new element of uncertainty and instability into the world capitalist system… further raising the specter of interruptions of supply, deterring needed investments… and adding to the risk of political enmities in the already uncertain world."

During his first term as Prime Minister, Manley began to advocate a form of Democratic Socialism as a means of raising the economy, health, education, and wages for his Jamaican countrymen. Manley's political party (the PNP) even adopted the slogan "Socialism is Love." Making matters worse in the eyes of the U.S., Manley established diplomatic relations with Cuba's Communist leader, Fidel Castro. Not only had Manley visited with Castro in Cuba, he was now looking to bring Cuban consultants to Jamaica to assist with domestic programs.

In the United States today, Bernie Sanders mirrors many of Manley's political views and ran popular primary campaigns as a Democratic Socialist Presidential candidate in 2016 and again in 2020. However, forty years earlier, the U.S. was still in the midst of the Cold War with the former U.S.S.R. and still vividly recalled the frightening Cuban Missile Crisis of years earlier. In the mid-1970s, the Ford Administration and Secretary of State Henry Kissinger were gravely concerned by Manley's political left-turn and feared another Caribbean island might fall prey to the "red menace" of Communism.

Kissinger flew to Jamaica in December 1975 to try to persuade Manley to change course from his current left-leaning policies, or else U.S.-Jamaican relations (including loans of financial assistance) "would be reviewed." Manley got the message but refused to back down from his mission to create a new political and economic system for his country.

Henry Kissinger, U.S. Secretary of State

Upon Kissinger's exit from Jamaica, American relations became frosty. The first change occurred with a sudden and mysterious increase of seven new members of the U.S. embassy staff in Kingston. According to investigative journalists Ernest Volkman and John Cummings, and other investigative sources, this move was "... a usually infallible omen of CIA agents moving in." It appeared that a U.S. movement was afoot to run a covert destabilization campaign against Manley's government and to support his conservative opponent, Edward Seaga. Manley's request for a $2.5 million loan from the U.S. Agency for International Development was quickly denied.

The CIA-planned destabilization operation in Jamaica had several components, including:

- Covert financial support for the opposition (JLP) party
- Creation of labor unrest
- Covert shipment of arms to opposition forces
- Economic destabilization
- Sponsorship of domestic media criticism of Manley's government
- Creation of anti-government middle-class groups to demonstrate against Manley
- Destruction of Jamaican tourism through inflated reports of armed gang violence

Manley was certainly wise to the CIA interference that rolled into his country. He knew, for example, that poor gang members in Kingston could not afford the machine guns and other strong arms that suddenly appeared on the island. According to Volkman and Cummings, Manley's security forces intercepted a CIA shipment of 500 machine guns being smuggled onto the island. The Prime Minister spoke out, albeit diplomatically, about American efforts to undermine his government. He indicated that, due to Jamaica's friendship with Cuba, in the course of exercising its "… rights of sovereignty and non-alignment, Jamaica was marked for punishment."

The Rock And Roll Detective uncovered a declassified "Top Secret" document prepared by the CIA that appears to confirm the rather close attention the CIA was paying to Prime Minister Manley. The April 1976 covert briefing document entitled "Intelligence Memorandum—Jamaica: In Pursuit of its National Identity" stated, "Prime Minister Manley's messianic commitment to bring about the social and economic assimilation of the black masses has pushed him steadily leftward. While claiming to be a democratic socialist, he has aroused fears that he has more revolutionary intentions… and has looked to Castro's Cuba for models and concepts of development as well as moral support in carrying out domestic reforms." The document detailed Manley's 1975 visit to Havana and his Cuban ties. It also set forth the political ammunition that the JLP used to exploit its opposition, cryptically concluding that the opposition party's "… electoral chances have greatly improved." Additionally, the document asserted that Manley will "choose multinational corporations [mining bauxite] as convenient targets for verbal blasts."

Throughout 1976, Jamaican citizens also became aware of the CIA's growing support for JLP leader Edward Seaga. Those who opposed the conservative politician and his alleged CIA connections began to write graffiti around Kingston that simply said "CIA-ga." The CIA took note of this fact in their Top-Secret assessment, stating Jamaica believed the U.S. was trying to destabilize the Manley government and noting that signs had popped up linking Seaga with the CIA.

Did the CIA try to destabilize Jamaica? Yes, according to former CIA operative Phillip Agee, who went so far as to detail the agency's Jamaican activities and to identify U.S. agents on the island. He wrote a book called *Inside The Company: CIA Diary*, which broke the longstanding code of silence on American intelligence interference efforts in other countries.

Agee went further in 1976, and publicly documented "how the CIA used money, guns and cocaine to undermine Michael Manley's administration." This did not go unnoticed at the top levels of the U.S. Government that were monitoring him. Again, the Rock And Roll Detective unearthed a declassified Top-Secret copy of the CIA's *The President's Daily Brief*, for September 17, 1976. President Ford's CIA dossier reported: "Agee arrived in Jamaica on September 9 for a highly publicized one-week visit. He appeared on television, held press conferences and made a number of speeches stressing the theme of US, and particularly CIA, efforts to destabilize Jamaica."

Behind closed doors, the CIA was quite annoyed at being outed in the middle of a clandestine campaign in Jamaica. The Rock And Roll Detective located one of these State Department attachés... err, CIA operatives. His diplomatic title was "Secretary for the Jamaican Consul," but Joey's (not his real name) real title was "CIA Deputy Chief of Station." Joey recalled Agee's visit: "Phillip Agee came to visit Jamaica under the sponsorship of Cuba's propaganda media arm, Cuban Prensa Latina. At his press conference [outing the CIA operatives in the U.S. Embassy in Jamaica] he screwed up a lot of [our] people." When asked if Joey was outed as a CIA agent by Agee, he laughed and responded, "That's what he [Agee] said. How do I dispute it? It is sort of like betting against yourself (laughing). So, I think it's safe to say my response is, 'no comment' (laughing)." The Rock And Roll Detective took that answer as an admission.

Publicly, the U.S. Government gave its official response to accusations of CIA meddling in Jamaica: "Contacted by the [*Jamaica*] *Daily News* yesterday after the disclosure made by Agee, the United States official mission in Kingston refused to verify or deny the former agent's charges. It is the policy of the United States Government not to comment on allegations of this kind."

Prime Minister Manley concluded the U.S. had interfered and had created destabilization. He emphatically stated, "They [the U.S.] deny it to this day, but I prefer the judgments of the heads of the Jamaica Security Forces at the time. Police, Army and Special Branch [internal security police] concurred that the CIA was actively behind the events. My common sense left me with no option but to agree." However, the CIA presence and covert operation in Jamaica did not necessarily include a plot to assassinate a reggae singer. Or did it?

Bob Marley—"You Got the Human Race/But This is a Rat Race"

Where did Bob Marley fit into the political rat race among the CIA, Manley's PNP, and Seaga's JLP? And did his music, politics, and lyrical expression make him a prime target for assassination by the CIA's operatives? Marley tried to walk a fine line between his country's two warring political parties. He had friends and acquaintances from both political parties and hosted representatives from both groups at his home on Hope Drive. He placed his belief in salvation for his country through his faith in the Rastafarian religion and God, not political leaders. He was heard to say, "Jah protect I [God will protect me]" on more than one occasion.

Dr. Gayle McGarry, a political scientist who followed Marley's political leanings, believes the reggae star leaned a bit more toward the leftist PNP party of Michael Manley. He told Marley biographer Roger Steffens, "But he did have some friends in Tivoli Gardens, which is the JLP turf. I remember some of those really seedy characters that would hang out at Hope Road." Tivoli Gardens is a West Kingston neighborhood in Kingston, Jamaica that was developed as a renewal project between 1963 and 1965. Unfortunately, the area has suffered from poverty, drug trafficking, violent gangs, and social unrest for decades.

Not unlike many pop, rock, and reggae stars of the 1960s and 1970s, Bob Marley occasionally used his public position—via his records, radio, and world tours—to express his political views. In April 1976, Bob Marley and the Wailers released an album to the world entitled *Rastaman Vibration*, which contained two songs that could be construed as political expressions of Marley's concern with the escalating violence in his country and desire for social justice for its most at-risk people.

One of these songs was called "War," and was based upon a speech by Ethiopia's emperor, Haile Selassie. Marley believed Selassie was the messiah of the Rastafarian religion to which he subscribed, and his close friend, Alan "Skill" Cole, suggested the idea of using the speech as lyrics for his song. The song is a plea for human rights and contains a powerful refrain. The original speech stated: "… And until the basic human rights are equally guaranteed to all without regard to race, there is war. And until that day, the dream of lasting peace, world citizenship, rule of international morality, will remain but a fleeting illusion to be pursued, but never attained… now everywhere is war."

The other political song on *Rastaman Vibration* was called "Rat Race." The lyrics were hard hitting and critical of the violence and bloodshed flowing in the streets of Jamaica in 1976. Marley was aware of the accusation that the CIA was supporting the JLP party, and he believed the CIA was likely involved in the sudden uptick in heavily-armed violence. He daringly name-checked the CIA in his lyrics as Marley sang that there would be political violence filling the city. And he was adamant that the Rastafarians would not work for the CIA.

If there was ever a moment for Marley to bring himself to the attention of the CIA, this would have done it! Interestingly, the lyrics to this song were never reviewed by CIA Deputy Chief Joey. When this author read him the lyrics, he responded, "That's reasonably political sounding, but I had never heard it. I still have reggae and calypso albums from the '70s and '80s, and they were all political." Apparently, it was no big deal to the CIA. The record—with these two political songs on it—reached the Top 10 on the album charts in the United States where Marley began to receive greater airplay on the radio.

Bob Marley was asked directly whether he thought the shooting at his home just days before the Smile Jamaica concert was political or not. In response, he said, "As for politics, I don't dabble in that. I stand up for my rights. I know what that is, see? I don't care who the guy [in power] is; because my right, is my right. My life, you know… all I have is my life." Although he was overtly apolitical in action, Marley's efforts to unify Jamaica would unwittingly draw him into the political arena.

The Smile Jamaica Concert—"Smile For Me Jamaica"

Politics aside, Marley deplored the unprecedented, escalating violence in Jamaica. Each political party wanted to run the island its own way, and if it meant blood running through the streets, so be it. Marley felt it was his responsibility to remain politically neutral as both the JLP and PNP attempted to sway him to their side. In earlier years, Marley had openly endorsed Michael Manley, yet he also remained good friends from childhood with Tivoli Gardens leader Claudius "Claudie" Massop, who was an enforcer for the JLP.

In his own way, Marley wanted to do something that would begin to heal the political violence and angry rhetoric that had spilled onto the streets of Kingston. He floated the idea of a benefit concert to be called "Smile Jamaica," and he recorded a song of the same name to promote the idea. It would be a peaceful, non-political concert. However, once word spread about the event, Marley was immediately approached by members of both political parties seeking his support via the concert. Although he sought a politically neutral concert, Marley soon discovered he needed government approval to put on the show.

By mid-1976, the Prime Minister had imposed a state of emergency and a gun ban on the island nation. The economy was sinking fast, and the ghettos were highly charged. "It was against this context that Bob felt he wanted to stage a show in Jamaica for Christmas," said Marley's manager, Don Taylor. "I saw this idea… as an opportunity to lift the spirits of the embattled, politically weary people."

As the famous saying goes, "No good deeds go unpunished." When Marley first approached Michael Manley in a meeting to seek approval, he explained that he did not want the Smile Jamaica concert politicized. Prime Minister Manley offered the Jamaica

House as a safe, neutral location for the show. At first, Marley agreed. However, in a year of political turbulence and turmoil, it was perhaps naive of him not to realize that others would want to spin the concert for their own political ends. Shortly after the announcement that Bob Marley and the Wailers would play the Smile Jamaica concert in several months' time on December 5, 1976, PM Manley called for a general election that would take place soon after the show. Clearly, this was a political move to make it appear as if Bob Marley and the Wailers would be appearing to support Manley's re-election campaign. After Manley co-opted the concert for his own political gain, Marley began to receive death threats from the political party opposing Manley.

According to Jeff Walker, who handled Marley's public relations, "Although there were efforts made on the Wailers' part to divorce it from politics, it was specifically announced as co-sponsored by the Ministry of Culture." Of course, once the general election of Manley was announced in conjunction with a government-sponsored Wailers show, Bob Marley was painted into a corner as an alleged supporter. It became difficult for him to back out or refute the political accusations he faced from Seaga's opposing party. The JLP opponents even began to politicize Marley's song "Smile Jamaica," claiming the lyrics were a partisan political slogan. They were quick to notice the similarity of the "Smile Jamaica" Tuff Gong record label artwork to PM Manley's party logo.

Bob Marley in association with
the Cultural Section
Prime Minister's Office
Presents
"SMILE
JAMAICA"
A public concert featuring
Bob Marley and the Wailers
Third World Light of Saba Drummers
Richard Ace Snr & Jnr St Anne's Dancers
M C's Winston Williams
Elaine Wint
Sunday December 5 at 5p.m.
NATIONAL HEROES PARK
(Kingston Race Course)
ADMISSION FREE!!!

In an effort to appease the JLP, who saw the concert as an endorsement of Manley and his Socialist government, Bob Marley was forced to compromise with the opposition party, especially given their early attempts to seek his endorsement. He agreed to move the concert away from Jamaica House to the National Heroes Circle. Using the Jamaica House seemed a slap in the face to the JLP because it was PM Manley's "home field." The move to a park with a graveyard honoring fallen Jamaican heroes appeared to appease the opposition somewhat, though it must have upset them when the concert posters appeared stating, "Bob Marley in association with the Cultural Section Prime Minister's Office Presents 'Smile Jamaica.'"

After a brief U.S. tour in the spring of 1976 in support of his *Rastaman Vibration* album, Marley had no more plans to tour that year. Walker, whose job it was to secure coverage of new releases for Island Records, needed to find another way to promote the Wailers' new album. The solution was to get them on TV. "This was still the pre-MTV era," said Walker. "The only way that you got rock and roll on television then was on *Don Kirshner's Rock Concert, Midnight Special,* or *Saturday Night Live*." Once Island heard about Marley's plan to perform a concert in December, they realized they had a promotional TV opportunity. Walker explained, "We knew that he would not be touring for a while, so it just made sense at that point to film the Smile Jamaica show so that we would have a tool to work with in promotion. So, getting footage on U.S. television was the strategy."

Meetings were held in London at Island Records' corporate office involving CEO Chris Blackwell, Charlie Nuccio (President of Island Records), and Jeff Walker to plan the concert film in Jamaica. Perry Henzell, who had directed the film "The Harder They Come," was tapped to direct. Peter Frank hired and managed a film crew that included cameraman Carl Colby. Walker met Colby for the first time once they all arrived in Jamaica. He recalled, "I did not learn of his background [as the son of former CIA Director William Colby] before that, but he was always very upfront about that. It was never an issue. And no one found it remotely suspect (laughing) that his dad had been in the CIA. Everybody's dad had been something. It doesn't mean that you were that as well." No one, including Bob Marley, gave it a second thought. Carl Colby was a recent graduate of Georgetown University where he studied philosophy. He was also a young filmmaker. Colby recalled, "I'd started making documentary films when I was at Georgetown… I became very interested in journalism and particularly documentary filmmaking."

Walker was with Blackwell at the Kingston Sheraton when word of the Marley shooting arrived via telephone call. They raced over to Hope Road within a half hour of the shooting and then on to the hospital. "We were with Bob when he was being treated. Taylor was in intensive care. The police were there, Michael Manley was there, and Chris Blackwell." Once Marley was released, he was hurried away under police escort and secluded in the Blue Mountains retreat called Strawberry Hill which belonged to

Chris Blackwell. The retreat was high above the chaos and violence of Kingston below, protected by 7,000 feet of rain forest and clouds that blanketed the mountains, and by machete-wielding Marley allies hiding in the trees surrounding the house.

The next morning Walker took Carl Colby to film and survey the carnage at Hope Road. They were provided an eyewitness account by Tyrone Brown (Wailers' keyboardist) and Aston "Family Man" Barrett (Wailers' bass player). The living room where the Wailers had been rehearsing was filled with bullet holes from wall to ceiling. In the kitchen, Walker noted that there was a lot of blood, yet not many bullet holes in the wall. He was told, "They had heard gunfire, then a gun appeared around the corner [of the kitchen door from the outside] and started shooting blindly into the kitchen," said Walker. "The bullets mostly happened to hit Don, not Bob. And only one bullet hit Bob." Marley associates Tyrone and Family Man indicated that the shooters were quite young—around seventeen—and they appeared as frightened as the people who were being targeted. They surmised that the gunmen appeared to fire randomly. They came in, did their number, and left quickly.

CIA Conspiracy Theory #1—Did the CIA Shoot Bob Marley?

Many conspiracy theorists believe that the Hope Road shooting was carried out by JLP puppets, directed and supported by the CIA. Essentially, this theory states that if Bob Marley (and the Wailers) were killed or severely injured, they would not be able to perform at the Smile Jamaica concert. The theory alleges that the CIA did not want the concert to go forward or appear to endorse Michael Manley for the upcoming election, and thus hatched a plot to kill Bob Marley in order to cancel the show.

Gunmen's night raid leaves Wailers manager Don Taylor, I-Threes Rita Marley wounded

MARLEY SHOT

As with all conspiracy theories, the proponents often sprinkle in a few facts, connecting the dots with a large helping of faith and fiction in order to make their argument. The following are the actual facts and eyewitness accounts that lead a reasonable person to conclude what really occurred in the assault on Bob Marley and his associates.

Interestingly, there are rules for setting up a proper CIA assassination. They were first codified by the CIA in a pamphlet for agents back in 1953. The booklet entitled *A Study of Assassination* was an essential training manual. Later a much more thorough study of proper CIA assassination rules was published in a book by former CIA operative and assassination expert Robert B. Baer, entitled *The Perfect Kill: 21 Laws for Assassins*. Baer was an accomplished and decorated CIA agent and winner of the Career Intelligence Medal. He authored a number of bestselling books on his career, including *See No Evil*, which was the basis for the film *Syriana*. He also served as a national security affairs analyst for CNN. The Rock And Roll Detective reviewed the pertinent rules for a CIA assassination in order to compare them to the facts of the Bob Marley shooting.

Addressing these rules one at a time, let's compare the actual facts of Marley's shooting to each rule in order to determine if his assault fits the CIA standards for a "perfect kill."

1. *The Bastard Has To Deserve It*

It would be hard to argue that Bob Marley deserved to be assassinated. First of all, Marley did not hold a position of elected or appointed power in the Jamaican government. He could not influence, promulgate, or perpetuate any policies for the people of his country. In the CIA's 1953 training manual, permitting a killing requires a justification for political assassination: "Murder is not morally justifiable…. [However] assassination of persons responsible for atrocities or reprisals may be regarded as just punishment. Killing a political leader whose burgeoning career is a clear and present danger to the cause of freedom may be held necessary." Under the CIA's own standards of justification, Marley did not qualify for assassination.

Marley did not belong to either political party. In fact, he spread the word that his Smile Jamaica concert was intended to bring both sides together to foster peace. Marley's lyrics in the song "Rat Race" also did not warrant a government-sponsored assassination; it was a harmless snipe from a pop star. If that was enough to trigger assassination, then why didn't the CIA assassinate its former operative, Phillip Agee, when he came to Jamaica and outed the names of fellow agents in the covert CIA operation?

Although PM Manley used Marley's politically neutral concert to create the appearance of promoting the Smile Jamaica show for his re-election, nothing could have been further from the truth. When Marley did eventually play the concert, there were no speeches, signs, or political party slogans on stage during his 90-minute performance. It was an entirely peaceful musical concert. Clearly Bob Marley was neither a "justified" target, nor did he deserve to be assassinated.

2. *Make It Count/Make It Final*

The act of assassination is designed to alter the calculus of power in your favor. If the CIA had assassinated PM Manley, the elected leader of the country, that would have clearly altered the calculus of power. Without a compelling leader to take his place, Manley's party was vulnerable to losing the upcoming election to Edward Seaga, his opposition candidate.

However, the goal here is to make the kill "final" in order to change power in the government. In this case, neither Bob Marley nor anyone else at Hope Road died, and none of them held positions of power. If Bob Marley had died, it would not have altered the calculus of those in power, and his death would likely have been spun by PM Manley to gain sympathy votes, thus harming the alleged objective. The balance of power would have likely remained unchanged because Marley's death would have served to make him a martyr in his country.

3. *Make Sure It Is an Efficient Act*
An assassination's purpose is intended to make sure the targeted individual is killed quickly and efficiently, and without the unnecessary taking of innocent lives. Marley received a bullet in the arm that did not kill him. The essential point of assassination is the death of the subject, and death must be absolutely certain. If Marley was the target, then the other victims were innocent. Why was Rita Marley shot in the head, and why did Don Taylor get shot five times?

According to eyewitnesses, the shooters did not spend time surveying their intended target(s) to see if they were dead. They left immediately after spraying the house with bullets. There was no police present, no guards, and no resistance or defensive return-fire that would cause them to leave without ensuring that the intended victim or victims were actually dead. This was hardly the model of a CIA or professional tactical assassination.

4. *Double Up On Everything*
In the case of the Marley shooting, eyewitness reports stated that only one shooter appeared in the kitchen. According to Rita Marley, he was distracted by her car starting up, and he was shooting around a doorway, even though Bob Marley was an easy, non-moving target. The small, narrow kitchen where Marley was standing would have been a simple, close-range kill shot for an experienced professional. Marley did not try to run, duck, hide, or move when the single shooter opened fire. Don Kinsey, a musician in the kitchen at the time, described the gunman aiming in a sort of vague, general direction. With no redundancy built in for bad aim or nerves, there was effectively no back-up plan or second shooter prepared to kill Marley.

5. *Employ a Trustworthy Assassin*
When the CIA employs a proxy to carry out an assassination, operatives do extreme vetting and use a professionally trained killer. Typically, they look for an experienced veteran who has marksmanship skills with all types of weapons and has been trained for assassinations (not local teenagers). The CIA manual demands expertise. "If special equipment is to be

used, such as firearms or drugs, it is clear that he must have outstanding skill with such equipment." The assassin has to be cold and calculating when executing the assassination under changing conditions.

In this case, witnesses described teenagers as young as seventeen carrying out the shootings. They were nervous, rushed, and randomly shot up the rehearsal space and kitchen. With absolutely no resistance from anyone in the home, they were unable to kill even one person, especially Bob Marley who stood tall and never moved. Clearly these attackers did not fit the mold of CIA assassins.

6. *Don't Shoot At Everyone In the Room*

As previously described, the shooters violated this rule by blindly scattering bullets throughout the rehearsal room. The shooter in the kitchen where Marley and Taylor were located reportedly shot blindly from around a door. Very unprofessional!

Ex-CIA operative Robert Baer opined, "When does blindly spraying bullets in all directions ever lead to a sought-after outcome?" His answer is that it doesn't; and it didn't work in the Marley shooting either. Baer went on to describe the "kill everyone haphazardly" plan as a sign of insecurity—certainly this is a profile that would fit a sloppy gang of inexperienced teens, rather than professionally trained CIA hit men.

7. *Keep Your Enemy In a State of Ignorance And Confusion*

Of course, the CIA does not tell its intended victim(s) it is planning or threatening to kill them. In this case, Claude Massop, leader of the Tivoli Gardens gang, had warned Marley (from prison) in advance that his lieutenant was coming after him. In addition, according to music journalist Vivien Goldman, who was staying at the Hope Road compound in the days before the shooting, "Around five-thirty, one morning I woke, restless, and looked out. Bob was standing in the otherwise quiet yard under the big mango tree, talking angrily to two men whom I couldn't see clearly. There was something ominous in their exchange." Apparently, the warnings began to increase shortly before the actual shooting. Bad guys, enforcer-types, and sketchy characters were observed hanging out near 56 Hope Road in the days leading up to the concert. Once again, this type of action is not the *modus operandi* for a CIA operation, especially if they planned to use the Tivoli Gardens gang as a proxy for their killing. Assassinations have a much higher degree of success when the intended target is not warned or threatened in advance.

8. *Leave the Country Immediately After the Assassination, and Never Revisit the Scene of the Crime*

The Jamaican police never solved the shooting case and never identified by name any of the alleged shooters. Witnesses, however, saw the getaway cars heading back to Tivoli

Gardens (downtown), Massop's gang territory. Conspiracy theorists lump the presence of filmmaker Carl Colby in with this assassination attempt because his father had once been the director of the CIA. This theory, however, falls flat regarding the shooting. First of all, Colby was at the hotel with the other filmmakers at the time of the shooting. Once he heard about it, Colby asked, "And I thought, shot for what? That was really my question: He's a musician, why would he be shot?" If Colby had anything to do with it, why didn't he disappear and fly back to the U.S. immediately? Why did he go with Jeff Walker the next morning to survey the scene of the crime? Why did Colby accompany Walker to Marley's hidden location after he checked out of the hospital? Why did he stick around to interview Marley the day after the shooting? And finally, why did Colby end up as the *only* cameraman onstage to film the first 75 minutes of Marley's Smile Jamaica concert before a second cameraman showed up to help? The facts just do not comport with the rule here. The CIA training manual emphatically states, The killer(s)' "safe evacuation after the act is absolutely essential." CIA assassins never stick around after the attack, *especially* when they have failed. In fact, mafia hitmen don't stick around either!

9. *A Failed Assassination Attempt Gives the Victim an Aura Of Invincibility and Power, While Diminishing the Assassin's. Don't Miss*!

Two days after the attempt on his life, Bob Marley bravely decided to perform at Smile Jamaica before 80,000 Jamaicans, all looking for salvation from the one man who could bring them together. He was a man who had survived a hail of bullets and was now singing like a wounded lion to bring justice to his island and salvation and comfort to the downtrodden. Marley was angry—fuming at being shot, enraged by "politricksters" who coopted his peaceful and apolitical intentions, and mad at the social injustice he saw in his country. His songs and words reflected his emotions.

On this special night, Marley's heroic performance catapulted him well beyond mere pop-star recognition to almost deity-like status. Filmmaker Colby remembers his impression of Marley as he filmed him onstage: "Shit! This is not a rock concert; this is like a religious experience, like they'd seen God or something." Marley's tough, gritty performance demonstrated his determination to follow through on his promise and to bring people together with his music. According to Jeff Walker, "The film of Smile Jamaica was an incredible piece of history and should have been released, but it wasn't." (Note: The almost complete concert is now available on YouTube). At the end of the concert, Marley bravely unbuttoned his shirt to show off the bandaged bullet wound on his arm, letting people see the sacrifice he had made for them... and then walked off the stage.

Once again, if the CIA was really concerned with Bob Marley, he never would have survived long enough to appear on stage. Surviving his brush with mortality gave Marley power, invincibility, and an almost biblical status that would remain with him the rest of

his life. He became known as a man willing to risk his life for the betterment of the poor and to speak up for injustice. On that night the *wounded lion* became Bob Marley the *revolutionary*.

In the words of former CIA operative Baer, "As is not the case in horseshoes, there are no points for coming close in assassination." It is common sense to conclude that the facts of Marley's assault pointed more towards sloppy gang-related violence than a professional CIA hit. Interestingly, in his book, Baer provides a historical chronology of known political assassinations, spanning from 44 BC (Julius Caesar) through 2008 (Hajj Radwan). Noticeably absent from the list is Bob Marley. He reiterated, "Conspiracy theorists are people who prefer their myths and beautiful lies to facts." In this case, to believe that the CIA tried to shoot Bob Marley is to believe in "myths and beautiful lies."

Yet another reason the CIA was not involved in the alleged assassination attempt of Bob Marley was the ongoing U.S. Congressional oversight scandal that erupted in 1975 and flowed into 1976. The concern over CIA agents running rogue operations around the globe led to parallel House and Senate investigations chastising the CIA for past illegal activities, including assassination attempts against foreign leaders. These Congressional investigations, headed up by House representative Otis Pike and Senator Frank Church, delved into all aspects of CIA operations.

During the controversial election year of 1976 in Jamaica, the CIA was under a daily virtual microscope back in the U.S. Although it was not held accountable for certain covert actions such as disrupting governments, it was called onto the carpet about foreign assassinations. The Pike and Church Commission completed its findings shortly after Jimmy Carter was elected President in the fall of 1976. Although the committees did not recommend abolition of all covert actions by the CIA, it called for an "absolute prohibition of assassination."

The Rock And Roll Detective interviewed Colonel Oliver North about the Pike and Church recommendations prohibiting CIA foreign assassinations, as well as his assessment of President Gerald Ford on the subject. North was a decorated U.S. Marine Corps Lt. Colonel during the Vietnam War, winning both the Silver Star and Purple Heart. In 1981, President Ronald Reagan appointed him deputy director of the National Security Council (NSC). Although many people recall he was implicated in the Iran-Contra scandal, involving the supply of arms to Iran in exchange for U.S. hostages, many are unaware that his convictions were overturned and all charges against him were dropped in 1991 by a federal judge. North went on to publish a number of books about his military career and hosted a military program called *War Stories* on cable television.

Despite losing the 1976 election to Jimmy Carter, Gerald Ford was still president of the United States when Bob Marley was shot. According to North, "All of the Pike/Church recommendations had been fully implemented by the Ford Administration by this time [prior to the Marley shooting] including an absolute proscription [ban] on assassination."

The other factor to weigh here is the legacy of an outgoing president. President Ford was *not* elected to office by the citizens of the United States. Instead, he assumed power when President Richard Nixon resigned from the presidency in an effort to avoid prosecution from the Watergate scandal. President Ford is remembered for issuing a full and complete pardon to former President Nixon, and many historians believe this was a significant reason Ford lost the 1976 general election to Jimmy Carter.

Surely, Ford would not have wanted to further tarnish his legacy by secretly authorizing the assassination of a reggae pop star (who held no elected or appointed governmental power) at the end of his only term of office. Colonel North echoed these sentiments. He recalled, "I did have several opportunities to interview him [Ford] during my tenure on the NSC staff. In my humble opinion, there is absolutely no way outgoing President Ford would have authorized any such [assassination] activity in his waning moments in the Oval Office." In fact, such an action seems patently absurd, especially considering Ford had been the one to adopt the rules prohibiting CIA assassinations in the fall of 1976.

It is interesting to note that *none* of the declassified CIA documents mention any ongoing surveillance of Bob Marley or any analysis of his lyrics, political action, domestic activities, travel within the country or to the U.S., or any other activity. The same holds true for declassified FBI records on the artist: nada... zero. Since mandatory 35-year declassification rules are now in effect, there would have been documents released on Marley if the CIA had been targeting him for surveillance or an assassination plan. None have turned up.

A CIA declassified document dated December 1976 mentioned Marley having been shot while rehearsing for the Smile Jamaica concert. The CIA report gleans this information from hearsay found in local newspaper reports and not firsthand source accounts from actual CIA agents stationed in its local consulate. One paragraph contains the erroneous opinion of the report's author, namely that the concert was part of the PNP's election campaign and Marley was a political ally of PM Manley. When shown this report, Marley's close friend, artist Neville Garrick, declared, "Its alla lie, a blood-clot lie!" He continued, "None-a this whole report is true. The concert was never political; it was never part of the PNP campaign!" Garrick is correct.

A review of the actual Smile Jamaica filmed concert footage (which remains commercially unreleased, but bootlegged) demonstrated that it took place as Bob Marley planned—a show of music and only music. No political speeches or propaganda were planned, prepared, or made during the entire program. There were also no political signs, slogans, or messages on or near the stage. It has been documented that Marley was upset when the Jamaican government stated it was sponsoring the event and again when PM Manley scheduled a general election to take advantage of the positive PR generated by the concert.

The CIA report (taken from newspaper accounts) also noted that the assailants had not been identified, and concluded, "The assailants may simply be enemies of Marley or one of his associates. Contributing to this view is the fact that, while the newspapers have given the shooting prominent coverage, the reporting has been curiously uninformative." The CIA was not concerned with a reggae star because it was too busy carrying out its own covert agenda against the person in power, PM Manley. The re-election of Manley was the U.S. State Department's biggest concern, and Bob Marley was simply not considered a relevant political target.

CIA operative Joey concurred. "Marley had no power," he said. "It doesn't make sense that he would be a target. He might have had some not too subtle political references in his music. But that doesn't rise to the level of assassination." In his conclusion, Joey revealed to the Rock And Roll Detective, "I would have known about any attempt on Marley's life if it had originated with the U.S. Government. I have no question in my mind that *if* this was going on, I would have known about it." The fact that the CIA report of the Marley shooting attempt came exclusively from a local newspaper account, and not first-hand from a CIA observer, certainly seems to confirm the credibility of Agent Joey's statement.

Some have also suggested that Bob Marley was not necessarily the target of the shooting assault at Hope Road. One theory for the shooting involves Marley's manager, Don Taylor. At a young age, Taylor was left on his own. He grew up hustling cruise tourists in Kingston and working deals with bar operators, selling cigarettes or washing cars—anything to get by. Even as his star rose and he became a music impresario, old habits die hard. He was alleged to have a bad gambling habit at the time. Rita Marley did not altogether trust Taylor, recalling in her memoir that he was "… a thief, unable to turn over what he should have [to Bob]." The shorting of his client's fees was alleged to have been due to Taylor's gambling debts. He also had another expensive habit according to Rita. She remembered, "Bob caught Don on cocaine binges many times, on the job yet unable to work properly under that influence." After the shooting, Wailers' keyboard player and eyewitness Tyrone Downie reflected on the assault and possible motives. He said, "And what was going through my mind was, what's going on? Who did this? Maybe they followed Don Taylor here, 'cause he was a gambler." Don was in the kitchen with Marley and Taylor at the time of the shooting and theorized that if the gunman had wanted to kill Bob, he would have. Instead, it was Don Taylor who took five bullets to his backside.

Yet another associate of the reggae singer was rumored to have been a target for the shooting. Marley was close friends with Allan "Skill" Cole, regarded by many as the most talented football (soccer) player in Jamaica at the time, thus earning the nickname "Skill." The Skill Cole rumor, as published in a number of sources, alleged that Cole was involved in a horse race that went wrong. The "plan" had allegedly been hatched at Marley's home on Hope Road. The angry participants took a financial drubbing and allegedly sought reimbursement from Marley. Again, Tyrone Downie wondered if Cole was the real target of the shooting. "There were so many things running through my head. Skill Cole was in some problem with horse racing, and we were just waiting." It is also interesting to note that Cole was AWOL at the time of the shooting and had apparently left Jamaica shortly before the night in question. Of course, common sense dictates that if gamblers killed Marley over a debt owed, the gamblers would never get their money!

If Marley was a target for elimination by the CIA, the spy agency certainly had multiple opportunities in its own backyard. Bob Marley played 93 concert dates in U.S. cities from 1976 through his last show in 1980. Adding in 14 more days for travel to and from the U.S., Marley spent a minimum of 107 days in the U.S. during this time period, not including any undocumented dates he may have entered for business or to visit his mother. Never once was an attempt made on his life in the U.S., nor was he ever arrested for his open use of marijuana, which was illegal at the time. Never once did the U.S. government try to revoke his passport, visa, or work permits in order to prevent him from touring or even visiting the U.S. According to Publicity Director Jeff Walker, who toured with Marley, "I had worked with Bob for years. We never had any problem with law enforcement or immigration on the U.S. tours. You know, he was easy to find. There was pot [marijuana] everywhere we went (laughing), and Bob was singing about 'Rasta don't work for no CIA.'" The U.S. government did not harass Marley or prevent the sale of his records or the radio and TV airplay of his music. He was free to go about his business and take advantage of the country's free speech rights, all without any U.S. governmental interference whatsoever.

In the lead up to the Smile Jamaica concert, the followers of the JLP and PNP were clashing hard. The JLP was angry after PM Manley had co-opted the concert for his own political purposes. Rita Marley felt that her husband was leading a dangerous life, simply because his music had brought attention to the island and fame to Bob. She commented, "You [Bob] may be up there, but you're also *out* there…. Eventually—inevitably—he was targeted for helping bring stabilization to the country, to appease the ghetto youth." Rita was aware of the scheduled election and the violence that was occurring. To her, it was a domestic matter between rival parties/gangs. "When it was time for politics," she said, "the party bosses would hand out guns and say, 'Go kill the opposition.'"

Claudie Massop was the leader and strongman of the Tivoli Gardens gang at the time of the shooting. His gang was later renamed the "Shower Posse Gang." They were politically aligned with Edward Seaga's JLP. There are two theories for the origin of the name "Shower Posse": one was that the gang was "showered" with gifts and promises of politicians, and the other referenced the manner in which the gang "showered" opponents with bullets.

Massop and Marley had been friends since childhood and were still good friends at the time of the shooting. However, Massop had been locked up in prison by the Gun Court at the time of the Marley assault, a strict measure instituted by Manley in mid-1976 to remove guns from the streets. Later, reggae singer King Sounds revealed to journalist Vivien Goldman, "I was in the room [during the recording of *Exodus*] when Claudie [Massop] said to Bob, 'True, Skip [Marley's nickname], this coulda never happen if me was outta jail.'" Claudie Massop, the enforcer, was sidelined and replaced by Lester Lloyd Coca-Cola (aka "Jim Brown"), and this prevented Massop from stopping his own gang from lashing out at Bob Marley. In fact, Massop even tried to warn Marley by telephone that Brown and his men were planning to get him (again, warnings are not part of CIA assassination protocol). It appears that Massop's absence provided a convenient opportunity for his number two man, "Jim Brown," to establish his street credibility and emerge from under the shadow of Massop. According to Laurie Gunst, author of *Born Fi' Dead*, an expert on Jamaica's gangland history at this time, The shooting "was a way for Jim Brown to show Seaga he was the boss while Claude [Massop] was in prison, to impress Seaga. However, it was not a Seaga-sanctioned hit."

When asked about the shooting in a subsequent television interview, Marley cryptically revealed his knowledge of the rogue gang shooting.

Interviewer: You never saw the gunmen?

Marley: At that time, no.

Interviewer: But you know who did it?

Marley: Yah, I know that.

Respected international Bob Marley scholar and historian Roger Steffens has studied this event for decades. He reached the same conclusion as this author, stating, "I have found *no proof* that the CIA was directly involved in the assassination attempt. It seems to have been a rogue operation organized by the JLP's gangsters. It was sort of, 'won't someone rid me of this troublesome priest' kind of operation."

Although there are many theories for the attempt on Bob Marley's life, the Jamaican Police never officially solved the crime. As for any CIA involvement, Jeff Walker is adamant in his conclusion: "It is absolute horseshit that the CIA had anything to do with the assault on Bob Marley's house. It is absolute horseshit. If anyone in the CIA really wanted him dead that night, he would have been dead!" This sentiment was also echoed by CIA operative Joey. "From everything else that happened that night, it didn't look like anyone actually intended to kill anyone. It was either inept or to send a signal," said Walker.

Had Bob Marley been killed and the Smile Jamaica concert cancelled, he would have likely been christened a martyr for social justice by the people of his country. The purpose or goal of assassination is for the killer's allies to gain power as a result of the political target's death, but in this case, a martyred reggae star would have likely caused the opposite effect.

A few conspiracy theorists believe that the bullet lodged in Marley's arm (which he refused to have surgically removed) ultimately killed him. The speculation is that lead from the embedded bullet seeped into Marley's bloodstream, causing lead poisoning and ultimately death. Decades after the event, Dr. Michael Hunter, a forensic pathologist, reviewed all of the medical records of the reggae star over his lifetime, including a subsequent event in 1980 where Marley collapsed while jogging in New York's Central Park.

Hunter concluded that there were no prior visits or reports that would give rise to a diagnosis of lead poisoning. He stated, "If Bob's collapse in Central Park was from lead poisoning, he would have experienced muscle weakness and vomiting years before. There is no evidence of this [in the medical records]." Therefore, Hunter concluded that lead poisoning was not the cause of Bob's collapse or ultimate death.

The judgments of CIA operatives Baer and Joey, Jeff Walker, Roger Steffens, and the NSA's Colonel North all confirm the conclusion reached by the Rock And Roll Detective. No primary evidence or any eyewitnesses exist to prove the causal connection or conclusion of CIA involvement in the shooting attempt on Bob Marley's life. Rather, all of the first-hand evidence leads to the exact opposite conclusion, namely that the CIA was not involved in or even aware of the shooting attempt. When closely analyzing the facts in this case, this conspiracy theory collapses. However, there is yet another conspiracy theory involving the CIA and Bob Marley…

Conspiracy Theory #2—A Second Attempt on Marley's Life?

Once Bob Marley's wounds were bandaged, and after a brief conference with PM Manley, he was cleared to leave the hospital. He was secreted out under heavy police guard and driven up to Blackwell's Blue Mountains retreat. "I went up there that same night and brought up a walkie talkie so that we could all be in touch," recalled Jeff Walker. Eventually, Marley went to bed to rest and recover from the traumatic ordeal.

The next morning, after Walker and Carl Colby spent time filming the aftermath at Hope Road, they returned to the compound where Marley was recuperating and considering whether to postpone or perform at the Smile Jamaica show scheduled for the next day. "After filming the aftermath of the shooting, Carl [Colby] and I went back to Chris [Blackwell]'s retreat to be with Bob. Carl was with me the entire time period between the Hope Road filming, back to the retreat, and through the time of the actual

Smile Jamaica concert," said Walker. This is important because Walker was witness to all of Colby's movements and activities at the compound, the site of the next alleged CIA attempt against Marley's life.

That same day, Walker joined Marley and his closest associates to discuss the impact of the shooting and whether Marley should still play the show. Was the objective to stop the show or some other message? Marley had to weigh his promise to perform against the fear of another attack when he would be unprotected and exposed to thousands of people up on stage. He relayed his fear to his friend, Neville Garrick, "Bwoy, dem say the concert say is a setup fe mek dem come finish the job. Tomorrow we will know what fe do."

Marley was clearly tormented by the assault and the realization that people he trusted and considered friends had tried to kill him. He had always moved easily among all of Kingston's gangs and differing political factions. It was a moment of great angst for the musician. He had until the next day to make up his mind what to do. During this crucial time, conspiracy theorists believe that a second attempt on Marley's life took place inside the seemingly secure Strawberry Hill compound.

Conspiracy theories are born from growing suspicion that institutions such as the government and mainstream media cannot be trusted, producing claims that certain events did not happen as officially reported, or that events that never occurred actually did. Today, in the face of lightning-fast social media platforms such as Twitter and Facebook, conspiracy theories can gain speed and momentum and reach a broader audience at a faster rate than traditional news, even if the story originated decades ago.

A form of alternative media ecosystem develops which births, coordinates, and promotes conspiracy theories that undermine the trust of readers with regard to a given story. In the case of Bob Marley, there is another dubious theory about CIA involvement in another possible assassination attempt.

According to his website, Alex Constantine is "devoted to exposing the CIA's unrelenting electromagnetic (EM) victimization of the world's preeminent anti-fascist researcher, Alex Constantine…. No other American writer has fought so tirelessly to expose such matters as CIA domestic terrorism, assassination, the mind control epidemic, controlled demolition of the World Trade Center, the innocence of O.J. Simpson, and the ultimate triumph of post-WWII Nazism." He claims that, for most of his life, he has been the target of the CIA's experts in EM mind control.

As part of this lifelong crusade, Constantine focused passionately on one conspiracy theory that asserts that the CIA deliberately gave Bob Marley cancer the day before the Smile Jamaica concert. In February 2002, he published an article for *High Times* magazine which has been widely and *wildly* spread throughout the internet ecosphere.

In a nutshell, his theory contends the following:

- A person *claiming* to be part of the Island Records film crew, who *didn't have a camera, talked his way past* machete-bearing Rasta guards to get to Marley
- His name was Carl Colby, son of late CIA Director William Colby
- The band (Bob Marley and the Wailers) prepared for the concert at Blackwell's compound
- A gift of a pair of boots (aka soccer cleats) was delivered to Bob Marley, according to "a witness" (no name was provided)
- Cinematographer Le Lew-Lee was "close friends" with unnamed members of the Wailers
- Lew-Lee "believes that Marley's cancer can be traced to the boots"
- Lew-Lee described the event (via hearsay from Wailers who were *not* present): "He [Marley] put his foot in and said, 'Ow! A friend go in [the boot] there'… he said, 'let's [get] in the boot,' and he pulled a length of copper wire out—it was embedded in the boot."
- Constantine asked, "Had the wire been treated chemically with a carcinogenic toxin?"
- The appearance of Carl Colby at Marley's residence was certainly "provocative"
- "And so was Colby's subsequent part in the fall of another black cultural icon, O.J. Simpson, 20 years later"
- After the shooting, *a rumor circulated* that the CIA was going to "finish off" Marley

If we understand this conspiracy theory correctly, Carl Colby snuck into Marley's hideaway, fooled machete-wielding Rastas, and claimed to be a cameraman without a camera. He was the son of then-retired CIA director William Colby, which made him guilty by association of being in the CIA and because "he snuck in." While the Wailers were allegedly rehearsing, Colby gave a gift of soccer boots or cleats to Bob Marley. Bob put them on and a copper wire embedded in one boot, tainted with cancer, cut his big toe and thus gave him cancer. Colby was also guilty because he later lived next door to murder victim Nicole Brown Simpson, and testified that O.J. Simpson was an abusive husband, leading to Simpson's downfall. Finally, this was all confirmed by an unattributed rumor that circulated, after the Marley shooting, that asserted the CIA wanted to finish him off. But wait! There's more.

Don Taylor, Bob's manager at the time, survived the shooting at Hope Road and was sedated in a U.S. Miami hospital having surgery at the time Marley was hiding out at Strawberry Hill in Jamaica. Despite his absence from these events, and without any eyewitness account, Taylor shared his conspiracy theory that the CIA tried to finish off

Marley. "I would later find out that among the crew hired to come to Jamaica was the son of a prominent CIA official who had traveled under an alias. This information convinced me that the CIA had been behind the plot to kill Bob Marley because of his influence on Jamaican politics and on the wider world."

Timothy White was a noted rock music journalist who began his career with the *Associated Press*, moved on to write stories for *Crawdaddy*, and later served as an editor at *Rolling Stone* magazine. He authored several books on rock and roll. At the end of his career, he served as editor of *Billboard* from 1991 until his death in 2002.

In White's book, *Catch A Fire*, his biography of Bob Marley, he added fuel to the conspiracy fire of this CIA theory when he stated, "One of the 'Smile Jamaica' film crew had also found his way up to the camp *minus his camera*. The Rastas had no inkling of it, but the cameraman was Carl Colby, son of CIA director William Colby." White's book does not provide a source for this comment and is possibly a rumor heard by the author while researching his book. No eyewitnesses were ever quoted.

For many years Keidi Obi Awadu (a writer, speaker, and researcher) has distributed his writings and videos on multiple conspiracy theories. He is involved with a think-tank called "Project for Africa" and founded the "7th Millennium of Consciousness." He has written numerous books, including *Dirty Work: The CIA in Africa*, and he authored the *Conscious Rasta Report*. In a documentary on the *Strange Universe* TV program, he provided his conclusion regarding the Marley/CIA cancer theory:

"It seems to be without a shadow of doubt that yes they [the CIA] had targeted Bob Marley for neutralization, and this [cancer by injection in the soccer boot] would be a prime vehicle for doing that."

Let us examine the actual facts of this event and see how they compare to the CIA conspiracy theory spread across the world by a number of convinced parties.

Alex Constantine claims the CIA has been shocking him for years with EM devices, so he clearly has a distrust of government and an axe to grind. The Rock And Roll Detective unearthed the facts of what really happened (and did not happen) at the time of Marley's stay at the Blackwell retreat before he decided to play the Smile Jamaica concert.

Constantine asserted that Colby was "claiming to be part of the Island Records film crew" and that he did not have a camera and talked his way past guards to get to Marley. He also noted that Carl Colby was the son of former CIA Director William Colby. In fact, Carl Colby was a young documentary filmmaker who personally knew Chris Blackwell, CEO of Island Records and the film's production director. He was legitimately hired by Island Records (under his real name) to be part of the crew. Therefore, no attempt was made by Colby to sneak in under false pretenses. Here is what Colby himself remembers from that day when he asked the film crew about their plans:

And suddenly Jeff [Walker] said to me that we're going up to [Chris] Blackwell's house, we're going to where Bob's hiding out. And I remember I said, "Well, what camera do I take?" Peter [Frank] said, "Well you're not taking the good camera." And he didn't want to go. He said, "I wouldn't go up there if I were you." And I said, "What are you worried about?" And he goes, "Well, he was shot at, I don't know who's up there." And I said, "Well, this is the movie, I mean, we came down here to shoot a movie about Bob Marley. Why wouldn't we shoot a scene with Bob Marley? I mean, what are you afraid of? I don't care." And I remember being very irritated and I said, "All right, so I'll take the other camera."… it was like an old, mildew-filled, humid, velvet box and couple of lizards run out of the box. And I thought; well at least it [the camera] worked.

Eyewitness Jeff Walker confirmed Carl Colby's story to the Rock And Roll Detective. Regarding the notion that Colby concealed his relationship to his father, this is another fiction. Once they reached the Marley hideaway, "everybody knew who Carl was (laughing). It wasn't like he snuck into the compound. He had a handheld 16mm camera that had a light leak…. Carl was with me the entire time period between the Hope Road filming, back to the retreat and through the time of the actual Smile Jamaica concert." Walker and Colby worked together to ensure they completed filming all necessary scenes for the project.

It is true that William Colby was Carl's father. However, in the mid-1970s, William Colby became embroiled in controversy following the Nixon/Watergate scandal. The press and Congress charged the CIA with widespread allegations of overall corruption. CIA disclosures, referred to as the "family jewels," revealed a pattern of illegality in areas of mind control, LSD experiments on unwitting humans, and other covert ventures. William Colby became the whipping boy during this upheaval. The result is that Colby was fired as director of the CIA on January 30, 1976, nearly a year before the Bob Marley assault on Hope Road and his son Carl's camera work in Jamaica. Therefore, Carl Colby was the son of the *former* CIA director. Given the disgrace of being fired from the CIA by President Ford, William Colby had no ability, resources, or credibility to involve his son in any covert operation. Carl Colby has explained that CIA operatives need a blank slate to operate effectively in a given country, and that openly sharing the same name as a *former* CIA director was not the cleverest method to use without being caught. This is common sense. CIA agent Joey also confirmed to the Rock And Roll Detective that Carl Colby was never employed by the CIA.

Constantine's theory claimed the Wailers were rehearsing when Colby arrived. He also implied that Colby gave a gift of soccer boots or cleats to Marley who subsequently cut his big toe on a copper wire within one boot that was tainted with cancer. All of this information was provided by a conveniently unnamed witness and allegedly told (via hearsay) to cinematographer Le Lew-Lee who wasn't even present at the compound. Without any eyewitness, medical, or factual evidence or explanation, Lee "believes that Marley's subsequent cancer can be traced to the boots."

Jeff Walker, an eyewitness who was with both Marley and Colby at the Blackwell compound, adamantly and emphatically denied this conspiratorial plot ever took place. He addressed Constantine's assertion that the Wailers were rehearsing with Bob at the compound:

> First of all, there was no [Bob Marley and the Wailers] rehearsal of music going on at Chris' compound as one theory reports. No. No. The band wasn't even there. No, there was no rehearsing. Rehearsing took place at Hope Road. In fact, when the concert had started, there were no Wailers around, and Bob finally decided to go down and perform. His backup band was Third World. I used walkie talkies to get in touch with the Wailers and let the family and all the Wailers know the concert was happening. And over the course of the show, they arrived.

Regarding the copper wire, allegedly tainted with carcinogens, that purportedly cut Marley's toe, Walker methodically detailed to the Rock And Roll Detective that this theory was also a Swiss cheese full of holes:

> Neither Carl nor anyone else took or gave any soccer cleats or boots to Bob. No one else gave any gifts of any kind to Bob while we were with him, up to and including the concert. Security up there was extremely tight. There were not people just coming and going and bringing him gifts. No one knew he was there—Bob was either barefoot or wore sandals at this time. If Bob had had any bandage on his big toe or had been bleeding, I would have noticed that. And he didn't. Of course, I saw Bob walk around the compound while I was there, and Bob did not walk with any limp. I did not see any boots or cleats in the house at all. And when you see Bob performing the next day at the concert there is nothing wrong with his feet. There was no copper wire and Bob did not cut his foot while I was there. The copper wire/CIA story is 100% fake!

Marley played the controversial Smile Jamaica concert on December 5, 1976. At the concert, Marley can be seen dancing and hopping around like a whirling dervish while he sings a 90-minute non-stop set. He is observed having no foot problem or limping. Walker explained that when you witness something in real time and know the truth, and then later hear stories about events that never happened, "it goes so far off the rails on facts, that it is so obvious that it was put together by piecemeal hearsay or parts were just wholly made up."

When asked in a TV documentary about Marley's death, Colby responded to the accusation head on, "It sort of perturbed me when I saw that I was supposedly this secret agent who would bring a poison darted football soccer shoe as a gift. I just thought it was absolutely ridiculous." Colby even discussed this wild speculation with his father, William Colby. The senior Colby responded to his son, "You certainly don't recruit the young son of a CIA director [for an assassination] who has now been booted out [of the CIA]."

In late 2017, another sensationalist clickbait website changed the conspiracy story ever so slightly when it quoted a deathbed confession from alleged CIA agent Bill Oxley. The fictional agent's alleged statement said, "I gave him [Marley] a pair of Converse All Stars. Size 10…. That was it. His life was over…. The nail in the shoe was tainted with cancer viruses and bacteria. It was goodnight nurse." In addition to Jeff Walker's eyewitness accounts that no one gave Bob Marley any shoes, The Rock And Roll Detective reviewed the unclassified CIA documents that listed all of the agents in Jamaica at the time. No Bill or William Oxley was found. In fact, no one by that name ever worked for the CIA. This was confirmed by Agent Joey who was in Jamaica at the time. There was no such man.

By the way, Bob Marley's foot size was not a size 10. It was larger. Additionally, the hospital in Mane confirmed that no one by the name of Oxley was registered as a patient at the time the fake news story interviewing "Mr. Oxley" was to have taken place. Of course, being fictional, the story contained not one corroborated document or firsthand statement to support its sensationalist headline. So we can say "goodnight nurse" to this conspiracy as well.

Forensic pathologist Dr. Michael Hunter also investigated this theory and discredited it immediately based upon his review of Marley's medical records. "When people have been assassinated using poisons, typically a small amount of lethal toxin is injected into the victim through stabbing or a tiny dart. However, there are no poisons that I know of that cause melanoma [skin cancer]. Therefore, I think this conspiracy theory is not true."

In addition, we cannot forget Lee Lew-Lee, the filmmaker who was not at the compound, yet who allegedly heard incredibly detailed hearsay from his friends, the Wailers, who were also not at the compound. Assuming Lee was in fact interviewed by writer Constantine, it was amazing he was able to conjure up an incident that never took place, including Bob Marley's yelling, "Ow!" when cutting his foot on the imaginary boot never given to him, with an imaginary copper wire embedded with imaginary cancer cells. Constantine was careful not to make a statement of fact. Instead, his article asked the question (cleverly planting the idea in the reader's mind), "Had the wire been treated chemically with a carcinogenic toxin?" No, because the event never took place, according to eyewitnesses Jeff Walker and Carl Colby.

Constantine's argument continued to be critical of Colby, describing his appearance at Marley's compound as "provocative." It wasn't. He was hired to be there and everybody knew it. Constantine also tried to bizarrely connect Colby's testimony on behalf of a woman who suffered documented domestic abuse at the hands of O.J. Simpson to his unsubstantiated account of Colby's (an alleged CIA agent) dosing Marley with cancer. To cement his Marley "cancer theory" and blame Colby, he linked it to bringing down another black icon. Colby actually testified to what he had seen and heard regarding O.J. Simpson's abuse of his wife, Nicole Brown Simpson, who herself left behind photos and 911 calls of her abuse at Simpson's hands. But Colby's testimony was at a preliminary hearing and had virtually no impact on the outcome of the one-year trial. Furthermore, because Simpson was found not guilty of murder in the criminal trial, what sense does it make to accuse Colby of bringing about the downfall of Simpson? In short, it is implausible that Constantine's theory can be believed on any level.

Don Taylor's theory falls flat as well. He would learn via hearsay from some unnamed, unknown person that Colby was guilty by association with his father's occupation. He seemed unaware that William Colby had been fired, and not with the CIA in any capacity, when his son Carl was known, hired, and paid to film the concert. This is strange since Taylor was Marley's manager at the time. Taylor also stated that Colby traveled under an "alias" and did not reveal his own real name or relationship with his father. This is also not true. Carl Colby traveled under his given name and was up front with Marley. He was part of a planned Island Records video team. Based upon Taylor's assumptions, and lacking any specific factual evidence, he also made an erroneous conclusion.

Timothy White discussed the CIA cameraman-son "minus a camera" theory in his book, and he believed the Rastas had no idea Carl Colby was the son of the former CIA director. If White had interviewed Jeff Walker, he would have learned that Colby and his relationship to his father was known to everyone, and that the handheld 16mm camera Carl brought to the compound to interview Bob Marley was also the same one he used to film the entire Smile Jamaica concert. Lastly, if White had researched the biography of William Colby when writing his book, he would have also learned that the senior Colby had been fired, disgraced, and lost all of his power almost a year before the assault on Bob Marley at Hope Road.

Keidi Awadu was convinced "without a shadow of a doubt" that the cancer from the soccer shoe was a "prime vehicle" to kill Marley after the shooting attempt had failed. (Author Note: the correct standard in criminal law is that a jury must be convinced "beyond a reasonable doubt.") By "prime vehicle," Awadu explained to the Rock And Roll Detective, "it is a means of creating cancer or cancer-like symptoms." In support of this theory, Awadu cited other conspiracy theories with "allegations of political assassination through cancer," including Hugo Chavez and Kwame Toure. If we were to believe Awadu's explanation, Marley was assassinated through cancer because he believes that other people have been assassinated the same way. Not very persuasive.

Awadu also cited Timothy White's book as proof of the CIA's interest in Bob Marley who, according to Awadu, "*seems* to fit their [CIA's] doctrine 'to prevent the rise of black Messiah.'" This author could find nothing in White's book or in the CIA declassified pages previously discussed, that support even the remote possibility that the CIA was surveilling Marley. Nor was information found that would suggest the CIA was ever concerned with Marley's political views, lyrics, racial profile, or ever considered killing Marley to try to prevent this so-called "rise of black Messiah."

Even if one clings to the fabricated theory that a copper wire in a boot cut Bob's big toe and caused cancer, one has to understand whether this is even medically possible. Professor Katherine Belov, PhD is an international expert on transmissible cancer. She noted that a healthy immune system will combat any shared foreign cells, including cancerous ones. "Only three types of contagious cancers have been identified, and all occur in non-primates," she said. Belov also noted that contagious cancer has not evolved in humans because of our "genetic diversity." When asked if cancer has ever been transmitted to another human, she replied, "We don't have any clear examples of transmissible cancers in humans."

When governments want to assassinate someone with a poisonous chemical, it is because they want that person dead *immediately* or in a matter of days, not years! Recent examples of this tactic employed poison, not cancer cells. Former KGB agent Alexander Litvinenko escaped from prosecution in Russia and fled to the UK. On November 1, 2006, he suddenly fell ill and died three weeks later in the hospital. He was the first confirmed victim of lethal polonium-210-induced acute radiation syndrome. The Russians repeated this lethal exercise again in 2018 when they killed a spy in England with the Novichok nerve agent. On February 13, 2017, North Korea's Kim Jong-un purportedly killed his half-brother, Kim Jong-nam. He allegedly hired two women who smeared Jong-nam's face with a later-revealed VX nerve agent at the Kuala Lampur International Airport in Malaysia. He died at the airport the same day.

Even if Marley had been successfully contaminated with cancer, which we now know did not happen, what was the point? He didn't die of cancer for another 4½ years. And further, Michael Manley's government was re-elected shortly after the concert, leaving the U.S. and its corporations with the same problems as before.

Marley continued to record and sell albums, receive worldwide airplay, and tour the world during his remaining years. Most importantly, an assassination could never shut down Marley's message or impact the sale of his records and worldwide radio airplay. In fact, his lyrics and musical message continue to entertain and inform the world decades after his death.

If the CIA Didn't Kill Bob Marley, Who or What Did?

Bob Marley's skin cancer began in his big right toe. That rather unique location provided Forensic Pathologist Dr. Hunter a clue regarding what happened to Marley's declining health from 1977 until his death on May 11, 1981. He noted that people with dark skin rarely develop melanomas. "But when they do," Hunter said, "70% have a very rare form called 'Acral Lentiginous (AL) Melanoma.' AL Melanoma develops on hairless portions of the body such as on the palm of the hands, the sole of the feet and even in the nail beds." From Marley's medical records, we know he was first informed by doctors in London in the summer of 1977 that melanoma cancer had developed underneath his big toe nail. According to Hunter, "I believe it was this form of cancer that killed Bob Marley. But it is not the full story."

Hunter's forensics team contacted the Marley family to learn if there was any family history on this form of melanoma, and the family confirmed his suspicion. Hunter emphasized, "This is highly relevant. All of the medical evidence points to a family history being one of the biggest risk factors for the development of melanoma skin cancer." Despite Marley's dark skin, he was still at risk for developing this cancer due to his family's medical background.

Hunter believed that, based upon the scientific medical evidence and the state of cancer research in the late 1970s and early 1980s, Marley's only chance to beat his skin cancer would have been to have his toe amputated at the time of diagnosis in the summer of 1977. However, Marley felt that losing his big toe would hinder his stage presence, playing guitar, dancing, and his love of playing soccer; as a result, he refused this type of surgical solution.

In the summer of 1977, Marley went to see a specialist in Miami. The British diagnosis of malignant melanoma was confirmed, and he was again advised to have his toe amputated. Once again Marley refused, but he allowed orthopedic surgeon Dr. William Bacon to perform a surgical excision to cut away cancerous tissue on the toe and have the cancerous skin replaced with a layer of skin from another part of his body. At this point, everyone believed the procedure had been a success.

Unfortunately, the cancer was metastasizing. According to Dr. Hunter, "The surgical excision failed to remove all of the cancerous cells, and over time they spread throughout his body, including to his lungs and into his brain. Sadly, it seems it was Bob Marley's undying love of music that ultimately led to his death [on May 11, 1981]." In conclusion, it is clear that Bob Marley's death was caused by the spread of Acral Lentiginous Melanoma.

VOID IF ALTERED OR ERASED

VOID IF ALTERED OR ERASED

07367

CERTIFICATE OF DEATH
FLORIDA

81-043381

DECEDENT - NAME — Robert Nosta Marley

Male — Date of Death: May 11, 1981

RACE — Negro — AGE 36

State of Birth — Jamaica — Feb. 6, 1945 — Dade — Inpatient

CITY, TOWN OR LOCATION OF DEATH — Miami — Cedars of Lebanon Hospital

Children of what Country — Jamaica

Married — Rita Anderson

Entertainer — Music

Residence - State: Florida — County: Dade — Miami — 12401 Vista Lane — No

Father - Name: Norval St. Clair Marley

Mother - Name: Cedella Malcolm

Informant - Name: Mrs. Rita Marley — 12401 Vista Lane, Miami, Florida

Kingston, Jamaica

Removal — Range Funeral Home, 5727 NW 17th Ave. Miami, Fl.

May 15, 1981 — 11:30 A.

Charles C. Bell — Sub-registrar

William L. Bacon, M.D., 1295 N.W. 14th Street, Miami, Florida 33136

Registrar — May 15, 1981

State Registrar

Date Issued: MAR 2 8 2007

23619998   CERTIFICATION OF VITAL RECORD

23619998

"Though the Road's Been Rocky, It's Sure Been Good To Me"

It is often difficult for people to deal with the death of a significant public figure, especially one who touches so many and brings joy to them. CIA expert Robert Baer believes that conspiracy theories are a fact of life when "… people get hung up on small, insignificant details and inconsistencies. With their abiding distrust of government, the facts surrounding an assassination are easily deflected, and then they quietly recede into infinite possibilities." The conspiracy that the CIA "killed" Bob Marley clearly follows this pattern. The Rock And Roll Detective dug into countless records and details to determine exactly what happened and why it did *not* include CIA involvement.

Jeff Walker provides the best explanation for all of the swirling, inaccurate details and speculation that surrounded the eventual death of Bob Marley:

> I think what it comes down to with all conspiracy theories is that when someone dies, people don't want to believe that someone as important and as much of a genius as Bob Marley could be taken down by something so random as cancer. So, a picture is painted where there is *something else at work*. And the saddest part about it is that it ultimately paints him [Marley] as a victim. And Bob Marley was *not* a victim.

There are a number of alternative history novels and articles that have surfaced over the years that also seek to paint a conspiratorial picture of dark forces bent on killing Bob Marley. Online fake news, fictional films, and phony documentaries are likely right around the corner. However, now armed with the facts and the truth, readers know the real story behind Bob Marley's early, unfortunate demise—one that most definitely did not involve the CIA.

Chapter Four
The FBI vs. "Merchants of Filth"

"How can we stamp out this menace?" wrote an angry father to Attorney General Robert F. Kennedy in a letter he received in early January 1964. Kennedy was still reeling from the assassination of his brother, John F. Kennedy, the president of the United States, just two months earlier. Sitting at his big mahogany desk in a modern executive leather chair, wearing a typical D.C. uniform—a white dress shirt, sleeves rolled up, and a slightly loosened tie —Robert Kennedy was reading his morning mail.

As Attorney General, Robert Kennedy had fought against organized crime and for African American Civil Rights legislation. With President Lyndon B. Johnson newly installed in place of JFK, Robert Kennedy was focused on bigger issues than a single citizen's complaint about a rock and roll record. He wanted to finish several of the projects his brother had been unable to complete. Most importantly, Robert Kennedy was mulling over a campaign for the United States Senate.

Nevertheless, he returned to his correspondence and became interested in a concerned parent's plea for assistance. The father explained:

> My daughter brought home a record of "Louie Louie" and I, after reading that
> the record had been banned from being played on the air because it was obscene,

proceeded to try to decipher the jumble of words. The lyrics are so filthy that I cannot enclose them in this letter.

Kennedy must have been intrigued by these "obscene" lyrics that were too "filthy" to be included in the letter. The troubled parent asked Kennedy to locate the artists, known as the Kingsmen, the record company, and the promoters, and make sure they were "prosecuted to the full extent of the law."

FEB 7 1964

CRIMINAL DIVISION

Mr. Robert F. Kennedy
Attorney General USA
Washington, D.C.

Dear Mr. Kennedy:

Who do you turn to when your teen age daughter buys and brings home pornographic or obscene materials being sold along with objects directed and aimed at the 'teen age market in every City, Village and Record shop in this Nation?

My daughter brought home a record of "LOUIE LOUIE" and I, after reading that the record had been banned from being played on the air because it was obscene, proceeded to try to decipher the jumble of words,
The lyrics are so filthy that I can-not enclose them in this letter.

This record is on the WAND label # 143-A and recorded by The KINGSMEN "a Jerden Production by Ken Chase and Jerry Dennon" and there is an address 1650 Broadway New York, N.Y.

I would like to see these people, The "artists", the Record company and the promoters prosecuted to the full extent of the law.

We all know there is obscene materials available for those who seek it, but when they start sneaking in this material in the guise of the latest 'teen age rock & roll hit record these morons have gone too far.

This land of ours is headed for an extreme state of moral degradation what with this record, the biggest hit movies and the sex and violence exploited on T.V.

How can we stamp out this menace? ? ? ?

As Attorney General, Kennedy was well aware that the suppression or limitation of allegedly obscene material raised an issue regarding Freedom of Speech, which is protected by the First Amendment to the Constitution of the United States. However, the courts would need to first determine factually whether the material in question (i.e., the lyrics to a rock and roll song) was in fact obscene. Therefore, Kennedy knew that he had to turn the complaint over to the U.S. Federal Bureau of Investigation (FBI) in order to determine, through investigation, if in fact the Kingsmen's recording of the song "Louie

FBI Director J. Edgar Hoover and Attorney General Robert F. Kennedy

Louie" contained obscenities. Kennedy dutifully mailed off the complaint letter to FBI Director J. Edgar Hoover, requesting that the FBI investigate the matter.

Ultimately, the Kingsmen's version of "Louie Louie" set in motion a two-year odyssey, a historic witch hunt through the halls of the FBI, occupying scores of G-men and spending inordinate time and taxpayer money, with the goal of symbolically "hanging" the rock band, record label, publishers, and producers for committing federal crimes and releasing a rocked-up sea chantey upon an unsuspecting public.

The Rock And Roll Detective (a former trial attorney) dug deeply into one hundred and twenty pages of FBI Freedom of Information Act (FOIA) records to dissect rock's most "menacing" song of this era. What was uncovered involves a predisposed probe, some intriguing techniques used by the G-men, and some unbelievable mistakes and omissions made by agents who blundered through this absurd bureaucratic hunt for obscenity. More importantly, what they *missed* is incredible in light of what they were attempting to find!

FBI Opens "Louie Louie" Investigation

In early February 1964, the FBI opened a file with the goal of investigating the Wand Records 45-rpm single "Louie Louie" to determine if the lyrics to the song were actually obscene. They proceeded to gather facts to support a case under the Interstate Transportation of Obscene Matter Statute (ITOM) since the record was being distributed for sale, airplay, and use in jukeboxes across the nation. Coupled with the FBI's legal responsibility was a morality initiative that flowed from the top down through the organization by its Director, J. Edgar Hoover. He believed that rock and roll was "a menace to morals" and a subversive movement that could and would foment revolt and social instability if left unchecked. With a predisposition by Hoover to find the "guilty" perpetrators of this allegedly filthy song, the FBI began its analysis of the actual recording and the lyrics, both the official and the unofficial "playground" (i.e., created by students) versions.

Later that month, the Tampa FBI mailed the record to its lab along with the official lyrics published by Limax Music and the "reported obscene lyrics for 'Louie Louie' [sent under Obscene Cover]." The FBI's prejudice was already transparent in the memo submitting these objects to the lab for analysis. The agent mentioned receiving the "obscene lyric" version from high school students, which was "very popular." He told the lab, "With a copy of the obscene words to refer to [while listening to the record] it sounds like the lyrics [sung] are identical with the enclosed obscene lyrics." He also concluded that the claimed official lyrics furnished by Limax Music Company "do not seem to be the same." Never mind that they were the federally copyrighted and officially published lyrics!

Meanwhile, in the same month, a parallel probe was launched by the Federal Communications Commission (FCC) to conduct its own investigation of the allegedly obscene song. The FCC wrote to the president of the record company requesting the

Louie Louie 45 RPM Single, Courtesy Of Author

official lyrics and copies of the record which were promptly sent to them. The label even offered, "Our record was made from a two-track recording. We will be happy to play the [isolated] vocal track for any of your representatives who would call on us, and this should clear any misunderstanding as to the lyrics on our record. They will find them to be exactly as on the enclosed lyric sheet." There is no evidence that the FCC ever accepted the offer of Wand Records to listen to the isolated vocals.

Simultaneously, the FBI lab began its analysis of the "Louie Louie" single to compare the official Limax-furnished lyrics to the obscene schoolyard lyrics, an examination which took eight days to complete. Their conclusion was fruitless and they admitted, "the lyrics of the song on the record, Q1 [the 45-rpm record], was not definitely determined in the Laboratory examination." In other words, the G-men in white coats had no idea what the lead singer of The Kingsmen was singing on the record. Of course, a thorough investigation should include identifying and interviewing the person who recorded the vocals in question.

When returning the materials to the Tampa FBI office, the lab suggested that agents contact the person who obtained (or created) the obscene-lyric version for an interview. The entire country learned from a United Press International (UPI) report on March 4, 1964 that not only was the FBI investigating "Louie Louie," but the FCC and the U.S. Post Office were joining the fray. The news release conveyed that the Governor of Indiana had complained about the song. Ultimately, the news stated that the FBI investigation was dropped because agents "were unable to determine what the lyrics of the song were even after listening to the records at speeds ranging from 16-rpm to 78-rpm." So, as quickly as the investigation began, it came to a swift ending (according to the media) because the lyrics sung by The Kingsmen's lead singer were too garbled to understand. Case closed? Or was this just the beginning?

"Indiana Wants Me..." Was "Louie Louie" Really Banned?

Meanwhile, the State of Indiana's governor, Matthew Welsh, received a complaint from a teen in late January 1964, who *felt* he had heard obscene lyrics in the song. As a form of evidence, the teen sent along "obscene lyrics" which seemed to fit with the verses of the actual song. At this point, no one knew if they were his own interpretive transcription or from an acquaintance.

The governor's executive secretary was immediately tasked with finding a copy of the record at a nearby record shop. Upon listening to the song with the teen's bootleg lyrics in hand, the governor made a decision for which he will forever be remembered. He too *felt* there may be some substance to the complaint of obscenity. Interestingly however, he never thought of seeking out the officially published, copyrighted lyrics to the song and comparing these official (non-obscene) lyrics to the recording. His press secretary issued a statement about "Louie Louie" stating the words were "… indistinct, but plain if you listen carefully." Huh?

As a result of *thinking* or *feeling* that the lyrics were obscene for a couple of days, Governor Welsh sent a letter to the president of the Indiana Broadcasters Association, Reid Chapman, *suggesting* that the record be removed from all radio stations in Indiana due to the purported obscene nature of the lyrics. There is no record of any cited legal authority that required or permitted a banning of this record from the airwaves. Nevertheless, a letter from the governor to the head of a statewide media organization *suggested* that the artists' constitutional freedom of speech rights be revoked based upon a feeling! Chapman, in turn, passed on the governor's "suggestion" to his membership (of radio and TV stations) by way of telegrams, *suggesting* they merely stop playing the song.

The Kingsmen, who were planning a tour of the Midwest for their hit song, were naturally incensed with this development. Band leader Lynn Easton protested to the

Indianapolis Star upon learning of the removal of their record from radio. "We took the words from the original version by [composer] Richard Berry and recorded them faithfully," he said.

The unofficial, but highly effective, Indiana ban caused great alarm and likely financial loss to the music publisher, Limax Music. Publisher Max Firetag had his law firm fire off a legal bombshell to Reid Chapman for taking their record off the air and vehemently stating that the lyrics were not pornographic as stated by the governor. At the time, "Louie Louie" had reached Number 14 on the Billboard Hot 100 record charts. Perhaps as more of a marketing ploy than an argument, Firetag told Billboard he "… would award a check for $1,000 to anyone finding anything suggestive in the lyrics as recorded by The Kingsmen on Wand Records." Of course, such a challenge would only entice more teenagers to purchase and listen to the record!

Attorneys for Limax Music further explained that the alleged obscenity and subsequent "suggested ban" should not be based upon suggested lyrics by listeners, but rather by a comparison of the official publisher's lyrics to the official recording. According to a review of the FBI records, the governor failed to do this before he suggested having the song pulled from broadcast. Subsequently, the office of the chief trial deputy of Marion County (Indianapolis) had to admit his investigators had found nothing obscene in the garbled words of the recorded song. Although "Louie Louie" was never technically or legally banned in Indiana, it was kept off the air long enough to negatively impact sales.

The final blow to the governor's censorship of "Louie Louie" came via an *Indianapolis Star* editorial on January 27th, which verbally took him to task: "As a music critic, Governor Matthew E. Welsh is probably a good lawyer…. The governor has no power to censor what goes over the radio stations of Indiana. Neither he nor any other public official should be given such a warrant." Not surprisingly, Governor Welsh failed to mention this First Amendment censorship in his memoirs. Apparently, J. Edgar Hoover did not subscribe to the Indy *Star*, because the Bureau continued on with its investigation of the song.

FBI Still on the Case—Verse, Chorus, Verse

Subsequently, the Bureau's hunt for "Louie's" obscenity continued in Indiana and Florida where the bulk of complaints originated. Concerned citizens were sending in the song containing lyrics they *believed* they were hearing. The FBI obtained an "official" copy of the Wand Records 45-rpm single in May and forwarded it to their San Diego, CA lab for analysis. After a quick listen, the lab concluded, "Because the lyrics of the song on the record Q1 ['Louie Louie'] could not be definitely determined in the Laboratory examination, it could not be determined whether Q1 is an obscene record." The lab ultimately disposed of the evidence on May 20, 1964, having nothing they could use to confirm a federal case against the artists or their label.

Back in Indianapolis, the local office reached its own conclusion about the record sold in Indiana stores, namely that the "record was publicly displayed, was routinely priced, and was not suspected of being obscene when purchased." Of course, one would have to listen to the record, and not just stare at it on a store shelf, in order to determine if it did indeed contain obscene lyrics. The FBI files also noted that UPI reported the "government had dropped investigations it had been conducting into the complaints that a popular rock-and-roll record has obscene lyrics." As we now know, this was an inaccurate statement on the part of the national media.

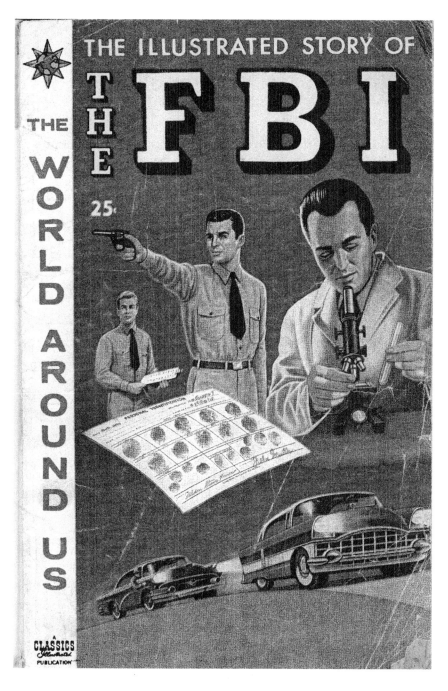

Indiana's FBI laboratory decided it needed to "determine its [the song's] obscene character when played at [a slower speed of] 33 1/3 rpm." They also listened to the record and compared the lyrics sent in by a concerned citizen who thought he heard the following verse:

Chorus: Oh, Louie, Louie, Oh No,
            Get her way down low…
Verse: At night at 10, I lay her again
            Fuck you girl, Oh, all the way
            Oh, my bed and I lay her there
            I meet a rose in her hair

Despite this alleged lyrical "proof" and numerous repetitions of phonograph play, the Indiana bureau concluded, "The record was played at various speeds but none of the speeds assisted in determining the words of the song on the record."

Over in Tampa, agents decided to detail (or justify) their continuing search for obscenity by outlining how they obtained an interview with a Sarasota college student. Somehow the agent (whose name has been excised) notes, "Portions of the lyrics on this record are slurred and not recognizable…. The obscene portions of the written lyrics [created by college students] correspond to the slurred portions of the song, 'Louie Louie.'"

So, if we understand this correctly, agents noted that the words to the song they listened to were not recognizable at any speed. Then they compared the unrecognizable vocals to some lyrics made up by a college student, rather than the official lyrics the FBI had received from the music publisher Limax. They then concluded there was a *correlation of obscenity* from what they could neither hear, understand, nor properly compare!

Ultimately, the Tampa lab determined that there was nothing obscene worth pursuing, although they did receive more salacious lyrics from college students:

Verse: Every night and day I play with my thing,
            I fuck your girl all kinds of ways,
            In all night now meet me there,
            I feel her low I give her hell

On April 17 another FBI laboratory advised, "… the record was played at various speeds but none of the speeds assisted in determining the words of the song on record."

In May 1964, the FBI declined to recommend prosecution after the Florida, Indiana, and California labs all failed to come up with a determination that the record's lyrics were obscene. Also, in May, Assistant United States Attorney Lester Irvin advised he would decline prosecution of the case since the FBI lab was unable to determine that the record was obscene. Thus, the initial investigation into "Louie Louie" that began with a single letter to Robert F. Kennedy came to an inauspicious ending. Or did it?

FBI Back on the Case—Reprise

The FBI took a year-long coffee break from its "Louie Louie" investigation, which lay dormant from May 20, 1964 until re-starting in April 1965. In the spring of that year, the FBI took up the case again because of a memo sent by the Detroit Bureau to J. Edgar Hoover in Washington, DC. Government documents indicated they enclosed a copy of the record along with "… an envelope marked 'obscene' containing the type-written words believed to be heard during the singing of 'Louie Louie,' when this record is played [at the slower speed of] 33-rpm." Sound the alarms!

An informant had walked into the Detroit office morally offended, reporting that when the song was slowed down to 33-rpm speed, "… obscene and suggestive words can be interpreted in this song." This person further claimed that teenagers were actually buying the record for the purpose of playing it at a slower speed in order to listen to the alleged obscenities.

J. Edgar Hoover responded to the Detroit office. He advised that they had already listened to a copy of the infamous record and were "unable to interpret any of the wording in the record and, therefore, could not make a decision concerning the matter." He also told them that the Tampa, Florida and Hammond, Indiana offices had declined prosecution as well. This information from FBI Headquarters did not deter the Detroit office, and they continued to send a flurry of memos regarding the obvious "obscenity."

In late May, some semblance of sanity returned to this case when a separate but related investigation performed by the FCC resulted in the clearance to broadcast "Louie Louie" on the radio. The representative explained that, for a long time, they had been receiving "unfounded complaints" concerning the recording "Louie Louie." She stated that, to the best of her knowledge, "… the trouble was started by an unidentified college student who made up a series of obscene verses for 'Louie Louie' and then sold them to fellow students." In her opinion, "a person can take any 45-rpm recording and reduce its speed to 33-rpm and imagine obscene words, depending upon the imagination of the listener." Had the FBI, which read and reported on the FCC's reasoned decision, never considered this possibility?

For his own investigative purposes and entertainment, the Rock And Roll Detective played "Louie Louie" at 33 1/3-rpm through headphones to get a flavor for the alleged filthy lyrics slowed down. All this author could decipher was the chorus: "Louuuuuuuuuie Louuuuuuie, meeeeeee gottaaaa goooooo." The rest was indecipherable.

In late June, Robert J. Grace, the U.S. Attorney for the Eastern District of Michigan, informed the Detroit FBI Bureau that he would "… defer his prosecutive opinion in this

COMBATING MERCHANTS OF FILTH:
THE ROLE OF THE FBI

J. Edgar Hoover*

In the Southwest last year, a 15-year-old girl was arrested following a series of promiscuous escapades with students from nearby colleges. To a local juvenile officer, she confided that she had begun selling her "favors" to teen-aged youths after reading a number of cheap novels in which the lives of prostitutes were glamorized.

On the West Coast, a young hitchhiker was picked up by two men and driven to an apartment where he was subjected to horrifying indecencies. When police, acting on information supplied by the victim, located the two men involved, a virtual storehouse of obscene photographs, literature and other pornographic material was seized.

In a heavily populated area of New England, a police officer issued a public warning against depraved sex offenders who had plied local children with intoxicants and pornographic material—then plunged them into wild orgies.

Near the nation's Capitol, a collection of "peephole" magazines and photographs of nude and seminude women helped confirm the identity of a vicious sex offender who had committed a series of atrocious crimes which led ultimately to his conviction for kidnapping and murder.

And in New York two young terrorists staged a violent crime spree which included the horsewhipping of teen-aged girls and a savage attack upon an old man whom they dumped into the East River to drown. Following their arrest, the youths admitted having devised the pattern for these sadistic assults from reading lurid books.

*Director, Federal Bureau of Investigation.

case pending advice of the U.S. Department of Justice." U.S. Attorney Grace then passed the case back up to Washington for more consideration. Despite these developments, or the lack thereof, Detroit persisted with its own inquiry and waited for the New York Bureau to interrogate Wand Records executives.

Just as things appeared to settle down in Michigan, a student sent a letter directly to J. Edgar Hoover complaining about the "pornographic" lyrics, requesting to know the status of the investigation, and expressing worry about the damage done by obscenity to teenagers around the country. In discussing the lyrics, the student wondered if "… there is perhaps a subliminal type of perversion involved? Even a conspiracy by records to pervert teens along with movies, magazines and paperbacks…"

Hoover replied directly back to the student and shared his concerns. He stated, "I strongly believe that the easy accessibility of such material cannot help but divert the

96

minds of young people into unhealthy channels and negate the wholesome training they have already been afforded by their parents." He declined to fill in the youngster on the status of the "Louie Louie" investigation because it was ongoing, but he assured him that the FBI was taking its responsibility seriously and with the "highest degree of thoroughness and dispatch." Hoover provided the teen with brochures entitled "Poison for our Youth" and "Combating Merchants of Filth: The Role of the FBI." Clearly, this is the label Hoover had for The Kingsmen. At this point, it would have benefited record sales if The Kingsmen *had* changed their band name to the "Merchants of Filth"!

Toward the end of July, the New York FBI office informed Detroit that it would interview an executive at Wand Management. The agent in New York stated that he would attempt to obtain a copy of the master vocal track (without instrumentation) in order to listen to the words actually sung on the record. He also stated that he would "attempt to locate the singing team, 'The Kingsmen' and interview them regarding the lyrics" they recorded in the song. Finally, after a year or so, the FBI had some leads. They went to Seattle and interviewed Jerry Dennon who was listed as a producer on the record.

The Rock And Roll Detective knew the late Jerry Dennon for 25 years. Dennon told this author that he was not present during the recording, nor did he technically produce the record. "My company leased the master recording of 'Louie Louie' to Wand Management which used Scepter Music to distribute it. My goal was to push the record and help get it played on the radio."

At the same time, perhaps because Hoover received so many letters still complaining about the record, Assistant United States Attorney for the Eastern District of Michigan Robert Grace was ordered to resume investigating "Louie Louie," and that "… additional investigation should be conducted in order to bring the case to a *logical* conclusion." He was also informed of efforts to obtain the isolated vocal track and compare it to the finished master, and that the FBI would interview someone at Limax Music, the publisher of the lyrics, in Los Angeles.

Meanwhile, the Michigan student who had written Hoover and received the "Merchants of Filth" prevention pamphlet asked for 50 more pamphlets for his club. The student also gave the FBI an interesting technical analysis of the song, stating "The 45-rpm 'Louie' was played at 78-rpm, taped at twice the regular speed and then slowed down so that it now plays somewhere between 45-rpm and 33-rpm. At this speed the obscene articulation is clearer."

Ever the suspicious director, Hoover was leery of the young man's technical concept of creating an in-between speed to study the alleged obscene lyrics, and he immediately ordered the Flint, Michigan FBI to investigate this youth who kept writing to him. The Michigan FBI agent advised Hoover that he knew of "no derogatory information concerning" the teen whose name is blacked out in the FOIA records. So Hoover wrote back to the student and thanked him for his thoughtfulness. He sent only 25 copies of the pamphlets requested, stating, "I regret, however, that budgetary limitations preclude furnishing the number for which you asked." Interestingly, the FBI had enough in the budget to run a nationwide investigation for two years into one rock and roll record, yet it lacked the funds to send the young man 25 more copies of its propaganda pamphlet.

The Kingsmen, 1963. From left: Top row Lynn Easton, Garry Abbott;
Bottom row Don Gallucci, Jack Ely, Mike Mitchell

Meanwhile, New York G-men received a direct copy of the requested "Louie Louie" master tape on August 23, 1965. Wand Records declined to let the government have the actual master without a court order, so the Feds settled for listening to a copy of the master. Jerry Dennon told this author, "That was a mono recording. There was only one track that contained the vocal and the instrumental performance together."

While at Wand Records, the agents were informed by an executive that she had been mistaken when she previously concluded the record had been made from a two-track recording. It was, in fact, a one-track recording—confirming what Dennon knew to be the case. There had been a simulated stereo master created that caused her to believe that it was a two-track recording. Although there was no separate vocal track, Wand prepared an *enhanced copy* of the "Louie Louie" master "… with the intent of bringing out the voice sounds to the best of their ability."

On September 16, 1965, the New York FBI lab concluded that a comparison of the Detroit 45-rpm specimen alongside the enhanced vocal specimen obtained from Wand Records yielded "no audible differences," However, the report makes no mention or conclusions regarding a comparison of the enhanced vocal version to the original lyrics or the alleged obscene lyrics. Wouldn't that have been a logical examination at this point?

Jerry Dennon recalled, "The FBI interviewed me around this time. I explained to them that the recording was made very quickly and the studio was quite archaic. Although the audio technique was poor, I told them the recording was definitely not obscene." Dennon found the visit intimidating. "It was surreal…. I told them nothing was done to 'Louie Louie.' That it was all in people's imagination. I found it pretty frightening."

Throughout the months of October and November 1965, the Bureau spread out its agents coast to coast to interview those involved with the writing, recording, distribution, or other business aspects of the song. Unfortunately, their names have been blacked out for "national security" or some other significant reason 50-plus years later. However, all of these nameless interviewees agreed there was nothing obscene in the lyrics as sung and recorded by The Kingsmen.

On December 2, 1965, Assistant U.S. Attorney Robert Grace again informed the FBI that he had reviewed the conducted investigation and "was of the opinion that there was no evidence of a violation of the Federal Interstate Transportation of Obscene Matter Statutes." Therefore, he recommended that no further investigation in this matter be conducted.

Finally, in late 1966, the FBI made what appears to be the last entry in its overzealous investigation—assuming it has indeed turned over all of the FOIA records in this case. On October 19, 1966, the New York City FBI lab finally returned the 45-rpm record of "Louie Louie" and the mimeographed copy of the song lyrics back to the Detroit FBI office, recommending they ask Assistant U.S. Attorney Grace whether they could return this material to Wand Management in New York City.

The Rest of the Story—Vocals

During the course of the investigation, in which Mr. Hoover took a personal interest, he sent his minions out to follow, listen to, and corral The Kingsmen—roughly a year and a half after the investigation began—while they continued to tour in support of their highly popular and controversial single. The agents no doubt hoped to "catch" The Kingsmen singing the "filthy" lyrics live in concert to please the audience. (Interestingly, when they finally asked to interview the band, the transcript was either deleted from the FOIA records or was on a page that was totally blacked out. This meeting was documented, however, by new drummer Dick Peterson, who was in attendance.)

After cornering the band in a hotel conference room, the agent read the entire band their Miranda rights, including the right to remain silent and the right to an attorney. However, before the band members could think or ask for an attorney, the questions began, according to Peterson. An agent immediately challenged band member Lynn Easton who had actually been the drummer on the "Louie Louie" recording date. The agent likely selected him for interrogation because Easton was now touring as the lead vocalist and singing "Louie Louie" each night.

Agent: What can you tell me about your recording of "Louie Louie"?

Easton: Well, I know that for the last year-and-a-half, certain people have professed to hearing obscene words on the record.

Agent: Are there any obscene words on the record?

(At this point, Easton was likely focused on the lyrics sung by the lead singer, Jack Ely, on the recording, and not on any spontaneous utterances that can occasionally be picked up on recordings. More on this later.)

Easton: As far as I'm concerned, the words they claim to hear simply don't exist on the recording.

Agent: You were present at the recording session?

Easton: Yes I was.

Agent: Where did you make this recording?

Easton: We recorded it on the West Coast over two years ago, in Portland.

Agent: What lyrics did you use?

Easton: We used the same lyrics Richard Barry wrote.... We only practiced the song a few times before we recorded it with vocals. There was absolutely no *deliberate* attempt to include any obscene words on the recording. [Easton chose his words carefully. The use of the word *deliberate* is cautious in that it does not convey what if any *spontaneous* words might have been used.]

After a couple more questions of little consequence, the agent asked the others if their answers would be the same. When they all answered in the affirmative, the agent thanked them for their time and let them go.

Interestingly, the agent (an attorney) did not ask Easton (a witness to and participant in the recording session) the names of the exact members of the band who participated in the recording session and whether any were absent from this questioning conference. In fact, the agent never even asked *who* sang lead vocals on the recording! Since the agents had been following the band to live concerts, they assumed Lynn Easton had recorded the vocals because he sang lead vocals at every concert they attended. But Easton did *not* sing on the track and had only played the drums on the recording of "Louie Louie."

The Man the FBI Never Interviewed

The late Jack Ely was born in Portland, Oregon in 1943. He began playing piano as a young child, but switched to guitar around 1956 after seeing Elvis Presley perform on TV. During high school, Ely met and started playing in a band with Lynn Easton. Later, the boys met other young musicians and formed The Kingsmen. They played mainly teen dances and eventually got a gig as the house band at a teen club called "The Chase," named after Ken Chase, a radio DJ.

In 1963, Ely heard a rival band playing the song "Louie Louie" and suggested that The Kingsmen learn and perform their own version of the song. It was a song they could stretch out and jam on while their teen audiences danced. In the spring of 1963, Ken Chase, now the group's manager, booked the band into a studio to record their cover version of "Louie Louie."

Ely recalled the studio in Portland as "… the only soundstage studio there was. There had been all kinds of recordings, commercials, demos, and overdubs done there. By today's standards it was a very modest studio." Depending upon what sources you check, or who you ask, the cost for the band to record "Louie Louie," plus the B-side, ranged from $36 to $50. Ely said, "It actually cost us $10 a piece, so $50 in all." Ely only sang on "Louie Louie" and certified he left the band shortly after it was finished. "I was gone by the time the album came out."

Jerry Dennon's company made it possible to get the song on the air when Jerden Records pressed up the recording onto a 45-rpm record. Ken Chase, also listed as the producer, actually produced the session. Chase truly wanted to capture the live, raw, and gritty sound of "Louie Louie" that the band had played over and over in his club. The night before, The Kingsmen with Ely on vocals had performed an extended vocal-straining marathon version of the song at the club.

On a Saturday morning at 10:00 a.m., The Kingsmen dragged themselves and their equipment into Northwest Records and began to set up. "In order to capture what Ken thought was our 'live' sound, he had us set up in a circle," recalled Ely, "… with me standing in the middle with a microphone." In a conventional studio setting, a microphone would have been situated on a microphone stand at mouth level for the ease of the singer and to assist in proper breathing technique.

However, according to Ely, the microphone placement, which ultimately contributed to the difficulty in understanding his singing, was in an awkward position. Ely explained, "So he [Chase] had a technician take the mic, put it on a boom, and stick it up on the ceiling! It was about a 15-foot ceiling. The mic was hanging down about 18-24 inches off the ceiling." This created an uncomfortable position for Ely to sing and strained his vocal cords and pronunciation. "I was directly under it [the microphone], leaning my head straight back, yelling up at this mic," he told the Rock And Roll Detective. The microphone placement was meant to also pick up the guitars, drums, and keyboards in an ambient manner that would make the performance sound more like the live nightclub setting. "The bass was the most important part of the song," relates producer Ken Chase. "The words didn't matter at all, so I didn't close-mic the song."

The late Robert Lindahl, who engineered the recording session, disagreed with this version of the microphone placement. "The Neumann microphone was on a boom," he said. However, Lindahl claimed, "We always placed the microphone off the corner of the guy's mouth, just a bit below his lower lip. I can only assume that Jack Ely was so inexperienced that he didn't know where the pickup element was… and he was maybe singing at the nameplate rather than at the pickup element."

The first take of "Louie Louie" was a breakdown, as Chase called to the band from the control room. He needed the engineer to reset some of the sound levels. While the band waited for another take, Chase and Lindahl argued over the sound balance. Chase won. Lindahl recalled, "I remember very well, he [Chase] didn't like my balance between the band [instruments] and the vocals. He had me reduce the volume of the vocalist." This fact would also make the vocals more difficult to decipher as they became buried in the mix. With the balance changes completed, Chase called for the band to do a run-through or rehearsal version of the song. The young band members were nervous and out of their environment, but pushed on as the famous organ sound started off the song's familiar 11-note-riff… "Duhhh, duh duh duh, duh duh, duh duh duh, duh duh."

At one point during the first full take, in order to cheer on the upcoming guitar solo, Ely yells out like a strangled chicken, "Okay, let's give it to 'em, right now!" This line clearly demonstrates how hard it was for the young singer to breathe and sing this song clearly.

Despite the difficulty in clearly hearing the verses, Ely swore that he was singing directly from the copyrighted official lyrics as written by Richard Barry. "What it [my vocals] really had to do with, is how words get annunciated when your head is tipped back and you're yelling up! 'Louie Louie,' when my head was all stretched up and back, came out, Lou-aye Lou-aye." Was anything sung dirty? "No, not a thing," confirmed Ely. "It was my inability to articulate the words. The words are the same as written by [Richard] Barry." Whether Ely was tired, hoarse, straining to sing upwards, singing into the nameplate instead of the microphone pickup element, and/or his vocal balance level was turned down for more instrumentation, the results were the same. The verses of "Louie Louie" as recorded by Ely were difficult to discern.

To the great surprise of The Kingsmen, Ken Chase decided this less-than-perfect first take of "Louie Louie" was perfect. He told the band, "Okay! That was great! What do you wanna put on the backside?" The band was incredulous. However, Chase was adamant. He said, "Yeah, Yeah. That was great man, you never did that song better." So the band proceeded to prepare the B-side. One must admit that history will confirm the great raw energy of the hit record "Louie Louie" from this one and only completed take.

Ely said he was paid $129.62 for singing perhaps the most famous (or infamous) rock and roll song of all time. He left the band shortly after the single was first released locally on the Jerden label. The record had only sold a few hundred copies at this point. However, Ely and Easton had feuded over who should be the lead singer which ultimately led to Ely's exit. From then on, he no longer appeared in photographs or toured with the group. The big question is, why didn't the FBI ever think to discover and interview the one and only person in the world who had sang and recorded the alleged obscene vocals to "Louie Louie"?

It is also fair to ask why the G-men never had a talk with producer Ken Chase. The producer was incredulous that the FBI had skipped him. "It's suspect. You'd think the man who recorded it ['Louie Louie'] in the studio... they didn't even talk to me?"

The Final Coda

Why didn't the FBI track down Jack Ely during this "crucial" hunt for obscene lyrics? When the Rock And Roll Detective asked him, Ely himself was in the dark: "The FBI spent about two years looking into this and never contacted me... ever!" The Bureau did track down Richard Barry, the writer of the song, and asked him about the Kingsmen version. He told them, "They sound like the original words to me, what are you talking about?"

We must recall that Ely left the band long before the song became a hit and before Attorney General Robert F. Kennedy received the first complaint letter about the lyrics. Ely had been ousted from the band in August 1963 by bandmember Lynn Easton. In the second year of the FBI investigation, it finally dawned upon Hoover and his minions to follow The Kingsmen on tour. Perhaps the band would make an inculpatory statement on radio or to the press admitting the obscene lyrics. However, it is more likely that the FBI hoped the band would slip the obscene words into the live version of their most highly demanded and infamous song—to the delight of the teenagers who came to the shows holding their version of obscene lyrics in their hands.

By the time the G-men began following the group, they witnessed Lynn Easton, and not Jack Ely, singing the lead vocals to "Louie Louie." Therefore, when the Feds cornered the band in a hotel banquet room to question them, they spoke to the *presumed* vocal leader. But as we learned earlier, the Feds never asked *who* recorded the vocals on "Louie Louie." In fact, they failed to ascertain the exact lineup and responsibilities of each band member in the recording of the song. Clearly, the FBI *assumed* Lynn Easton recorded the vocals because he sang them live every night on tour while being tailed by G-men. The simple reason Jack Ely was never investigated by the FBI over those two years is that the FBI (by investigative omission) didn't know he ever sang and recorded the controversial track with The Kingsmen.

Perhaps the biggest blunder of this inquisition was that, despite playing the song at every speed upside down, backwards, inside out, and with headphones on—the FBI missed the utterance of an actual obscenity. Labs in New York, Florida, Indiana, and California played this 45-rpm single over and over, wearing out the grooves, only to miss a stray obscenity actually yelled in frustration by drummer Lynn Easton, but not as part of the song's lyrics upon which the Feds were so focused.

If you listen closely to the song at the 0:55-mark, after Ely sang the first chorus, the microphone picked up Lynn Easton clanking his sticks. In frustration, he clearly yells out, "Fuck!" Producer Chase confirmed the obscenity. "He [Easton] was doing one of those runs on drums where he plays around all of the drums on a fill and he hit the cymbal. And one of his sticks instead of hitting the face of the drumhead went clank on the metal rim, and you can hear him say, 'Fuhh…' (laughing). I'm not going to repeat what he said."

Although he was off the microphone, the obscene word clearly registered on the tape. From this point on, his drumming never quite got back into sync with the song. The little vinyl record that the FBI studied for two years, during which it never found an obscenity in the lyrics at any speed, did in fact contain a swear word. The word "fuck" was never mentioned or observed in the one-hundred-and-twenty-page probe of FBI FOIA records. Ironically, the FBI never heard the one swear word actually on the record!

Finally, the Rock And Roll Detective wondered what the FBI investigation might have cost taxpayers in modern day dollars. According to *The FBI: A Comprehensive Reference Guide*, the FBI's total budget in the middle year of this investigation (1965) was $161,080,000. The nationwide investigation took the better part of 30 months. Based upon the convolution of multiple legal jurisdictions, prosecutors, the Indiana "ban," interstate travel, multi-state Bureau involvement, and the ongoing press interest and airplay, I assumed conservatively that this case consumed an average of 2% of the FBI annual budget. At this rate, 2% of the budgeted $13,416,666 per month yielded an expense of $268,333 per month spent investigating "Louie Louie." Multiplied by a 30-month period, "Louie" cost taxpayers $8,050,000 in 1965 dollars. If we dare to use an inflation calculator to measure this government boondoggle, "Louie Louie" cost taxpayers a grand total of $62,903,783.65 in present day dollars! Simply amazing... and truly obscene!

It is fair to conclude that the FBI's two-year investigation was confounding, highly amusing, and a colossal waste of time and taxpayer money. Perhaps FBI Director J. Edgar Hoover should have been awarded an RIAA Gold Record Award for keeping "Louie Louie" on the radio, in the charts, and selling out at record stores. Hoover also deserves credit for assigning The Kingsmen's version its "dirty" mythology. The Bureau failed to prove the unprovable (obscene lyrics) and also failed to prove the provable (an actual swear word heard on record). Perhaps their greatest omission, however, was not investigating the actual vocalist and producer involved in the recording production. No FOIA records reflect any real conclusion to the "Louie Louie" case. The government witch hunt into the "Merchants of Filth" just quietly vanished as if it had never occurred.

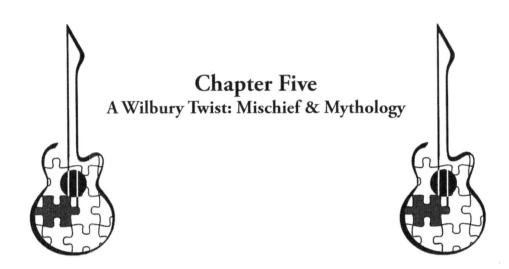

Chapter Five
A Wilbury Twist: Mischief & Mythology

Whatever Wilbury Wilbury…

This is a simple phrase that, once upon a time, was uttered by a band of mischievous traveling musicians in the late 1980s. Or perhaps it was an homage to Doris Day's thoughtful hit song, "Que Sera Sera." Regardless, the intriguing research of Hugh Jampton, E. F. Norti-Bitz (Reader in Applied Jacket, Faculty of Sleeve Notes, University of Krakatoa, East of Java) sheds light on the origin of the special musicians who coined this expression. We learn these special musicians commenced as "… a stationary people who… began to go for short walks—not the Traveling [kind] as we now know it, but certainly as far as the corner and back." We also discover that a musical culture emerged in this tribe, predating the interference of "managers and agents," thus promoting a more adventurous musical sound. The wise Elders of these Traveling Wilburys believed this music "… had the power to stave off madness, turn brunettes into blondes, and increase the size of their ears," says Jampton. As they traveled further, the musical and cultural journey of the Wilburys ran into some unsavory, lesser-developed species such as "night club owners, tour operators, and record executives," not to mention "… wives, roadies and drummers."

In order to better understand the secret origin and reasons for the numerous pseudonyms and fictional high jinks employed by the Traveling Wilburys, as well as the covert rationale behind their faux history, it is essential to examine the artifacts, eyewitness accounts, and clues left behind at the time of the group's formation.

What began as "a stationary people," according to Hugh Jampton, would eventually morph into one of the most fantastic collaborations in music history, one that included members of the Rock and Roll Hall of Fame classes from the 1950s, 1960s, and 1970s. The band was formed by George Harrison (The Beatles), Jeff Lynne (ELO), Tom Petty, Roy Orbison, and Bob Dylan. *Wow*.

When word first arrived on radio and MTV, we were told of a band comprised of Nelson, Otis, Lucky, Lefty, and Charlie T. Jr. These were the clandestine covers selected for the fictional musical family known as the Traveling Wilburys, all sons of Charles Truscott Wilbury Sr., 1901 to 1955. In a promotional photo released in the fall of 1988, we learned that Charles Truscott Wilbury, the "father" of the brother Wilburys, was in fact their first manager… and [was] pretty good at playing darts! "… Fond of a drink and notoriously unreliable with women, Charles had to be replaced when the children were only minors and his successor Cecil 'Sissy' Wilbury could reasonably claim much of the credit* (*and some blame) for the fabulous early deals that led to so much wealth and near-disaster."

Some have called it a "happy accident," while others have described the group's formation as providence written in the stars. In reality, the formation of the group was part pipe dream, part drunken thought, and part premeditation. Jeff Lynne related the early concept and first pseudonym considered for the name of the band. "It was *Trembling Wilburys* at one point. Me and George [Harrison] were doing George's album *Cloud Nine* and we had this fictitious sort of group that we might have one day called the Trembling Wilburys. It's just what you do in the studio, you know about 4 o'clock in the morning. And little did we know it would become Traveling Wilburys."

Of course, the art of transforming a "4:00 AM pipe dream" into a finished album, written, played, produced, and sung by five of the greatest artists in rock history is somewhat of a wonder. George Harrison explained, "It's sort of a miracle… it's unique and maybe more so because I realize you couldn't put it together if you tried. It was totally by accident or we had some sort of creative astrology happening that weekend… I was in L.A. at the time…. So, if I hadn't been there doing that video it wouldn't have happened. Then again, if I hadn't gotten born, none of this would have happened." So how did this secretly formed supergroup with super pseudonyms originate? And why was there so much secrecy and clandestine activity behind the scenes?

Anthropology of the Alias

The pseudonyms used by the Traveling Wilburys and their inner circle are part of a long and mysterious history of secret alter egos utilized in music by many artists, including two of the Wilburys. In order to better understand the unique derivation and motive for the Wilburys' surreptitious travels, we need to travel back in time to the early 1960s to discover where George Harrison and his first band, along with Bob Dylan, first independently developed the concept.

In May 1960, London concert promoter Larry Parnes was assembling a package of pop and rock stars to tour Scotland. The Silver Beatles (as they were known at the time) passed a Liverpool audition on May 10, 1960. They were chosen to serve as instrumental backing for teen singer Johnny Gentle. The tour of Scotland began on May 20, 1960.

Paul McCartney explained the rationale behind the band's first use of "stealthy" names on that tour:

> Now we were truly professional, we could do something we had been toying with for a long time, which was to change our names to real showbiz names. I became Paul Ramon, which I thought was suitably exotic. I remember the Scottish girls saying, "Is that his real name? That's great." It's French, Ramon. *Ra-mon*, that's how you pronounce it. Stuart [Sutcliffe] became Stuart de Stael after the painter. George became Carl Harrison after Carl Perkins, our big idol, who had written "Blue Suede Shoes." John was Long John. People have since said, "Ah, John didn't change his name that was very suave." Let me tell you: he was Long John. There was none of that "he didn't change his name"; we all changed our names.

This early use of alternate identities was partly for showbiz reasons but also, of course, to attract the girls who came to the shows. However, as time went on, The Beatles as a group (and later as solo artists) began to expand the use of pseudonyms for a variety of creative and business purposes.

Paul McCartney was an early adopter of pseudonyms and has continued to use them throughout his career. In the mid-1960s, he used the name Bernard Web to disguise his authorship of the song "Woman," penned for the British pop duo Peter and Gordon to record. McCartney's intent was to see if the song could reach the top of the charts without the help of The Beatles' songwriting reputation and stand firmly on the merits of the song and the performance of Peter and Gordon. The single was released in both the United States and England in early 1966. In this case, "Bernard Web" did not fare as well as The Beatles' singles. Although the song reached number 14 on the charts in the U.S., it stalled at number 28 on the British charts. Regardless, McCartney had discovered a business rationale to use surreptitious names.

In 1967, McCartney found yet another use for an alternative name when he produced a song for the Bonzo Dog Doo Dah Band called "I'm The Urban Spaceman." In this case the name was used because McCartney was exclusively under contract to the EMI Parlophone record company, and The Bonzos were signed to a different label. In the sixties, record labels and their attorneys had yet to create the language and policies of loaning out artists to collaborate on other labels. As a result, many artists who wished to collaborate would either work uncredited or use an alias to receive clandestine credit. It became a game for fans to figure out the real names behind the alter egos.

Also in 1967, Paul McCartney explored yet another technique to employ an alter ego for The Beatles. He was inspired to create a new persona for the group, one which would free up the band to experiment in musical expression and to shed their mop-top image. McCartney wanted the band to find a new way to reveal to fans and critics how their music had matured. Thus, the fictional group of Sgt. Pepper's Lonely Hearts Club Band was created. The imaginary group would also use the name for its title track, reprise, and the album's title. McCartney explained, "We were fed up with being The Beatles. We really hated the fucking four little mop-top approach. We were not boys, we were men… and thought of ourselves as artists rather than just performers." Indeed, *Sgt. Pepper's Lonely Hearts Club Band* would be widely considered the first rock and roll "concept" album, based upon the fictional name, Sgt. Pepper costumes worn by the group, and the experimental music which was bookended by the album's opening track and reprise. The group even added a hidden track (for dogs!) and published their lyrics on the back cover, all to demonstrate their artistic maturity. Even the album cover has become an iconic work of pop art.

McCartney would continue to use *nom de plums* throughout his solo career for a variety of purposes, with names such as Billy Martin, Percy "Thrills" Thrillington, and the Fireman to name just a few. John Lennon would also take up the fictional name game in his solo career. Names such as Mel Torment, Dr. Winston O'Boogie, and The Reverend Fred Gherkin would adorn his solo records. Ringo Starr got in on the act too, appearing with the not-so-secret alter ego of "Ritchie Snare" for his drum sessions on Harry Nilsson's 1972 song, "Spaceman."

Future Wilbury George Harrison also utilized fictional names on his individual projects. In 1969, Harrison used the name L'Angelo Misterioso to disguise his participation with Eric Clapton as a guitarist on Cream's hit song "Badge" (co-written by Clapton and Harrison). Returning the favor to Clapton, who had played uncredited on Harrison's 1968 Beatles song "While My Guitar Gently Weeps," Harrison had to disguise his name due to legal reasons because no permission was granted for Harrison to guest on another label. "In those days," recalled Harrison, "the record company, both my record company and his [Clapton's], they didn't like you to have your name on other people's records, very possessive."

That same year, Harrison released an experimental solo album on the Apple Records/Zapple label titled *Electronic Sound*, on which he secretly credited himself as Artur Wax.

On a brief liner note, he poked fun at his avant-garde music with the line, "There are a lot of people around, making a lot of noise, here's some more."

Throughout the late 1960s and into the 1970s, George Harrison continued to use various pseudonyms to let fans and friends know he had secretly played sessions on the albums of other artists. The many names used by George Harrison during his solo career are long and humorous, including George Harrysong, George O'Hara, Son of Harry, Harry Georgeson, P. Roducer, Jai Raj Harisein, L'Angelo Misterioso, and many more. On George Harrison's own solo record, *All Things Must Pass*, he even supplied his own multi-tracked background vocals, using the *nom de plume* "George O'Hara-Smith Singers."

Perhaps one of the funniest alter egos adopted by Harrison was displayed during a surprise appearance at a Sydney, Australia concert in 1984. When Harrison's friends in Deep Purple brought him onstage as a guest, George introduced himself. "I am Arnold Grove from Liverpool," said the guitarist, in a humorous reference to the street name of the house he grew up in.

Bob Dylan was also no stranger to the use of an alter ego. Born Robert Allen Zimmerman, the young man started playing music in his home state of Minnesota while still in high school. Having grown up in the 1950s, Bob was familiar with short, snappy names for pop musicians such as Chuck Berry and Elvis Presley. While still only a teenager, he created his first pseudonym for a stage-name persona, and thus "Bob Dylan" was born.

As legend would have it, the pundits often repeat the myth that the name "Dylan" came from Bob's love of Dylan Thomas' poetry. However, the musician himself refutes this myth. In answer to a related question in a 1978 interview, Dylan stated, "No, I haven't read that much Dylan Thomas…. It wasn't that I was inspired by reading some of his poetry and going 'Aha!' and changing my name to Dylan. If I thought he was that great, I would have sung his poems and could just have easily changed my name to Thomas…. I just chose that name and it stuck." When Bob Dylan moved to New York in early 1961, he left Zimmerman behind forever, except for the fact that this legal name was still on his driver's license. In October 1961, John Hammond signed Bob Dylan to his first exclusive recording contract with Columbia Records.

Robert Shelton, a folk music critic of *The New York Times* and early fan of Dylan, recalls Dylan's early interest in writing songs with social commentary. "He was influenced by the whole *Broadside* magazine scene which included Pete Seger, and this was probably his period of greatest political involvement…" In late 1962, Dylan was asked to contribute some songs to *Broadside's* record project. Since Dylan was already signed to Columbia, it would have been a breach of contract for him to record for another company. In 1963, the Broadside/Folkways record label released an album titled *Broadside Ballads Volume 1*. The album contained three interesting songs with the titles "John Brown," "Only a Hobo," and "Talking Devil." The songs were credited to a musician named "Blind Boy Grunt."

It was fairly obvious at the time that the voice behind the songs belonged to Bob Dylan using this pseudonym. In this manner, Dylan was able to record anonymously, apart from his contractual obligations to Columbia.

Blind Boy Grunt was not the only pseudonym Dylan used in his early career. He appeared as piano player "Bob Landy" on the 1964 anthology album called the *Blues Project* for Elektra records. "Bob Landy" can be heard tickling the ivories on the song "Downtown Blues." Also in 1964, Dylan adopted the name "Tedham Porterhouse" in order to secretly play harmonica on Rambling Jack Elliot's album track, "Will The Circle Be Unbroken." He also lent a hand to Steve Goodman, adding piano and harmony vocals on Goodman's song, "Somebody Else's Trouble," in the early 1970s. On that song he became "Robert Milkwood Thomas." In each case, Dylan was clearly trying to avoid any contractual disputes with Columbia while still lending a hand to other musician friends in the studio.

Handle With Care

In 1988, Warner Brothers' international records division asked George Harrison to create a new song to serve as a B-side to a single they planned to release from his *Cloud 9* album called "This is Love." The new song would provide the single with additional value for Harrison's fans, giving them an extra track not heard on the new album. That evening, Harrison and his co-producer/friend, Jeff Lynne, were out to dinner with Roy Orbison. Lynne was currently producing a new album for Orbison who was a huge recording star from the 1950s, having been first discovered by Sam Phillips. Orbison and Harrison were old friends from 1963 when Roy and The Beatles toured England together on the same concert bill.

That night, while Harrison, Lynne, and Orbison dined out, they discussed Harrison's need to record another song for Warner Bros. When Lynne informed Harrison that one could not find a studio on such short notice, George suggested that he call Bob Dylan who had a home garage studio. Again, through a coincidence, Bob Dylan, who was planning for his 1988 "Never Ending Tour," and who would play 71 shows that year, was actually at home! He invited them to come over to his home the next day, and Orbison was invited to come along.

The next day, Harrison swung by Tom Petty's house to pick up a guitar he had loaned him. Harrison explained that he had to record a B-side and that they were headed to Bob Dylan's garage studio. Tom said, "I wondered what I was going to do today." So Petty tagged along and all five rock and roll legends found themselves hanging around Bob's garage, helping George write and record his B-side. Once the song, "Handle With Care," was written, George figured there was no point in wasting all of this assembled talent, so he put them to work sharing lead vocal duties. No doubt, Harrison and Lynne realized they had formed the group they often joked about during the *Cloud 9* sessions. This was the silly, imagined group they had originally tagged "Trembling Wilburys."

According to Mo Ostin, who was then CEO of Warner Brothers, Harrison came by a few days later to play his new "B-side." Ostin said, "We went next door to A&R head Lenny Woronker's office so he could hear it too. George played 'Handle With Care.' Our reaction was immediate," said Ostin. "This was a song we knew could *not* be wasted on some B-side. Roy Orbison's vocal was tremendous. I really loved the beautiful guitar figure George played. The guys had really nailed it. Lenny and I stumbled over each other's words, asking, 'Can't we somehow turn *this* into an album?' I also had a suspicion that perhaps George had been hungering for another band experience." Ostin's suspicion was prescient, and thus a new supergroup was born of friendship, dreams, and talent with a little help from the stars (astrological and otherwise).

A Name By Any Other Name Is Still A Wilbury

Clearly, the concept of a band of "friend-burys" was on Harrison's mind before the "Handle With Care" sessions of 1988. There is significant evidence (including the existence of a special, tiny artifact) that Harrison had been plotting and planning for a while. Sidebury drummer and longtime friend Jim Keltner said, "I was very used to George being able to do anything, so while others may have been astonished, I thought, 'Okay, this is another one of George's deals.' George just had that way about him."

The first time Harrison really let the cat out of the bag to a third party was in the fall of 1987. Harrison was asked to create an extended mix of his *Cloud 9* hit song "Got My Mind Set On You." The tape engineer, Bill Bottrell, had been given only a two-track tape. In order to extend the song, Bottrell needed Harrison to record a new guitar solo to create a third track. Harrison agreed to record the part, but didn't have a guitar. The studio, Village Recorder, did not have a spare guitar available. However, a staff tech offered to go get his guitar and loan it to Harrison for the session. It was a red Hamer prototype, solid-body electric guitar.

Bottrell confirmed that the idea of forming the Traveling Wilburys surfaced in their discussions while they were waiting for the tech to run home and fetch the guitar, and the first piece of Traveling Wilburys "forensic evidence" surfaced at that time as well. Bottrell recalled, "We were sitting around, and George said, 'Yeah, I guess we're gonna have a group or something.' Then he handed me a Traveling Wilburys guitar pick." Oddly, the group name was purposely misspelled on the pick. Harrison confirmed this first revelation of the group name even before he had secured the members of his band. "Yeah," said Harrison. "Somebody was making these [custom] picks and they said, 'What shall I put on them?' Everybody has some smart little thing written on the pick. So as we'd [Jeff Lynne and Harrison] just been talking about this Trembling Wilburys, I had *'Travelling Wilbury's'* misspelled on this guitar pick.... But at that point it was just a drunken thought..."

It was the lack of ego by five superstars that gave way to the Traveling Wilburys' alter ego. So many other supergroups had crashed and burned before takeoff due to the clash of super egos. Jeff Lynne affirmed, "Nobody [in the group] thought that they were better than anybody else really. I actually made up the name Traveling Wilburys." Bob Dylan was unsure if he liked the name at first. He had a different idea. "I don't think Bob was that keen," recalled Lynne. "He wanted to call it 'Roy and the Boys.'" Dylan must have been outvoted.

This "drunken thought" took on even more reality in a nationwide radio broadcast for *Rockline* in February 1988, when George publicly revealed for the first time, "But, what I'd really like to do next, is you know, not particularly my own album. [I'd like] to do an album with me and some of my mates. That way we could do something different." Pausing to ponder the concept, George clarified, "You know, a few tunes... maybe the 'Traveling Wilburys'. This is the new group I got.... It's called the Traveling Wilburys. I'd like to do an album with them, and later, we can all do our own albums again."

As plans for the new group and album were being made, Harrison began to create the characters, faux history, and imagery for his utopian world of the Traveling Wilburys. What began as an idea to create a fictional band morphed into a real band of superstars who were then transformed back into an imaginary world with funny aliases. Harrison conjured up a faux family tree with a humorous backstory, names, and custom guitar picks for his bandmates. He even wrote out a funny little business card design, reminiscent of the early, pre-Beatles Quarrymen, hoping to get a local gig. The card read "Functions, Party's [sic], Dances... the Traveling Wilburys," along with a telephone number. It was hand-printed in red ink on a yellow lined legal pad.

Significantly, George Harrison wanted his friends and the recording sessions to be relaxed, casual, fun, and productive. To this end, Harrison had had an experience in The Beatles in which many of his own contributions to Lennon-McCartney songs (both lyrically and musically) were never credited or acknowledged with compensation or publishing credit. Harrison knew that the best way to preserve harmony in his new group was to acknowledge each songwriter's input on each song in a fashion commensurate with his contribution. "I know now, writing with friends, that when you're all sitting around and a song comes out, you have to think carefully about assigning how many percent each person gets," said Harrison. "Cause there's nothing worse than being involved in a situation [like The Beatles] where you think, 'Wasn't I there?'"

The Wilburys began with the democratic concept that everyone who helped write the lyrics and/or music of a song would receive a proportionate share of the publishing revenues. This system of revenue sharing went a long way toward preventing arguments that have been the cause of many rock bands breaking up or suing each other over the years. Publishing deals were prepared and implemented by the group. In examining copies of Traveling Wilburys' publishing agreements (made public at memorabilia auctions over the years), the documents demonstrate the practice of the group's democratic pro-rata compensation plan, based upon actual creative contributions for each song. On the song, "Rattled," for example, the contract between EMI Publishing and the members of the group specifies, "… any and all profit from the song is to be divided as follows: Bob Dylan 14.17%, George Harrison 24.79%, Jeff Lynne 39.79%, Roy Orbison 7.08% and Tom Petty 14.17%." The band's egalitarianism ensured that each member was equitably rewarded based upon his input on each song.

The group's name, Traveling Wilburys, also served another important purpose—to diffuse any possible ego issues among the five superstars. Imagine the potential problems if the band had decided to call itself Harrison, Dylan, Orbison, Lynne & Petty. And imagine the discussion within the group of what the order of billing should be for those five names! By utilizing a humorous, easy-going name, the group could immediately downplay its relative stardom and get down to collaborating on songwriting, vocals, guitar lines, lyrics, and arrangements.

The band also recognized that there would likely be incredible pressure from very high expectations by fans, the music industry, and the media, if word of the sessions leaked out. Harrison was aware of this potential pitfall. "Well, first of all, you can blow a good thing or the press or somebody can. All you need is somebody to say, 'We know about this thing that's happening,' and it just takes the wind out of it." The Wilburys' name was the perfect solution to creating a relaxed, creative, and private environment in which to make a record.

"We did this on our own. No managers involved," affirmed Tom Petty. "He [George] wanted to be in a band but he wanted to avoid all those pitfalls that a band has." Jeff Lynne attested, "We just were having fun being these other people [Traveling Wilburys]." Roy Orbison summed it up the best, "We did it for the music's sake. And I feel very honored to be with this bunch." Mo Ostin, who had told George Harrison that his collaboration on "Handle With Care" was too good to waste on a B-side, understood Harrison's move to create a relaxed atmosphere conducive to creating a cohesive collaboration with five superstars. He explained, "The group was born: five guys with star stature in their own rights, but it was George who created this Wilbury environment where five stars could enjoy an ego-free collaboration. Everybody sang, everybody wrote, everybody produced—and had great fun doing so."

Harrison was very clever in creating a pseudonym for the band to secrete it from discovery until he could "clear the way first" with each member's record company. Just how did Harrison convince the corporate label CEOs to play nice and lend out their members? "I went to MCA and talked to them," said Harrison. "I said, 'I was thinking of doing something with a few friends, more like a group thing, and I know Tom Petty's on your label but would it be any trouble if he was on the record because, if it is, maybe I'll just use somebody else.' I went with that kind of attitude and they said, 'Oh no, we're an artist-oriented label, fine, fine, fine.'" Harrison's clever strategy worked for each member and his respective record company.

Someday Everybody Gonna Be A Wilbury

In April 1988, Nelson… err, George Harrison set about jotting down ideas for this new, self-contained, imaginary Wilbury world in which his band of mega-stars would truly become a band of whimsical brothers. But beyond musical comradery, Harrison was thinking of the project as one in which everyone—including family, friends, and fans—would feel like they too could be a happy Traveling Wilbury.

He began creating pencil drawings of band logos, business cards, and other ephemera. He drafted a little promo handbill poster with pictures of early 1900s airplanes with a message directed at fans, but with a jab at the record industry. It read simply, "Just when you thought that real music was gone forever…THERE CAME the TRAVELING WILBURYS. No Computers—all done by hand." He made sure to create rays of sunshine around the band's name to underscore the positive vibes the band's music would bring to each other and to the world.

The chief Wilbury had recently received a thank-you note from Dinah Gretsch of The Gretsch Company, thanking him for posing on the cover of his recent album, *Cloud 9*, with his Gretsch guitar. Dinah Gretsch related the story to the Rock And Roll Detective: "He [George] called me directly at our office. He thanked me for sending the thank-you card." George told her a little about The Beatles' history with his black Gretsch guitar. Then to Dinah's great surprise, George said, "I've got this new group called the Traveling Wilburys and we are going to be recording at Dave Stewart's house. I was wondering if you and Fred [Gretsch] could come here because I have some ideas I would like to discuss with you." So, Dinah and Fred went that weekend to meet initially with Tom Petty, Jeff Lynne, and George Harrison—a mystery trip that would be revealed only upon their arrival.

The timing of this meeting was fortuitous for the Gretsch family. Gretsch was founded in 1883 by Friedrich Gretsch, a German born immigrant who had moved to Brooklyn at the age of sixteen. The young man was a guitar maker and innovator. As the company was handed down through generations, it became known for its precision and superior quality in the craftsmanship of guitars.

In 1960, George Harrison of the young and relatively unknown Beatles purchased a used 1957 Gretsch Duo Jet guitar. He used it on some of The Beatles' earliest recordings and live concert tours. Later, in the mid-1960s, during the height of Beatlemania, Harrison would use his new Gretsch Chet Atkins Country Gentleman guitar on the Ed Sullivan show, which caused thousands of Baby Boomer aspiring guitarists to go out and purchase the very same guitar from Gretsch.

By 1967, owner Fred Gretsch, Jr. (the uncle of current owner Fred Gretsch) had retired and sold the company to the Baldwin Music Company. Over the next eighteen years, the company did not fare well under non-family ownership. Production of Gretsch guitars became more limited and was shut down completely in 1980. According to great-grandson Fred Gretsch, "During all that time, it was my fervent desire to return the company to Gretsch family ownership." In 1985, Fred achieved his goal of buying the company back for his family from the Baldwin group. "When we bought it," says Dinah, "they had not made any guitars in like six years because their factory had burned down. So, when we bought it, guitars had not been made…" Enter, the Traveling Wilburys!

After making "Handle With Care," The Traveling Wilburys reconvened at the home-studio of ex-Eurhythmics' guitarist/producer Dave Stewart, on May 7, 1988. "So we left that weekend," recalls Dinah. "We met with Tom Petty, Jeff Lynne and George Harrison at Dave Stewart's house. They had all these guitars there, with the idea to make a *Wilburys* guitar!" They told the couple, "We want Gretsch to make them for us."

The band members excitedly used the guitars they had brought to the session to share their ideas for the size, shape, tuners, headstock, neck, fret markers, finger board, tone, and volume controls. Dinah said, "Tom, Jeff and George all had a lot of input. They had already talked about it before we got there and all had good [design] ideas." So the Wilburys and the Gretsch's worked out four basic designs that would turn into six total Traveling Wilburys' models (with a couple having minor changes like a tremolo bar added).

The interesting artistic look and concept for the guitars was revealed to Fred and Dinah by Harrison. He told them, "There should not be two alike." Harrison had already figured out how to achieve the unique look of every Wilburys' guitar. "George created this really large graphic design for the production of the guitars. It was like 3 x 5 feet. And he did all the drawing and coloring himself," recalls Dinah. The huge graphic would be turned and positioned differently on top of each guitar produced to create a different unique design on each Wilburys' guitar. Dinah confirmed, "George did all the drawing and coloring himself, but each guitar would have the Traveling Wilburys name on it. And it was George's idea that all of the Wilburys' family member names—Nelson, Otis, Charlie T. Jr, Lefty, and Lucky—would be autographed [and reproduced] on the back of each guitar."

The Gretsches were in store for another surprise that day, consistent with Harrison's master plan of sharing the Traveling Wilburys' fictional world and faux-family history with fans around the globe. Dinah recalls that she and her husband assumed the band wanted Gretsch to make expensive custom guitars. However, the Wilburys had a different

Traveling Wilburys poster designed by George Harrison.

idea. Dinah explained, "They wanted to have everybody be able to play a Wilburys guitar. They wanted to price it so that everybody could afford one." This would tie in nicely with Harrison's desire to share the fun Wilbury "family" with their fans. To emphasize this point, he later had promotional posters made stating, "Someday, Everybody Gonna Be A Wilbury."

Harrison's master plan for his imaginary family forming a fictional band, and keeping it fun, was now in play. Ironically, he had the first piece in place for fans long before the album had even been recorded. Dinah summed up their time sitting in on writing and recording sessions with the Wilburys as follows: "The Wilburys wanted the whole thing to be fun: the music, the names and the custom guitar. You knew it from the minute you were there. They would sit around and laugh." The Gretsch [guitars] were present at the time the group was working up the hilarious song "Dirty World." Dinah said, "They would make up some lyrics for example, then laugh and say, 'No, no, we can't say that... ha ha ha.' They showed us all the Gretsch guitars they were using. It was barefoot, jeans and hair all over the place, recording and recording and having a fun time."

The Wilburys' custom guitars were ultimately manufactured in Korea to keep the retail cost low for fans. "So, in 1988, the Wilburys' guitar was our first custom guitar project," said Dinah, "but we hadn't even made any guitars yet." By the end of 1988, the band had signed the Wilbury autographs to be used on the guitar backs, the artwork and models were all approved, the contracts were signed, and all of the attorneys had agreed. The guitars began their manufacture in Korea at the start of 1989. But at least one prototype had been created in advance. Gretsch had made one model TW-300 for a special event in the fall of 1988. More on that later....

We Love Your Sexy Body…

One of the first songs recorded at Dave Stewart's home was a full-on band collaboration of a down-and-dirty song that started with Bob Dylan. Dylan, a native of Minnesota, was fascinated with fellow Minnesota artist Prince, and his sexy/dirty songs. George Harrison described the scene as the Wilburys were just starting to throw around ideas for the song "Dirty World." "We just sat down and we said, 'Okay, what are we going to do?' And Bob said, 'Let's do one just like Prince.' And he just started banging away, 'Love your sexy body, ooo, baby.' I love that track. It's just so funny, really." The other band members immediately jumped into the scheme, throwing out ideas from car magazines and off the top of their heads. Each lyrical idea was duly written down by Harrison and Dylan. The suggestions ranged from mere sexual innuendo to hilarious in-your-face dirty comments, normally reserved for construction workers watching pretty girls walk by at lunch break.

Recalling Dinah Gretsch's comments that the band had to reject some of the racier lyrics, The Rock And Roll Detective examined copies of the original lyric sheets. This documentary evidence clearly showed lines drawn through some of those rejected lyrics

Traveling Wilburys guitar back with alter ego autographs.

from "Dirty World" that were too funny, too on-point, and perhaps too naughty to include in the song: "We love your… Added Stiffness… We love your… Shakey Cockpit…. We love your… Pointed Pyramids…"

One line clearly illustrates Dylan's enjoyment with being in this fictitious brotherhood, telling his fictional girlfriend that he wants to, "… 'introduce you to the other' members of his gang. As Dylan sings the line, the astute listener can hear each of the other Wilburys vocally introduce themselves, singing a Beatles "Twist and Shout"-like vocal run. You can absolutely feel the collective glee of a band of brothers up to mischief.

The high jinks continued as the band recited a number of hilarious sexual innuendos to be sung, in turns, by each Wilbury standing in a circle around the microphones. "We just wrote this random list and had it on the microphone," said Harrison. "… and then we just did the take. And whoever sang first, sang the first one, and we just sang around the group until we'd done them all." There was one lyric that paid tribute to Lynne and Harrison's original secret group name from the *Cloud 9* sessions, the group's name check of the original pseudonym for the band. Jeff Lynne picks up the story. "And every time it came around to Roy Orbison [to sing], he always got the line 'We love your… Trembling Wilbury.' We almost collapsed every time. And no matter how we rearranged it, he always ended up with 'Trembling Wilbury' (laughing)."

Orbison jokingly felt the "Trembling Wilburys" line was rigged for him to sing. In the Wilburys documentary, *The True Story of the Traveling Wilburys*, he spoke about it to Lynne and Harrison. "Not even Traveling. [It was] Trembling. Whichever way it went around it was a conspiracy (laughs)," he said. "If we sang [in the circle] to the left, I got the duff line, if we started to the right, I got the duff line." Laughing out loud, Lynne replied, "It was just meant to be I think."

The band name also came up in another prenatal form during the pre-Wilburys' sessions for Tom Petty's *Full Moon Fever* album. Petty recalled, "When we were making *Full Moon Fever,* we did a lot of it in the same studio." On the track "Zombie Zoo," Petty, Lynne, and Orbison combined to sing the song. "… We used to do background vocals, me and him [Roy Orbison] and Jeff Lynne, and we called ourselves the Trembling Blenders." Yet another variation of the Traveling Wilburys name had surfaced.

Another Wilbury briefly made his singing debut on the *Wilbury 1* album, although uncredited. Harrison's son Dhani actually got to sing background vocals on the album at the young age of only nine. This secret was recently revealed by Dhani himself in an Instagram post to Jeff Lynne following their successful 2019 tour together. Dhani recalled, "You are my family and I have been standing right next to you during some of the greatest moments of my life. From the first time we sang 'Margarita' together on *Wilbury 1*."

Pickin' Plectrum Names

The unique Traveling Wilburys alter egos served a special purpose, one in which each individual in the band could free himself from previous fame and the self-imposed standards each had employed to write and record on his own individual albums. Harrison explained, "We wanted it to be like a proper group. But at the same time, to have a bit of a rough edge and it gave us all a way [to do it]. Maybe it's like safety in numbers. You can hide behind each other a little bit and get away with a little bit more that you wouldn't allow yourself to get away with on your own, where you become so critical."

The real names of the five band members did not appear anywhere on the finished first album. However, it was easy enough to spot their true identities by listening to the individual members' distinctive voices and seeing their faces on the album cover. The *Sgt. Pepper's Lonely Hearts Club Band* album had featured The Beatles "disguised" on their album cover, dressed in special silk coats and newly-grown mustaches; however, just like the Wilburys, their unmistakable voices were instantly recognizable on the record. For the Wilburys, this was all beside the point because their alter egos served a broader, more psychological purpose—to free up creativity and share brotherly friendship for everyone's sheer amusement. On early copies of Traveling Wilburys posters and albums, the band members even went so far as to sign autographs using their Wilburys nicknames.

The band was truly intended to be a collaborative effort. "Nobody really outranked anybody. It was a group effort," recalled Petty. When Harrison asked each member to come up with his own special Wilbury name, each fashioned their own creative identity. Petty observed, "Everybody picked their names because we didn't want to sound like Crosby, Stills, Nash & Young, like a bunch of lawyers." Petty continued, "And maybe we could lessen that [pressure] a little bit by taking on different identities. We didn't want to kind of slide on who we were…. And we wanted to keep a sense of humor about it." Harrison added his take on the use of make-believe names. "There were always these groups in the 70s, these superstar groups, and we hated that. All these famous people trying to make a record. You know, it doesn't mean it's going to be good, just because you get these famous people together," he said. "I wanted to avoid that totally."

Early on, there were quite a few silly Wilburys nicknames created for sheer amusement, but not actually chosen. Some of these were memorialized by Jeff Lynne on a T-shirt, and included Hagerty F., Hagerty R., Tomkins, Crapper, Dewhur, and MacInty Wilbury. In the end, the original Wilburys chose Nelson (George Harrison), Otis (Jeff Lynne), Lefty (Roy Orbison), Lucky (Bob Dylan), and Charlie T. Jr (Tom Petty). Interestingly, Harrison had created a family tree sketch with the five mothers who bore Charlie T. Wilbury Senior's sons. The hilarious list of "moms" included Alma Belvedere, Cahuenga Shoe Box (Betty Crocket), Eufrosyne Savalis, Ann Tenor (Gladys Ormsby Jones), and Pearl Talbot.

George Harrison's choice of Nelson Wilbury found its origin in his beloved hobby of following Formula One race car drivers and competitions. Harrison recalled how he came to love car racing from a very early age. "I used to go to watch motorcycle racing at Aintree, in Liverpool, and I saw a poster advertising sports car racing," he said. "I used to go up to the railway straight at Aintree and my earliest memory of a car is a Jaguar XK120 racing [against] a Mercedes-Benz 300SL." Harrison never had one favorite driver. He was a fan of many drivers, including Jackie Stewart (who was memorialized in Harrison's song "Faster"), Emerson Fittipaldi (who Harrison honored in a get-well version of "Here Comes Emerson" to the tune of "Here Comes The Sun"), and Damon Hill.

Harrison was not only a fan of race drivers, he also counted them as his friends. Long time Monty Python friend Michael Palin recalled a party at Harrison's Friar Park in July 1983, and meeting a Brazilian driver who had just raced in the British Grand Prix the day before. "We met Nelson Piquet, the Brazilian driver who came [in] second at Silverstone yesterday…. Piquet's a little, perky, pleasantly ambitious Brazilian. He loves his work. No doubts, no fears, from what he says," recalled Palin. Harrison would often invite Grand Prix drivers who he liked over to the house. Harrison enjoyed Piquet's spunky nature and sense of humor. In 1985, Piquet posed in a hilarious photo in the pits of the European Grand Prix with George Harrison, Ringo Starr, and driver Jackie Stewart. In the photo, Ringo is trying to fix Stewart's nose with a mechanic's wrench as the others look on in laughter. Known as a practical joker on the race circuit, it is not a surprise that Harrison might have taken his Wilbury name from Nelson Piquet.

Tom Petty had an alternate origin for "Nelson Wilbury." He revealed that it was Derek Taylor who first took a crack at writing the fictional account of the Traveling Wilburys. "He [Harrison] had him write an entire history of the Wilbury family," said Petty. Taylor, a long-time friend of George Harrison's, had been The Beatles' press relations man during part of their touring years in the 1960s and later joined the group's company, Apple Corps Ltd., as their press officer. He later went to L.A. for a couple of decades to work with artists and record labels there and authored several great books before returning to Apple in London in the 1990s. Petty recalled, "Derek Taylor wrote this huge history of the Wilburys. There was extensive (laughs) extensive work done on it; you know. Derek's thing was really funny.... It didn't make the album." However, both Petty and Lynne believe George Harrison's selection of the name Nelson Wilbury originated in Taylor's faux Wilburys' history. He recalled Harrison naming everyone a Wilbury name for laughs, but "he just used to crack up with 'Nelson,'" said Petty. He continued in conversation with Lynne, "What was it? He [Derek Taylor] had some General Wilbury?" Lynne replied, "Oh, you mean Lord Nelson?" Petty replied, "Lord Nelson, yeah!"

Lord Nelson was one of Britain's greatest naval commanders. He had a long and distinguished career, during which he earned a reputation as a master war strategist and for his bravery. But something else about Lord Nelson likely appealed to George Harrison. Nelson possessed the characteristics of a daring and bold commander. At one point, Nelson was blinded in one eye. When he was given a command to withdraw his troops at the Battle of Copenhagen, he ignored the command with a cheeky move. He placed his telescope up to his blind eye and pretended not to see the enemy. His mischievous move paid off with his gaining victory in the battle. No doubt, Lord Nelson's naughty but humorous nature likely appealed to Harrison. Although an interesting theory, Dhani Harrison definitively confirmed that his dad had created his Wilbury moniker after the race car driver. "My dad had chosen Nelson Wilbury after Nelson Piquet, the racing driver."

Jeff Lynne decided to choose "Otis Wilbury." The story behind his choice is not as in-depth or personal as with the other members of this brotherly tribe. Lynne told journalist Matt Hurwitz that the origin was really based upon treating the whole group formation lightly. "Well, because we didn't want to be taken seriously, like... or too seriously, you know. Or take ourselves too seriously about what we were doing," recalled Lynne. "I think it was George's idea, that we all should have silly names." When asked how he had chosen the name Otis Wilbury, Lynne replied simply, "I just thought, 'What's the opposite to me?' Otis (laughs)?!" As simple as that, we all now know that the name "Otis" is the opposite of "Jeff."

Tom Petty credited Derek Taylor's writing of the Wilburys' history with influencing his choice of a Wilbury name on the first album. In the course of Taylor's history, Petty recalled, "... the Wilburys' father was named Charles Truscott (laughs). And I thought that was so funny that I decided I'd be Charles Truscott, Jr (laughs)." Being the youngest member in the group, "Charlie T. Wilbury Jr" made the most sense to Petty.

Roy Orbison was surely the first of the Traveling Wilburys to create his Wilbury persona. As a young man and budding musician, Orbison idolized American country music singer/song-writer and guitarist Lefty Frizzell. Back in high school in 1954, young Roy Orbison signed a yearbook for his friend, Charles Evans, as follows: "Roy 'Lefty' Orbison," the same name he would choose on *Traveling Wilburys Volume 1*. In searching for his style and voice as a teenage singer, Orbison was an early fan of the style of Lefty Frizzell. Orbison recalled, "The first singer I heard on the radio who really slayed me was Lefty Frizzell. He had this technique which involved sliding syllables together that really blew me away." And thus, "Lefty Wilbury" was born.

On June 20, 1966, Bob Dylan released his classic album *Blonde on Blonde*. He was at a creative and popular peak in his career, yet he was also burned out from touring and all of the attention paid to him by fans, stalkers, and the media. One of the songs on his new release was called "Pledging My Time." The song contained some interesting lyrics that foreshadowed a dramatic life-changing moment in Dylan's life. The last verse of the song talked about an accident, including "somebody got *lucky*."

Just one month later, on July 29, 1966, Dylan was riding his Triumph motorcycle on a winding stretch of road near his home in Woodstock, New York, when he lost control and crashed. Dylan broke his neck and had to wear a brace on it for at least six weeks, and he was very "lucky" to escape death. The lines of "Pledging My Time" seemed to foreshadow his accident. And Dylan's theme of good fortune would reappear in future songs such as "Minstrel Boy" ("Oh, *Lucky's* been drivin'...") and "Idiot Wind" ("... can't help if I'm *lucky*"). The moniker would become a lifelong alter ego for the artist who knew he had barely escaped "knockin' on heaven's door." So it is not at all surprising that Dylan would choose "Lucky Wilbury" as his fictitious name in the group.

When Dylan's old friend George Harrison came onstage at Bob Dylan's 30th Anniversary Concert Celebration at Madison Square Garden in 1992, George introduced him, referencing Dylan's song "Serve Somebody," but adding his Wilburys moniker. "Some of you may call him Bobby; some of you may call him Zimmy. I call him Lucky," he said. "Ladies and gentlemen, please welcome Bob Dylan!"

In keeping with Harrison's sense of humor, Harrison dubbed saxophone player Jim Horn a "Sidebury" and pronounced that Wilburys' drummer Jim Keltner would henceforth be forever known as "Buster Sidebury."

When George asked his guitar tech to make up custom guitar picks with the Traveling Wilburys' names on them, there were twelve different picks made for the first album sessions: Traveling Wilbury, Travelling Wilburys, Nelson Wilbury, Otis Wilbury, Lefty Wilbury, Lucky Wilbury, Charlie T. Wilbury Jr, Gladys Wilbury, Biff Wilbury, Betty Wilbury, and Cyril Wilbury.

There has been a lot of conjecture about the last four Wilbury names and if they actually belonged to anyone involved in the project. One Harrison insider remarked to the Rock And Roll Detective, "I know it's always been a bit of a mystery. As far as I know, some of these were 'Wilbury spares' in case anyone else needed to join the Wilburys and weren't actually assigned." Despite being unassigned, the names were quite funny.

"Biff Wilbury" was never officially assigned to a musical Wilbury, but was likely a Harrison homage to *Biff Comics*, which ran as a multi-panel comic strip in the UK's *Guardian* newspaper from 1985 to 2005. It was well known for its ironic cultural commentary, a style of humor closely akin to Harrison's own. According to film director David Leland, a creative colleague of Harrison's, "If Biff is on the pick, then you can bet George was familiar with the comic." Another Harrison insider commented on the Biff Wilbury pick, telling the Rock And Roll Detective, "That is such a funny name. I can see why George would have liked that one."

Klaus Voormann, the great artist and bass player, believes he knows when and why George came up with the names "Cyril" and "Betty Wilbury." The names surfaced during the recording of Harrison's solo album *All Things Must Pass*. Voormann recalled, "The two girls in question were Doris Troy and Madeline Bell. They were session singers in London in those days." The girls were fun to hang out with and Troy even took Voormann to a gospel church in London. However, he explained that "she was a bugger when it came down to money, royalties or session fees. If she had to stay 10 minutes over, she would charge an extra session fee." This type of behavior did not sit well with Harrison. "So, I remember," said Klaus, "this was the reason he did not mention their [real] names in the credits on *All Things Must Pass*. Thus, the anonymous singers became Cyril and Betty [in the album credits]." It is quite likely that Harrison may well have resurrected these two silly names for the spare Traveling Wilburys' guitar plectrums.

The Wilburys' picks made George smile at their sheer Python-like silliness. It was Harrison himself who had taken the name "Jack Lumber" [recalling the famous Monty Python sketch, "I'm a Lumber Jack"), put it on a pick, and reportedly used that alter ego to check in anonymously to hotels during his 1974 U.S. solo tour. When asked about these extra names he liked to create, Harrison replied, "We could have the Wilbury B-team. Like 'We Are The World'—we could have 'We Are The Wilburys'! I'd love to do that." Continuing the running joke about the benchwarmer Wilburys names, Harrison concluded, "Maybe it won't be the Wilburys, maybe it will be... the Trundling Wheelbarrows. Or the Smegmas: Betty, Doris, Gladys and Cyril Smegma... Volume 7."

Now that the band had created an anonymous persona and had written and recorded the songs for their first album, *Traveling Wilburys Volume 1*, it was time to surprise the world with this gift of music and good cheer. In promoting the album, Harrison had a number of *norti-bit* ideas up his sleeve.

By the Light of the Wilbury Moon

With the album completed, Harrison, who had the greatest claim to the band, signed them to the Warner Brothers label. Then the "Legalburys" went to work, first creating a company called T. Wilbury Limited Corporation United Kingdom to *handle* their business *with care*. Once that was completed, Harrison created a boutique record label for the group, Wilbury Records, that would appear on all media and music released by the group. Harrison had great experience in this area, having co-created The Beatles' boutique label Apple Corps Ltd. in the 1960s and his own Dark Horse Records label in the 1970s.

At the end of a quiet evening on August 13, 1988, the doorbell rang at the home of ex-Monty Python, Michael Palin. It would be highly unusual to expect visitors at this time of night. Palin's wife Helen cautioned Michael to look very carefully through the spy hole before opening the front door. "I look through the spy hole. There, beside the scaffolding, clutching an envelope is one of The Beatles," recalled Palin. "It's George, with the Wilburys' sleeve notes he wants me to have a look at." Palin invited in George, Olivia, and Dhani Harrison, along with Dominic Taylor (the son of Derek and Joan) and his girlfriend. Harrison explained the assignment and likely shared Derek Taylor's early mythology of the group and his desire for Michael to tell the story on the sleeve of *Volume*

Michael Palin of Monty Python performing the Lumberjack song with Carol Cleveland.

1. And thus, Hugh Jampton, E. F. Norti-Bitz (Reader in Applied Jacket, Faculty of Sleeve Notes, University of Krakatoa, East of Java) was created, as Palin humorously tells the Wilburys' faux backstory. In recalling the process of writing the sleeve notes for the first album, Palin said, "I'm quite proud of that."

Ironically, George Harrison, the alleged "quiet Beatle," became the de-facto "manager" to navigate the shark-infested waters of five different managers and record labels. "… Cause in a way I was the Wilburys' manager," affirmed Harrison. "In the recording studio I was doing everything, all the art work and coordinating publishing deals so everyone was happy, trying to get the record deal…" And of course, Harrison was also co-writing, playing, recording, and co-producing the album.

During the recording of the album, Harrison took a number of home videos (both at Dave Stewart's house and at Friar Park) of the group writing, playing, singing, and relaxing. The resulting footage would be used by Harrison to extend the mystery and the joke to the marketing and sales team at Warner Bros. Records at their nationwide summer convention in New Orleans. The film was entitled *Whatever Wilbury Wilbury*, and was dripping with Monty Python influences and references. One of the things that instantly bonded the five members was their love of Monty Python's sense of humor, especially between George Harrison and Roy Orbison, the latter of whom seemed to have memorized every skit. Harrison, whose company had produced Monty Python's film *The Life of Brian*, played up the Wilburys' style of humor in the promotional film which was never released to the general public.

The film featured a funny cartoon-like version of Nelson Wilbury talking and welcoming the Warner Bros. brass in jaw-drop, Terry Gilliam-animation style. The home movies were shown with the songs from the album played over the footage. Each half-brother Wilbury was introduced only with his alter ego name. The conventioneers were privileged to watch the band singing and recording the sexually-charged song "Dirty World," comparing sex to automotive parts and service. The band was shown singing vocals and cracking up whenever Lefty Wilbury sang, "She loves your Trembling Wilburys." At one point in the film, Harrison features a close up of a squirrel and labels him "Eddie Wilbury."

Even the ending credits of the film were hilarious, if you got the joke. Harrison credited himself as "Director" under the name "Cecil Bidet Wilbury," and as "Cameraman Norris Fault." Some of the funniest non-assigned credits included "Lighting" by "Edison Wilbury" and "Catering" by "Big Mac Wilbury." Harrison's sense of humor shined throughout the film and likely endeared the entire gathering at this convention to support the Wilburys' forthcoming album. The film ended with the inclusive message, "Remember, someday everybody gonna be a Wilbury." Aside from the film's humor, the theme of inclusion and letting everyone be a Wilbury was a major ongoing message in Harrison's Wilbury folklore creation.

Now came the fun part of expanding the promotion and marketing of the clandestine band in anticipation of surprising the world with the release of a secret supergroup record album.

The Wilburys Are Coming!

In early October 1988, Wilbury Records Inc. put out a somewhat mysterious press release to the media. It announced a strange musical group: "The Traveling Wilburys, a famous band of brothers, with years of struggle, strife and triumph in their knapsacks, are launching into a new phase of their journey, their voice raised to a level of awareness sharper than ever would have seemed possible." The presser goes on to tease out the question of the identity of the band in typical George Harrison-style humor. "So! What are their names? Is it not enough to be Wilburys? In a new group, names are rarely fascinating. Rather, they are empty, unconvincing." And on and on went the release with the big tease. Finally, at the end of page we find: "Wilburys Records Inc. proudly present: The Traveling Wilburys. For the record, as it were, they are Lucky, Otis, Charlie T., Lefty and Nelson, but this may not be all… (There will always be a few Wilburys around)." This must have baffled

TRAVELING WILBURYS, From left: Roy "Lefty" Orbison, Jeff "Otis" Lynne, Bob "Lucky" Dylan, Tom "Charlie T. Jr" Petty, and George "Nelson" Harrison.

record reviewers, radio programmers, and critics, at least until they saw the album cover of *Traveling Wilburys Volume 1* and listened to the music in utter astonishment. Thus began the promotion of the alter ego band of brothers.

In the 1980s, record labels continued to expand the marketing concept of using a variety of promotional posters, record store standees, and promotional-only toys to incentivize stores, radio programmers, MTV, and VH1 to push their musical product ahead of their music competitors. In the case of a surprise superstar collaboration, not a lot of toys were needed to get radio, TV, reviewers, and record stores onboard. Given the enormity of the supergroup being promoted, the marketing campaign for *Traveling Wilburys Volume 1* proceeded without a major hype rollout.

In fact, these industry pros quite literally got "onboard" plugging the first Wilburys album. Not coincidentally, they were all given a yellow, square, plastic window tag, just like those then in vogue alerting us there was a "Baby On Board" the car. Only this promo item stated, "Traveling Wilbury On Board." Once again, Harrison's theme made everyone feel "Wilbury-welcome" and onboard. It was genius! Who wouldn't want to be a Wilbury after hearing this amazing music? The onboard tags were serviced to record label pluggers, promotions people, DJs, programmers, journalists, and record store chains.

A poster of the band all sitting together with their guitars, along with old-time "traveling themed" pictures surrounding them, was hung at radio stations and in record stores. The message on the poster was simple, "Where there's a way, there's a Wilbury." A three-dimensional record store counter standee featured each of the "brothers'" five guitar cases standing up against a backdrop of the soon-to-be-famous Traveling Wilburys' logo.

On October 17, 1988, the Traveling Wilburys' sonic surprise was unleashed upon the world. The album appeared in stores and the first single, "Handle With Care," was released along with a group video of the song featuring George Harrison playing the first prototype Gretsch Traveling Wilburys guitar. The continuing imagery was carried through to Buster Sidebury's (Jim Keltner's) bass drum head which featured the band's logo front and center on his drum kit. In his Nelson Wilbury identity, Harrison even introduced

"Handle With Care" to the United States, appearing on MTV: "Hi I'm Nelson Wilbury of the Traveling Wilburys," he said. "And now our new video is coming up on 'Now Hear This'—Time to get traveling." If people knew their classic rock icons, their jaws surely hit the ground once MTV put the first video into rotation. To see George Harrison, Roy Orbison, Bob Dylan, Tom Petty, and Jeff Lynne playing their guitars and singing a new song together around a single microphone was surely heart-attack-inducing!

Promotion for the first album continued with the release of "Heading for the Light" as a second single one day later. While records were flying out the door, Gretsch Guitar had sent the artwork and prototypes for six different models of Traveling Wilburys guitars over to Korea to be manufactured. The guitar had a white finish with Traveling Wilburys' graphics (no two alike) on the front. On the back were reproduced autographs of each Wilbury signed in full alter ego Wilbury names. The guitar was made of Masonite like the Danelectro guitars of the 1950s and 1960s. The model numbers reflected better quality and features as the numbers increased. The models were TW-100, TW-100-T, TW-200, TW-300, TW-500, and the deluxe TW-600 which was produced in extremely limited quantities. The guitars would eventually be sold in the first quarter of 1989 through musical instrument stores.

While appearing on the NBC *Today Show* to plug the album, George Harrison was asked where the name of the group came from. Harrison delighted in spoofing the entertainment host, "The name of the group came from our talk with the Duke of Edinburgh," said Harrison (looking deadly serious into the camera). "And he said, 'If you guys did form a group, it should be called the Traveling Wilburys!'" For emphasis, Harrison added, "So, it [was] Traveling Wilburys by appointment of his Royal Highness, the Duke of Edinburgh." The host timidly inquired, "Is this true?" Harrison replied, "Yeah, of course." Then in unison, Harrison, Petty, Orbison, and Lynne all said, "Would we lie to you?" Of course, the answer was *yes*! But it was all in keeping with the wit and whimsy of being a Wilbury.

The *New York Times* fell hook, line, and *Wilbury* for this phony story when pop critic writer Stephen Holden incorrectly echoed the funny fib to his readers as gospel. He wrote, "The group, whose name was suggested to Mr. Harrison by Prince Charles at a Prince's Trust Concert, claims to have a whimsical family history dating back to the sixth century." Not only did he fall for the joke and repeat it without checking the facts, he also made the mistake of naming Prince Charles as the Duke of Edinburgh. In fact, Harrison was referring to the late Prince Phillip, the actual Duke of Edinburgh, who was married to Queen Elizabeth. Additionally, the critic seemed to have made up the "Prince's Trust" story as well. Oops! Nevertheless, Nelson Wilbury had the last laugh spreading his fictional band's bio throughout New York and the rest of the country.

Harrison loved how easy it was to spoof the U.S. media, so he continued his fake backstories on a morning program in Britain, telling the host, "I think it [the Wilburys] started as the Trundling Wheelbarrows. That's what we thought. And then we were having a party with [U.S. late night talk show host] Johnny Carson in America. And he said, 'No, you should change it to the Traveling Wilburys… something like that.'" The Brit TV host was amazed, remarking that Harrison had received advice from somebody "pretty high up." The response delighted Harrison who went even further with his joke. "Oh yeah, the Pope… he sent us a telegram and he said, 'Maybe it should be the Trembling Wilburys lads,'" cracked Harrison, hoping some sanity would flow into the interview. He finished by turning down the Pope's suggestion. "But we preferred the Traveling Wilburys."

On MTV, Charlie T., Nelson, and Otis joked with host Laura Gross about just who could, or could not, be Wilburys:

Nelson: Little Richard and Jerry Lee Lewis, they could be Wilburys. Hall & Oates couldn't.
Charlie T.: Jerry Lewis couldn't.
Nelson: Keith Richards is a Wilbury, but George Michael isn't.

After cracking up the interviewer, Nelson explained that the whole world of Wilburys is "… just a little joke really… something to lighten up show biz which is so serious…. It's just amazing that it happened really." However, Harrison *was* serious about the idea of creating a fun film around the Wilbury family. He backtracked a bit, stating humorously, "We're saving it. There's too much interest [in us] now. We want to wait till it dies down a bit." In fact, Harrison had asked Eric Idle, Michael Palin, and director David Leland if they would help him make a film for the group. Palin recalled, "George asked if we'd help make a spoof film for a group of himself, Tom Petty, Roy Orbison, Bob Dylan and Jeff Lynne. They called themselves the Traveling Wilburys."

Film director David Leland was meeting regularly at the Bel Air Hotel in Los Angeles to discuss George Harrison's interest in creating a Wilburys film. Leland, who had directed Harrison's HandMade Films production of *Checking Out*, was also directing the Traveling Wilburys music videos. He recalled, "I think we saw it as a feature length (fictional) documentary for general release. The inspiration for a Traveling Wilburys film often found its way back to Monty Python. George [Harrison] was a mega Python enthusiast and we certainly wanted to involve Michael [Palin] and Eric [Idle]. I don't think there was ever a written film treatment, but there was certainly a concept." The thematic conversations between Leland and Harrison centered on creating the history and legend of the Wilburys, going back over centuries. Leland explained the backstory, "They [the Wilburys] were one of the first migratory tribes that travelled from country to country, crossing continents, playing their music and picking up songs along the way. Travel and music was in their blood that is easy to detect if you listen to the recordings of their music. The contemporary Wilburys were reincarnations of their ancestors."

Why is it that such a promising mock-umentary film was never made? Michael Palin merely related, "We never made the film." Looking for an explanation, the Rock And Roll Detective inquired of director David Leland. He said, "I think the key reason was that we lost Roy [Orbison]. That's my recollection. I also believe trying to put a deal together involving all the participants was complicated because individuals were signed to different record labels, and so on. Those kinds of negotiations took some of the fun out of it. It went against the Wilburys spirit."

However, there was one more reason that the project was doomed: HandMade Films' studio-head Denis O'Brien. While Harrison and Leland were brainstorming ideas, they asked the London film office to research old film and TV shows from the '30s, '40s and '50s. O'Brien was not keen on the project. He wanted to make big Hollywood blockbusters, not small arty documentaries about a fictional rock group. "As it evolved, we were frustrated in the process of getting the materials we requested," said Leland. Harrison was at first unaware his own executive was slow-walking the process. "We later learned that in London, Denis O'Brien had insisted that he vet any material we requested before it was sent to us in Los Angeles. Obviously, this slowed the process, frustrated us, and it did not go down well [with George]." The friction caused by O'Brien earned him the nickname "Denis the Menace" for sabotaging the film.

In late November, Warner Bros. Records released a double-colored vinyl (red and green) set of albums as a promotional release to U.S. radio stations. The compilation was filled with holiday greetings from the Warner roster of artists along with holiday songs sung by select artists. George Harrison had not done such a "holiday greeting" since the 1960s when The Beatles released annual flexi-disc 45-rpm records to their fan club members during the holidays. However, he would repeat this exercise for his beloved Wilburys in order to keep the promotion and the faux folklore moving forward.

Harrison's holiday greeting was straight to the point. "Ho, Ho, Ho, Ho, Happy Christmas everybody from Nelson Wilbury of the famous Traveling Wilburys. Clap, clap, clap, clap [applause heard]. Cue the music ['Handle With Care' plays in the background]. I hope you have a wonderful Christmas and a Happy New Year, and get lots of little things in your stockings. Keep on traveling folks. Bye-Bye." Harrison had one more Wilbury greeting up his sleeve when he convinced a famous TV comedian to record another greeting. "Hello, this is Pee Wee Wilbury," said Pee Wee Herman (aka Paul Reubens), "wishing you the very merriest, Wilburyiest of Christmases (laughs)." Herman was only too ready to earn his stripes as an honorary Wilbury for George Harrison.

The charm and huge success of *Traveling Wilburys Volume 1*, released on October 25, 1988, was a blessing for this band of buddies. Sadly, however, it was marred by the sudden and unexpected death of Roy Orbison, aka Lefty on December 6, 1988, shortly before the band was to create a music video for the song "End of the Line." The band was deeply shocked and saddened. The video was filmed on a soundstage intended to look like a train boxcar. Their fallen friend and hero, Lefty, was honored in the video with the prominent inclusion of his framed photo and a rocking chair displayed with his signature guitar during Lefty's vocal solos. Drummer Keltner described the sorrow felt by all the Wilburys during filming. "It was surreal, actually," he recalled. "Because you're there for hours and hours doing multiple takes, and there was that chair with the guitar on it the whole time by itself." George, Bob, Tom, and Jeff were all enormous fans of Orbison. The loss was truly a shock to all of them. Brother Lefty would not be replaced by another artist, despite rumors in the press. The year 1988 ended with both laughter and tears in the Traveling Wilburys camp.

Will The Wilburys Ride Again?

In 1989, George Harrison continued his promotional cheerleading for the *Traveling Wilburys Volume 1* album, while the other members of the band began working on their own solo projects. *Volume 1* was so commercially and critically successful that it boosted the careers of the individual members. Just as Harrison had planned, the organic, rhythm-guitar-based, rough-edged sound of the Traveling Wilburys had proven it could compete successfully against the then popular synth-pop, hip-hop, and the rest of the lip-synched, shiny musical crap that was being cranked out for MTV at the time. Harrison and company had laid down the musical gauntlet believing their band would dominate the conveyor belt pop of the era with their organic 5 rhythm guitar sound. They had proven themselves admirably with the immense success of *Volume 1*.

As 1990 arrived, many fans and members of the media began to wonder if there would be a follow-up album, given Orbison's death and the busy individual schedules of the remaining band members. Harrison was patient, but clearly wanted his Traveling Wilburys to ride into the studio for another group effort. He told one journalist, "Because I'm really waiting for Tom to get off the road and for Bob to finish his never-ending tour and for Jeff to finish his album. I don't want to do another solo album at the moment. I want to be in a band."

Harrison was also hounded by media questions inquiring if the Traveling Wilburys might ever go on tour. Although the band had discussed it many times, it usually sounded like a good idea late at night over quantities of beer. However, the morning hangover usually quashed the idea in the bright sunlight. Of course, Harrison loved to keep the jokes and mystery going about his beloved Wilburys. He told a TV journalist in Holland that the group *was* touring. "We're going over Niagara Falls in a barrel of beer," he said. Then he got down to the real answer. "It's too tiring… it's not my idea of fun." The group never did tour, despite some of Harrison's hilarious ideas such as touring via aircraft carrier around the world, docking in a port and playing on the ship. The costs would be offset by calling the craft "Sponsor-Ship." Each show would be sponsored by a corporation whose name would be painted on the side of the ship. Then, after leaving a port, the hull would be repainted with the next corporate sponsor. The idea of touring by train was also hatched, but ultimately rejected. The Traveling Wilburys would always and exclusively be a studio band.

In February 1990, The Traveling Wilburys lost the *Album of the Year* Grammy Award for *Volume 1* (to Bonnie Raitt). However, they did walk away with a Grammy statue for

"Best Rock Performance by a Duo or Group with Vocal," beating out stiff competition from Living Colour, The Rolling Stones, U2, and U2 with B.B. King. This well-deserved award came as no surprise to Tom Petty who remarked about his favorite part of being in the Wilburys (aside from the friendship), "We had a very nice group vocal sound. And that was something else that you couldn't have planned, because everyone's voices are so distinctly different. And when we sang together, we made this really nice blend of voices. I enjoyed that a great deal, sort of having a harmony group. It was almost too good to imagine."

While giving an interview in Europe, Harrison was asked if he thought there was the possibility of another album and, if so, what the title might be. Harrison wisely replied, "We won't know what to call it until we make it." Then he quipped, "… Probably *Traveling Wilburys Vol. 13B*." It was clear to see that Harrison relished pulling off another surprise on the unsuspecting media, fans, and the record industry.

As for the rumors that swirled around which artist could replace Roy Orbison, the media speculated on Roger McGuinn, formerly of The Byrds, as well as Carl Perkins and Duane Eddy. Tom Petty put the stories to rest in a definitive statement. Realizing that the media did not understand the origin of the band and the group dynamic, he said, "We wouldn't try to replace him [Roy] because you can't replace him. All the rumors about who is joining the Wilburys are just rumors. The Wilburys, I promise you, haven't picked anyone to replace anyone." And that settled things down as the band reconvened in March 1990 to work on a follow up to *Volume 1*.

A "Wilbury Twist"

The four remaining brothers and their Sidebury drummer, Buster, reconvened at a rented, fully-furnished, Spanish-style mansion high up in the hills of Hollywood that had been built in the 1920s. The group flew a Traveling Wilburys flag from atop the mountain where they would write, record, and hang out. It was dubbed "Wilbury Manor," according to Petty. However, Harrison would later dub it "Wilbury Mountain Studio" on the credits of the album.

Harrison was cautiously optimistic as he mused about a second album which would not be a surprise like the first record. He told *Musician*, "I think the songs can be just as spontaneous. We can make it with the same vibe and atmosphere. But there is gonna be an element where people are already primed for it." Recalling his first group, George said, "I mean, I remember the second Beatle single that ever came out. And the *New Musical Express* wrote, 'Below Par Beatles.'" And, of course, there was also the absence of friend and singer, Roy Orbison, to whom the band would dedicate their forthcoming album. "It's too bad Roy won't be part of it," he mused.

The second album began with a different feel from the first. Tom Petty spoke about the vibe. "Yeah, I mean, he [Roy] was certainly missed. The second album was a different scene, because by then we were a big successful group." He continued, "I wouldn't say the vibe was bad, it was still good, but it had changed a little bit. That's what success does. We still had a lot of fun on the second one too."

Given Bob Dylan's limited ability to participate, due to his schedule of never-ending touring, the songs had to be written and recorded with economy. Each song usually began with a group meeting around the lyrics. "It was something you won't see again, probably," said Petty. "It was a very unusual project. And I just felt really lucky to be part of it." Even Dylan, who rarely did any interviews, admitted that writing with the Wilburys was unique. "Of course, unless you find the right person to write with as a partner... (laughs) … you're awfully lucky if you do." Referencing his "Lucky Wilbury" name in a humorous double entendre, he continued, "To me, unless I have another writer around who might want to finish it... outside of writing with the Traveling Wilburys, my shared experience writing a song with other songwriters is not that great." The second album was dominated vocally by Bob Dylan's voice. The loss of Roy Orbison's amazing voice was clearly missed, as well as a more group-oriented vocal exchange. Jim Keltner observed the absence of Orbison, "It was Roy's presence [that] made them rise to the occasion."

The band continued to work on songs around the dinner table in the kitchen with their four acoustic rhythm guitars. Meanwhile, they borrowed a sound deck and recording machine and moved it into the home's library. Petty described the scene, "The tracks were cut with Jim [Keltner] playing the drums, and for separation, we turned the sofa over in front of the drums. And then on the other side we had the four Wilburys with acoustic guitars. And we would track everything with four acoustic guitars, and then we'd build the track from there." The sessions were quite enjoyable. "And nobody ever went home when the sessions were over," laughed Petty. "We hung out all night and all day."

Towards the beginning of the sessions, Harrison was contacted by his wife, Olivia. She had visited Romania and had become deeply alarmed by the plight of thousands of orphan children who were being severely neglected. Olivia decided she had to do something to raise awareness and money to provide basic necessities to make these orphans' lives more tolerable. Olivia related, "The appeal was launched by Barbara Bach [Ringo Starr's wife], Yoko Ono [John Lennon's widow], Linda McCartney [Paul's wife], and myself in April, 1990 to develop a committed long-term programme of aid for the thousands of orphans in Romania who suffer varying degrees of deprivation. On my recent visits, even the best conditions I found heartbreaking." Olivia asked George if the Traveling Wilburys would consider donating a song to the fundraising cause. The group quickly recorded the song "Nobody's Child," a song The Beatles had performed with Tony Sheridan decades earlier in Hamburg. Since they had forgotten some of the words, the group wrote some new lyrics for an additional verse. George went further to enlist many of his musical acquaintances (Ringo Starr, Elton John, Van Morrison, Stevie Wonder, Eric Clapton, and others) to donate songs for a charity album. In a unique twist, "Nobody's Child" became the only song that credited "The Wilburys" *group* as the producer of the song.

Perhaps the most humorous song recorded on the second album used the group's fictional name in its title, "Wilbury Twist." The song was most unusual given the upbeat dance style of the track which contrasted with the other mid-tempo rockers on the album. The irony was not lost on fans of the group. Harrison, Dylan, Lynne, and Petty were not known for using backup dancers, performing their own clever dance moves, or writing dance songs. "Wilbury Twist" was an actual dance tune, and it certainly reflected the band's sense of humor. The music video, originally created to support the release of the "Wilbury Twist" single, featured silly cameo appearances by Eric Idle, Cheech Marin, Whoopi Goldberg, Woody Harrelson, and Milli Vanilli. Eric Idle recalls being placed on camera behind Bob Dylan as the band performed the song. Idle related, "It is normal in these circumstances, when filming, to lean slightly left or right to find the camera. I leaned right; Dylan leaned right. I leaned left; he leaned left. He [Dylan] was preternaturally aware of where I was behind him and determined to stay in front. He seemed to have extrasensory vision. I was impressed and gave up. Hey, it was their video."

While working on the second album, Harrison again suggested the Wilbury "brothers" create a new set of nicknames. In George's words, "Let's confuse the buggers." Tom Petty quickly took on the new identity of "Muddy Wilbury." The name's origin came from Petty's love of blues musician Muddy Waters. "When I was a kid," said Petty, "we didn't have any blues stations. I never heard Howlin' Wolf or Muddy Waters or any of those people until the [Rolling] Stones had come along, and I took it upon myself to find out who these people were that they were covering." In the 1970s, Petty and his band would jam with Muddy Waters at a club called Dooly's in Tempe, Arizona. Petty loved to cover Waters' signature songs in concert, including rocking blues versions of "I'm A Man," "Baby Please Don't Go," and "I Just Want to Make Love to You." One tribute, written after his death, described Petty's music this way, "He rubbed blues all over '70s rock, he dragged Chuck Berry and Muddy Waters into a sound that crossed Florida swamp with California beach, and he never for one second did it with any sense of pretention." In 2010, Tom Petty released his *MOJO* album which telegraphed to the world that it would be a bluesy record. It was influenced by Petty's love of Muddy Waters and Chicago blues. He covered the song "Got My Mojo Working," and made it his own. It is not surprising, therefore, that the youngest member of The Traveling Wilburys chose the name of "Muddy," his blues hero, known as the "father of modern Chicago blues."

George Harrison adopted "Spike Wilbury" as his new nickname. The name Spike came from George's love of the British comedian Spike Milligan. As a lad, Harrison was a huge fan of the British radio comedy "The Goon Show," which ran from 1951 to 1960. Spike Milligan was the creator, co-star, and main writer of the show which also featured

Harry Secombe and Peter Sellers. The Goons were equivalent to rock stars on British radio in the 1950s. Before The Beatles, George Martin produced Spike Milligan and Peter Sellers comedy records. In fact, it was Martin's work with these Goon alums that attracted The Beatles to working with him. Martin famously recalled, "I didn't know them [The Beatles] from Adam, but they knew me, because they were Goons fans." By the early 1970s, Spike Milligan was among several comedians who formed a part of George Harrison's inner circle of friends at Friar Park. Years later, George gifted one of his used and played Stratocaster guitars to Spike; so it is no wonder that the chief Wilbury would honor his friend's name by using it as his pseudonym on the next album. Commenting on the name changes for his band of brothers, Harrison remarked, "You know it's just a joke really. I mean the newspapers get a little cocky… so I thought, let's change the names, just to keep them on their toes."

Bob Dylan took on the name "Boo Wilbury" for the second album. Dylan never publicly revealed in any interview why he chose the name Boo, but if one takes a very close look at a unique turning point in Dylan's career, it reveals the significance and origin of the name. On July 25, 1965, Dylan released the iconic single "Like A Rolling Stone" to radio and record stores. Unlike his past works of acoustic folk, this song featured an electric rock and roll sound. Five days later, Dylan, backed by members of the Paul Butterfield Blues Band, played his first electric rock and roll set, including "Like A Rolling Stone," at the Newport Folk Festival. Many fans *booed* along with a mixture of some scattered cheers. The crowd was clearly agitated, hearing the cacophony of electric guitars at an acoustic folk festival. Allegedly, folk artist Pete Seeger tried to cut the electric cable to the stage with an ax. Folkies believed that the use of anything but acoustic instruments at this major folk festival was blasphemy. The booing of Bob Dylan continued for some time, boosted by the media which loved spreading the story of folkies rejecting one of their own as a traitor, simply for going electric. Al Kooper, who played organ on "Like A Rolling Stone," and who toured with Dylan, argued that the media created a myth which encouraged more booing from fans, stating "that's what the journalists told the lemmings to do." But the booing of Bob was just beginning.

Almost a year later, on May 16, 1966, Bob Dylan came to the Free Trade Hall in Manchester, England as part of the European leg of a world tour. Backing guitarist Robbie Robertson vividly recalled the reaction to Dylan's conversion to amplified rock. "It was very dynamic, very explosive and very violent. We traveled all over the world," said Robertson, "and people booed us everywhere we went." The first set went well since it was all acoustic and what the fans expected. The second set was all electric and one could feel the agitation in the crowd with each song Dylan played. For the closer, Dylan chose his hit "Like A Rolling Stone." Before launching into the song, a clearly upset fan brought the audience tension up on stage by yelling "Judas!" Dylan responded angrily with, "I don't believe you…. You're a liar." Dylan turned to his rock band and yelled, "Play fucking loud!" A book about the events of that year even uses Dylan's eventual Wilbury nickname: *Judas: From Forest Hills to the Free Trade Hall, A Historical View of The Big Boo.* The boos continued to haunt Dylan throughout this period until he took time off from his career after his bad motorcycle accident later that year. But the negative reaction to Dylan's simple transformation from acoustic to electric would remain with him for life. Thus, Bob Dylan would take another page out of his storied musical history by showcasing his humorous side and christening himself Boo Wilbury.

Jeff Lynne chose the name "Clayton Wilbury." He has yet to reveal the origin of the name and why he chose it. The album would later be credited to Spike and Clayton Wilbury as producers.

Many have wondered what alter ego Roy Orbison would have selected had he lived. Roy's son, Alex, revealed the answer to the Rock And Roll Detective, "Oh, for sure my dad would have picked either 'Orville' or 'Wilbur Wilbury'!" When asked why he would have chosen one of those names, Alex replied, "He loved Orville and Wilbury Wright, the flying Wright Brothers. He was always talking about them. So I am sure he would have chosen one of them for his next Wilbury name."

Few guitar picks directly connected to the Wilburys surfaced during the second album sessions. However, Harrison did have a plectrum especially made for Garry Moore who played a couple of lead guitar solos on the album. He was dubbed "Ken Wilbury." Harrison was also seen using another funny pick during the recording sessions, "Sir Edmund Wilbury," a reference to the first man confirmed to have reached the summit of Mount Everest, Sir Edmund Percival Hillary. Harrison, in his notes, even doodled a sketch of the remaining four Wilburys in which he wrote "Sir Edmund Wilbury" on his character's jacket

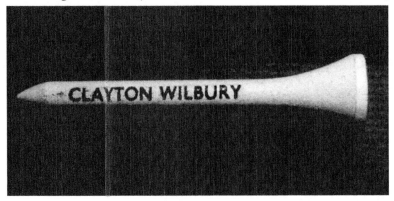

lapel. Jeff Lynne, who had transformed into Clayton Wilbury, had custom-made golf tees made with the name "Clayton Wilbury" printed on the side. One would imagine that a golf tee could also be used as a guitar plectrum in a pinch.

Volume 3

With the second album almost complete, it was time to give it a proper name. One interviewer asked George if he would name the album *Volume 2.* Harrison replied, "I thought of that [title]. Because it's obvious you know, *Volume 1*, *Volume 2*. It's too obvious you know, you had to make it Volume 3, just for the change." Perhaps an unspoken reason that *Volume 2* was not used as a title was that bootleggers had secured stolen rough mixes from *Volume 1* and had already released an underground LP under the title *Traveling Wilburys Volume 2*. Harrison also joked that "there was so much pressure, we decided to avoid *Volume 2* and just go straight to *Volume 3* where there was no pressure." That's one way to avoid a sophomore slump.

Once again, another Monty Python alumnus, Tiny Hampton (aka Eric Idle), was asked to write the liner notes for *Volume 3*. Mr. Hampton was unafraid to dig into the "etymological origins of the Traveling Wilburys" and the ensuing "controversy" in academic circles. He argues that the group may have evolved from "Ye Traveling Willyburys... who were popular locksmiths during the Crusades, used to picking or unlocking jammed chastity belts (rather like today's emergency plumbers)." However, we also learn that Dr. Arthur Noseputty of Cambridge "believes they were closely related to the Strangling Dingleberries, which is not a group, but a disease." On and on goes this silly family mythology of the band, causing anyone with a sense of humor to laugh out loud.

Finally, Tiny Hampton took a swipe at the music media as he listed his brief bio: "Professor Tiny Hampton is currently leading the search for Intelligent Life amongst Rock Journalism, at the University of Please Yourself, California." This dig at rock journalists caused at least one sour writer to return semantic fire at the Traveling Wilburys. When *Entertainment Weekly* (hardly a credible source for critiquing rock music) printed a review, the author snarked, "Why the dumb joke of the title, calling their second release *Volume 3*? Why a whole new set of silly pseudonyms (Dylan, once 'Lucky' is now 'Boo')?" Clearly, Harrison was right to change the names of the group and goof with the title, just to see who had a sense of humor and who did not. The *EW* writer lamely attempted another unsuccessful dig at the band, trying to get his readers to join sides with his stupid position. "… You realize that it's only by indulging in all that coy Wilbury malarkey that these duffers can throw off their heavy fame…"

Released on October 30, 1990, Traveling Wilburys *Volume 3*, while not as popular as the original surprise release with Roy Orbison, was still well received and was certified Platinum (1 million units sold) on January 8, 1991. Not bad for some old duffers indulging in musical malarkey! Three music videos were created to promote the album and support the corresponding singles: "She's My Baby," "Inside Out," and "Wilbury Twist."

Lacking the surprise factor of the Traveling Wilburys' *Volume 1* on the second album, Warner Bros. executed a bigger promotional campaign. They prepared a number of interesting and humorous promotional items that were scooped up by record store merchants, radio programmers, DJs, critics, and VJs to get them all excited about pushing the new album. Most promotional items usually consist of cardboard or plastic items that

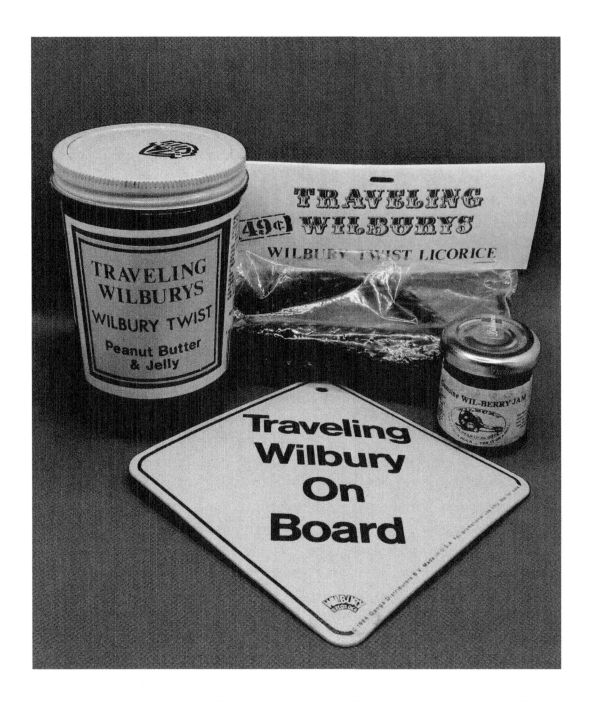

are imprinted with the name of the band and/or the album title. However, the Wilburys took this a step further by developing promotional food items to tie in to the single "Wilbury Twist."

The first was a big jar of actual peanut butter and jelly, twisted… err, mixed together. The yellow label on the side of the full glass jar stated "Traveling Wilburys, WILBURY TWIST, Peanut Butter & Jelly." The yellow metallic screw-on lid featured a Warner Bros. logo. Another "Wilbury Twist" item was a small Dickenson's jar of jam. This product collected all of the Traveling Wilburys' humor on a tiny label. The product was called

"Genuine WIL-BERRY JAM." The famous photo of a Wilbury guitar case and suitcase is pictured above a make-believe corporate motto, "Try it on a rock… Try it on a roll." The side label, in Python-esque style, explains how the jar "contains only the freshest WIL-BERRIES, plucked from the walls of damp caverns [a sly reference to Liverpool's Cavern Club where George and the early Beatles played 292 times] with ancient wooden tongs and dried by the breath of a young marsupial named 'RED.'" The Wil-berry jam ingredients provided yet another inside-joke opportunity to introduce the members of the band in a delicious way: "Ingredients: lynneseed oil [Jeff Lynne]; savoy truffles [a reference to George Harrison and his Beatles song of the same name]; gator juice [a reference to Tom Petty's home state]; absolutely sweet marie [a reference to Bob Dylan and his song of the same name]; and, of course, Wil-berries." And for dessert, the band offered up "*Wilbury Twist* Licorice" for 49 cents.

The "Wilbury Twist" vinyl 45-rpm records came with postcards of old black and white, silly travel pictures, all carrying the message that "The Wilburys are coming." These antique photos were similar to George Harrison's early sketches for the band. Another version of the vinyl record contained individual postcards of the four remaining Traveling Wilburys in their alter egos. Finally, there was an inflatable globe mobile with a Traveling Wilburys logo, hung in many record stores to attract buyers to the new album. Despite all of these clever promotional toys, the singles failed to chart in the United States. Harrison offered an explanation for the second release and its less than stellar charting. He recalled, "I think a lot of people who liked the first album didn't get the second one, *Traveling Wilburys Volume 3*. Unfortunately, it came out just when the Gulf War was starting and the economy was going down. I remember we were going down to choose outfits for our first video and we heard that they'd just bombed Baghdad." Although the album was enjoyed by millions, it appeared that the Traveling Wilburys were quietly walking into the sunset like the end of a Charlie Chaplin silent film.

Wilbury Sightings

Although the Traveling Wilburys never toured and never recorded together again, there would be more clues for fans of George Harrison's cherished supergroup to discover. In late 1991, George Harrison agreed to tour Japan with Eric Clapton and his band. In honor of the tour, Harrison created a guitar pick which he named "Nakahama Wilbury." He did not perform any Wilburys songs, but they were in his heart and his fingers as he strummed. Later, when Harrison's *Live in Japan* album was released, the credits read, "Produced by Nelson and Spike Wilbury," which were both Harrison.

In 1992, as previously mentioned, Harrison introduced Bob Dylan as "Lucky" at the "30th Anniversary Tribute to Bob Dylan," perhaps hoping to spur Dylan (and Petty who was also there) to think about another "Volume" of Traveling Wilburys music. Later that year, Harrison was awarded the *Billboard* magazine Century Award. He was introduced by his old buddy, Charlie T. Jr. In his acceptance speech, Harrison reminisced about his favorite supergroup. In describing the Traveling Wilburys, he told the audience that they were "the band that made me remember how much fun it was to play rock and roll."

In Harrison's last ever TV performance on VH1 in 1997, he was handed a guitar and chose that moment to perform the only known live version of the Traveling Wilburys' song "If You Belonged To Me," which had appeared on *Volume 3*. And, in 2001, after digitally remastering the album *All Things Must Pass*, for re-release with bonus tracks, Harrison recorded a promotional conversation for Capitol Records. The interview, conducted by Chris Carter, was provided to radio stations to promote the new edition of the album. On the back of the CD booklet is a picture of George in the foreground holding his beloved ukulele. However, lurking in the background is a ventriloquist's dummy in a smart suit wearing a Traveling Wilburys pin on his lapel—very subtle, but clearly visible to those looking for clues.

Tragedy struck Harrison on December 30, 1999. After being attacked and nearly killed by a crazed knife-wielding man who broke into his home, Nelson Wilbury still had a sense of humor. When addressing the media, he harkened back to his fun band of brothers when he explained from his hospital bed that his would-be assassin "wasn't a burglar, and he certainly wasn't auditioning for the Traveling Wilburys." Even the horrendous, shocking attack could not dishearten Harrison to abandon his sense of humor or his love for his Wilbury brothers.

Congratulations

After Harrison's passing on November 29, 2001, Eric Clapton organized a tribute concert in his honor at the Royal Albert Hall. On November 29, 2002, Tom Petty, Jeff Lynne, Jim Keltner, and George's son Dhani paid tribute to Harrison's love of his Traveling Wilburys by playing "Handle With Care." Dylan was noticeably absent, although he had been invited.

There was yet another Wilburys sighting that took place on March 15, 2004, when George Harrison was posthumously inducted as a solo artist into the Rock & Roll Hall of Fame. With the song "Wilbury Twist" wafting in the background, Nelson's "brothers," Otis and Charlie T. Jr, gave speeches to induct him. That evening, Petty, Lynne, Dhani Harrison, and Traffic alums Steve Winwood and Jim Capaldi gathered on stage to play another rousing tribute of "Handle With Care."

In 2007, Jeff Lynne, with more than a little help from Dhani Harrison, re-released a three-disc box set of the Traveling Wilburys' albums, singles, B-sides, unreleased tracks, and music videos. It was well received, given that the albums had gone out of print in the 1990s. For this special project, a newly discovered Wilbury brother would surface, Ayrton

Wilbury. Ayrton would provide a guitar solo and backing vocals on George Harrison's previously unreleased Wilburys bonus track, "Maxine." He also added background vocals with Otis Wilbury to the unreleased Lucky Wilbury track, "Like A Ship." As you might have guessed, Ayrton Wilbury was Dhani Harrison who had been a young kid hanging around the original sessions of *Volume 1* and *3*. Dhani, who had been turned onto auto racing by his dad, chose to honor another great Brazilian racecar driver. "I chose Ayrton Wilbury after Ayrton Senna, the Brazilian racing world champion," recalled Dhani. "So that was kind of a nod to my dad as well." Ayrton Wilbury's guitar pick was the last of the official Wilbury plectrums to be fashioned.

The box set included a DVD with a newly-created documentary called *The True Story of The Traveling Wilburys*. Again, founder Nelson Wilbury's humorous influence was felt when the credits flashed on the screen for each member in reverse style. (e.g., "Nelson Wilbury" as George Harrison; "Otis Wilbury" as Jeff Lynne, etc.) The box set was lovingly produced by Nelson and Otis Wilbury, and was subsequently certified with an RIAA Gold Record Award as a huge worldwide seller.

In conjunction with the release of an anniversary picture disc LP of *Volume 1* in 2018, the Traveling Wilburys' website added a feature that would have made Nelson Wilbury proud—a "Wilbury Name Generator." Reinforcing Harrison's theme of inclusion and his slogan "Someday everybody gonna be a Wilbury!" the site encouraged fans to input limited personal information and learn, "What's Your Wilbury Name?" For the record, this author was honorably dubbed "Obediah Wilbury."

End of the Line

At the end of the line, as the closing song on the first album promised, everything will work out fine, and it did! The experience for each of the five original members and their Sideburys was a fun, brotherly, creative flash in time that will never be recreated. It was magical, mysterious, surprising, and filled with a lot of laughter among friends. It was also meant to be inclusive to the world. "Someday, everybody gonna be a Wilbury," said Nelson. And he meant it (except perhaps *not* for George Michael, Daryl Hall, or John Oates).

There were a number of mysterious and funny Wilbury names that were left on the cutting room floor by Nelson and Spike. In his own handwriting, George Harrison listed scores more that went unused, but not without a lot of laughter. Some of these unsung Wilburys included Zeke, Drinker, Buddy, Lonnie, Little, Zsa Zsa, Diego, Zog, Duggie, Blister, Mister, Hoagy, Bing, Gomer, and Memphis Wilbury.

The Wilburys themselves knew how precious, unique, and significant this brief moment in time meant to them. "It's kind of like [the Wilburys] had a life of their own," said Roy Orbison, aka Lefty Wilbury, "and we all worked differently than we would have under other circumstances. We all play guitar, which helped, so by the time it was to go to the next stage, why, we all knew what we were doing."

In the words of Tom Petty, aka Charlie T. Jr Wilbury, "We wanted it to be something that warmed the heart. We wanted to make something good in a world that seemed to get uglier and uglier and meaner and meaner. The Wilburys was this nice friendly thing. And I'm really proud that I was part of it. Because I do think that it brought a little sunshine." Anyone who was surprised to discover the identity of the Traveling Wilburys and their music can attest that the band did bring the sunshine. "The thing I guess would be hardest for people to understand is what good friends we were," said Petty. "It really had very little to do with combining a bunch of famous people. It was a bunch of friends that just happened to be really good at making music."

Jeff Lynne, aka Otis Wilbury, also understood the unique nature of the special relationships and creative partnerships that grew organically within the supergroup. "You could never capture the sheer enjoyment we all got from the Wilburys," he said to a reporter. "The fun of it all [and] the freedom from pressure. Then there was the sheer surprise in what we did. Nobody expected it."

It is best to let the founder and "Quiet Wilbury," Nelson, summarize the mischievous and mythical world of the Traveling Wilburys which he used to unleash a little sunshine and happiness into the world. In the Limited-Edition Genesis Book titled *Traveling Wilburys*, Harrison summed it up beautifully. "It's an attitude of, let's get back to the reason we liked doing this in the first place. Get through all the jadedness of the music business and have that fun in the music that started us all out in the first place," he said. And taking a swipe at the plastic pop music dreck in the world, Harrison opined, "The kind of attitude that it's more important just to do some good, fun tunes that are not surrounded by some kind of electronic madness that doesn't relate to reality. To get the same feeling we did when we first started, which was very simple, direct guitar playing and drumming. That's all we were trying to do." Harrison and the Wilburys can certainly declare "mission accomplished," which is why the music continues to resonate decades after it was recorded.

For George Harrison, there were other benefits and relief for him and his famous "band of brothers" by virtue of their collaboration. "I just loved playing with the Traveling Wilburys. It was such fun doing that," said Harrison. "Oddly enough, with a band that included, besides myself, Bob Dylan, Jeff Lynne, Roy Orbison, Tom Petty, and Jim Keltner on drums, I felt less pressure than I had on many smaller projects, because none of us had to worry about the solo performance thing so much. There was so much input from everybody, and we were all relieved to be in a band of equals where no one had to worry about doing all the lead [guitar] and vocals or all the writing."

It was clear to Harrison that the Traveling Wilburys had to be kept a secret at the outset. The names of the band members were changed, and none of the recording was done in a proper studio where word could leak out. Roy Orbison Jr. recalled being sworn to secrecy after actually witnessing his dad secretly joining the band. Harrison knew from his many years in the music business that he had to make the experience equal parts fun, irreverent, rebellious, equitable, and somewhat mysterious to achieve not only a comfortable environment for musical creation, but to assure that the internal friendship would not be disturbed by outside forces like record labels, managers, and the media. Today, with the secrets and mysteries of the Wilbury brothers now revealed, we can see why the legacy of the greatest supergroup that never broke up will carry on for generations to come.

Sadly, Roy Orbison, George Harrison, and Tom Petty are no longer alive, and there will never be another Traveling Wilburys new album. But take heart. The music and videos live on. In the words of the Bhagavad Gita, which Harrison quoted in his posthumous album, *Brainwashed*: "There never was a time when you or I did not exist. Nor will there be any future when we shall cease to be."

Long live the Traveling Wilburys. Thy Wilbury be done.

Chapter Six
A Blues Marvel—Unmasked

On the morning of September 7, 1929, readers of the *Chicago Defender* were greeted with a screaming ad headline posing the mysterious question:

"Who sings this great new Paramount record? Who is The Masked Marvel?"

Puzzled but curious, readers were surveying a drawing of "The Masked Marvel" that depicted a dapper man in a tuxedo with an eye mask covering the top of his face. The 78-rpm vinyl record in question was called "Screamin' and Hollerin' the Blues," backed with another song called "Mississippi Boweavil Blues." Neither the song titles nor the drawing offered much of a clue, which was the idea, of course, behind this clever marketing ploy. The ad did offer one teaser: "Here is a hint. The Masked Marvel is an exclusive Paramount artist." This was not much help, since no one in the 1920s had access to Paramount's artist roster; if they did, they would have found a number of blues artists on that list. One would have to purchase and listen to the record to try to recognize the mystery singer's voice. Readers were encouraged to go to their local record shop, procure the record, and send in the coupon to Paramount with their guess as to the alter ego of this blues artist. If they guessed correctly, the label would reward them with their choice of another Paramount record.

Musicologists often romanticize the blues music genre as a reflection of the larger black culture. However, early recorded blues music was also part of a careful marketing strategy intended to reach a niche audience, from its inception in the early 20th century. In 1922, Paramount Records, a small record label based in Wisconsin, realized it could target and attract people of color to their "race" records by advertising in the *Chicago Defender*. A "race" record was a term used to categorize practically all types of African-American music. Race records were the first examples of popular music recorded by and marketed to black Americans. Reflecting the segregated status of American society and culture, race records were separate catalogs of African-American music. The *Defender* was a widely-circulated

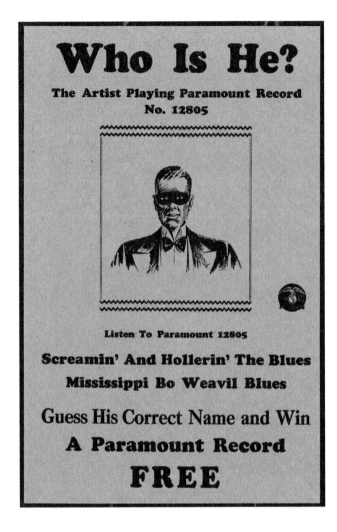

Who Is He?

The Artist Playing Paramount Record No. 12805

Listen To Paramount 12805

Screamin' And Hollerin' The Blues

Mississippi Bo Weavil Blues

Guess His Correct Name and Win

A Paramount Record

FREE

black newspaper, reaching both urban African-Americans and those living in the rural South. Founded in 1905, the paper was very important to African-Americans because it reported and campaigned against Jim Crow era violence and segregation, and urged black people in the South to migrate North.

Was The Masked Marvel the first ever marketing nom de plume used in the fledgling music industry? And just who was this Masked Marvel? What was the rationale behind the use of pseudonyms by this blues musician who sang in different musical styles and different voices on record? And why did Paramount Records choose to advertise *this* particular record in such a mystifying manner?

The Audition

During the 1920s, the stock market in America was expanding at an overly optimistic and lightning pace. As the decade neared its end, wild speculation was rampant as investors believed their stocks would only continue to rise. However, behind the scenes, labor production was declining and unemployment was rising. Stocks were overvalued, wages were low, and the nation's debt was rapidly increasing. A recipe for disaster was brewing in the overheated stock market when an unknown black singer-songwriter sent off a letter of inquiry to a record store owner who served as a talent scout for Paramount Records and other music labels. The blues singer invited talent scout Henry Speir to visit him at Dockery Farms, a plantation in Sunflower County, Mississippi for an in-person musical audition.

At the age of 24, Henry Speir was living in Louisiana where he enjoyed listening to the live music being played and sung by African-Americans in New Orleans. He got a job assembling phonograph record players and was interested in seeing if this race music could be recorded for others to enjoy around the country. He eventually moved back to Jackson, Mississippi and opened his own record store in 1925.

Speir soon began scouting talent for record companies as a way to supplement his store revenues. Using this extra money, he installed his own recording equipment above the store in order to record audition demos he could then send up North to record companies. If the company liked what it heard, they would reward Speir financially and forward a train ticket and expenses to send the artist up North to record. The record label required Speir to buy 500 advance copies of a record from any artist he recommended, likely to insure Speir chose his artists wisely. At the time, the average sales figure for a successful hit race record was 5,000 copies.

One day, in late winter of 1929, according to Henry Speir, he received a letter of inquiry from a nearby blues artist, expressing interest in a recording audition of his original blues songs. That spring, Speir made the trip by car from Jackson to Dockery Farms to locate and audition this young artist. Speir was at first taken aback by the confidence of this young man when the singer told the talent scout that he considered himself the equal of any Delta blues singer who had ever made a record. Sara Garrett, the cook at Dockery Farms, recalled the musician's attitude, "He just thought he was the biggest and best in makin' music, you know, and thought everybody oughta look on him [according] to *who* he was."

It took nearly two hours of playing and drinking alcohol for the young man to get warmed up, but Speir's patience paid off when the young artist at last got into the "swing" of his music. When Speir finally heard him sing the completed song called "Pony Blues," he recalled, "I knew that voice would carry [on record]." The key to success in the record business was the marketability of a significant amount of original material from an artist. This young artist seemed to have this potential. Speir recalled, "[He] was big, because he had a lot of material." Speir was also struck by the rhythmic pulse of the guitar that drove the song along. It was different and unique from anything he had ever heard. The youth had a booming voice that was perfect for the recording studio. In fact, his nickname in the neighborhood, where he regularly performed on Saturday nights at Dockery's for workers and their families, was, "Old Wide Mouth."

On the recommendation of Speir, Paramount Records quickly responded and wanted to record "Old Wide Mouth" up North at Gennett Studio in Richmond, Indiana as soon as possible. On June 14, 1929, the young man recorded fourteen titles at his first Paramount recording session, far more than the average artist who typically produced four songs in a day. One cannot underestimate Speir's talent for discovering so many musical gems of the Mississippi Delta. According to pre-war blues historian Gayle Dean Wardlow, "Speir was the godfather of Delta Blues. H.C. Speir was to the Twenties and Thirties country blues what Sam Phillips was to Fifties rock & roll—a musical visionary.

If it hadn't been for Speir, Mississippi's greatest natural resource might have gone untapped."

Within six weeks, "Old Wide Mouth" would be a major selling artist for the label. Two of the fourteen songs recorded that day were "Screamin' and Hollerin' the Blues" and "Mississippi Boweavil Blues."

Paramount Records

Paramount Records began its corporate existence in rural Grafton, Wisconsin as a chair manufacturer, aptly named Wisconsin Chair Company (WCC), specializing in rocking chairs for the relaxation of a hard-working nation. In the early part of the 20th century the company became involved in making phonograph cabinets for famed inventor Thomas Edison; this

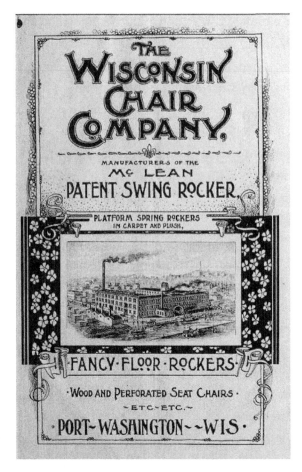

led WCC to contemplate another business… that of making records to go with the phonograph into its cabinets. Company executive Fred Dennett reasoned, "… to sell a phonograph, you had to produce the records to go with it." By 1917, the company had begun remodeling its building in Wisconsin to record and manufacture records. With that major change, out went the rocking chairs and in came the rocking blues!

Not unlike other industries manufacturing products, the role of the music industry is to transform its products into financial revenues. Unlike the streaming format popular today, recorded music in the 1920s was a purely physical product that required manufacture, marketing, advertising, distribution, and purchase. Early marketing efforts were directed towards creating and retaining a loyal consumer base for artists and rewarding that loyalty. Creativity was essential to achieve sales objectives. In short, the goal was simple: develop a campaign to target the audience base for each type of music, and then sell the suitable music product to each appropriate niche group.

In the 1920s, black-oriented radio was nonexistent and there was no television. The only medium in the home for blacks to enjoy their culture was to own a wind-up phonograph record player. They listened to records to relax and to dance to. According to Wardlow, "Ninety percent of Speir's [record store] customers were black. Of that 90%, probably 90% were women." The cost of a 78-rpm record containing two songs was $0.75 each, which was a lot of money. (Note: given today's inflation, that would be the equivalent of $11.27 in 2020). "But sharecroppers didn't buy records," said Wardlow. "The woman who worked for the white man as a cook or a maid in his home bought the records—she had the money." It was also the women who purchased the highly prestigious record players for their homes.

According to blues historian and film director Bernard MacMahon (*American Epic*), "Paramount set up a whole system where they had a bunch of civilians going door-to-door as salesmen. They put an ad in the Chicago Defender in the mid-1920s to set up a distribution network." Ultimately, there were 2,000 people in the South selling Paramount records. "People would commit to buy these records. Sometimes they wouldn't have a cent to put down for a record, but the [sales]person would come back and collect payment in installments on these records," said MacMahon.

To market its records far and wide, Paramount turned to the *Chicago Defender*. Although expensive at $1,000 for one full-page ad, Paramount's race records appealed to African Americans to enjoy in their own homes. The music spoke to them personally, describing the hardship of life down in the Mississippi Delta. These hardscrabble stories touched listeners who began to buy up titles, and Paramount started selling records around the country. Former Paramount record executive Art Satherley recalled, "It was so new for people of America, both black and white, to be able to buy what they understood and what they wanted, that we quickly had several thousands of these records [selling] daily."

Pseudonyms, Disguises, and Alter Egos

The use of an alter ego or pseudonym is in many ways a deception, offering a layer of mystery and a "mask" regarding the true identity of the artist. According to Joyce Carol Oates in the *New York Times*, "Choosing a pseudonym by which to identify the completed product simply takes the mysterious process a step or two further, officially erasing the author's [or musician's] identity and supplanting it with the pseudonymous identity." An artist, disguising his or her name, can produce a single work and then drop that clandestine identity like an old pair of shoes. There are many reasons for using a *nom de plume*. These include humorous obfuscation, preventing market oversaturation by a prolific artist, hiding overly personal work, legal or marketing reasons, a lack of confidence in one's work, and in many cases, creative freedom from the artist's true identity.

During the 1920s, Paramount Records began to expand its revenues by selling or licensing the recording masters of its blues artists to other companies. Often the record label would change the actual identity of its artists appearing on other labels using name disguises. This was a practice that allowed Paramount to fool both its consumers and competitors into thinking its roster of artists appeared larger than it actually was. However, the label soon discovered a new marketing strategy to implement with its own customers, namely, using mystery to create an entertaining method of promoting and selling a new record. In May 1924, Paramount placed a headline ad in the *Chicago Defender* inviting "Every Member of the Race" to create the title for "*Ma Rainey's Great, New Mystery Record.*" The first, second, and third place winners would walk away with a Wisconsin Chair Company phonograph. Given this incredibly generous contest reward, thousands of blues and Ma Rainey fans bought the mystery record and sent in their ideas for a title. This mystery marketing scheme was highly successful.

Paramount's "new release" ads placed in the *Chicago Defender* were critical to record sales and often contained coupons to be mailed back to the record company in exchange for the music. These ads were beautifully illustrated with images evoking the old South in a nostalgic manner. They typically depicted timeless blues music themes of love lost, plantation blues, fights, floods, and other events such as traveling to and from the South by car, train, or boat.

Paramount Records promotional photo
of Charley Patton

Stock prices across the board began to take a dive in September 1929. The plunge continued into October as a selling panic began to set in. Finally, on Black Thursday, October 24, a record number of shares were traded, mostly in a downward direction, and within days, stock prices collapsed completely. It was against this backdrop that Henry Speir's new protégé, "Old Wide Mouth," released his third single on the Paramount label.

His first single, released in July 1929, was called "Pony Blues" b/w "Banty Rooster Blues" (Paramount 12792). This blues record sold well, earning the young musician the right to release another song later that fall. Just one month later, Paramount was trying to shift records of their prolific new artist in various ways. According to MacMahon, "They'd done this blues record. Now let's test the water with a gospel song and see how that goes." Paramount decided to release the young man's gospel song, "Prayer of Death Part 1 & 2." However, in an attempt to differentiate the artist and to prevent oversaturation so soon after the "Pony Blues" hit had been released, the company named the gospel artist under a suitably pious pseudonym, "Elder J.J. Hadley." MacMahon said, "Sometimes they [Paramount] used pseudonyms to get more records out than a market could stand under your own name."

This young bluesman was not the first musical artist to be listed under a pseudonym on a professionally made record. Composer George Gershwin was credited with producing dozens of piano roll songs under assumed names in 1916, including the names "Fred Murtha" and "Bert Wynn." According to blues archivist John Tefteller, known as the "Sherlock Holmes of the Blues," "Pseudonyms were very common long before he started his career. Many such artists would record with another name in order to record for another company. It was moonlighting." However, record companies also had a number of reasons to use alter egos for their artists.

The Masked Marvel

"The Masked Marvel," said Paramount Records historian Alex van der Tuuk, "was just a way of attracting customers to buy the record and guess the name of the artist." Seven thousand ad posters were sent to record retailers showing the mysterious "Masked Marvel" as the artist, wearing an eye-covering mask, promoting his new record, "Screamin' and Hollerin' the Blues," backed with "Mississippi Boweavil Blues" (Paramount No. 12805).

The winner who correctly guessed the real name of The Masked Marvel would win another Paramount record by a different artist. That meant the customer could potentially buy one record for $0.75 and get one free. The ad promoting the Masked Marvel contest (published in the *Port Washington Herald* on August 24 and in the *Chicago Defender* on September 7 and 14) had been produced by a local Grafton, Wisconsin printer a month before the release on August 24, 1929, according to Van Der Tuuk, who found the document buried in a Wisconsin library. Another ten thousand entry forms were tucked into record sleeves for customers to find, listen to the blues singer, and send in their guess to Paramount. The label was anticipating the record would be a big seller based upon the quality of the music and the mystery behind its true artist. In some ways, this idea presaged The Beatles' own clever effort, 38 years later, to create and release an album under the alter ego group name, *Sgt. Pepper's Lonely Hearts Club Band*.

Record sales for The Masked Marvel surpassed all expectations, spurred by all the buzz. The initial pressing of 10,000 records quickly sold out, more than double the sales of a typical hit race record in this era. "The fact that they printed 10,000 slips to tuck

Paramount Masked Marvel
Contest Entry Blank

I have listened to one of your Paramount Records No. 12805 by the Masked Marvel and am herewith listing what I think is his correct name. It is understood that if I have given the correct name you will send me free one Paramount record and my choice in case I win is

NO...........

Name of Artist

_____

My Name and Address

_____

_____

_____

This Blank to be Mailed on or Before Oct. 15, 1929

The New York Recording Laboratories,   :-:   Port Washington, Wisconsin

into the record of The Masked Marvel tells you that this was a teaser [promotion] to make it a hit, following on the successful sales of Pony Blues," said van der Tuuk. When the 10,000 records had been sold, and the contest was over, there was no need to hide the name of the mystery hitmaking blues artist anymore. When Paramount re-pressed the record in a quantity estimated in the low thousands, they confirmed the winning answer by posting the name of their hit-making blues artist on the newly produced record labels… Charley Patton, soon to be known as "King of the Delta Blues."

Who Was Charley Patton?

Born in Mississippi sometime between 1885 and 1891, Charley Patton would become the most extensively recorded blues and folk artist of the Mississippi Delta, releasing an enormous body of 52 recordings between 1929 and his death in 1934. Historians assert that Patton's music reflected the events he witnessed or experienced in his short life. He was always traveling around the Delta playing at Dockery Farms, on street corners, in juke joints, and at private parties. Once he began recording, Patton's travels took him to Illinois, Missouri, Wisconsin, Indiana, and New York. In the early 20th century, most black males made their living off the land, and therefore were tied to one location for most of their lives, but not Patton. Patton was clearly the product of a mixed racial ancestry, thus he did not feel tied to the land as other black men of his era. He felt different and unique. Although he had helped his father in the fields as a youth, he was not a typical sharecropper. He pursued and planned a career as a traveling musician and was able to earn a decent living at it. Based upon accounts from contemporary blues artist "Son" House, it is quite likely that Charley Patton earned on average fifty to one-hundred dollars per week. In comparison, it would take a black sharecropper an entire year to earn fifty dollars. Patton even owned his own automobile. Add to that the money Paramount would pay him for recording sessions and Patton was far ahead of his peers financially.

Patton did have several years of formal education, religious learning, and a lot of street smarts. These tools served him well as he learned to write and play songs on the guitar. Clearly, the fact that Henry Speir recalled receiving a personal letter from Patton is yet another piece of compelling evidence supporting Patton's claim to literacy. Many of his musical themes were similar to other blues artists of the era. He wrote about travel, different towns, floods, trains, trouble in the world, spirituality, Jesus, and difficulty with the law. According to John Tefteller, "Patton was actually torn between being a religious preacher, and basically a hard-drinking blues singer. He had this war going on within his soul, about what do I want to do with my life? Do I want to live the blues and sing the blues, or do I want to preach the Lord's gospel?"

For Patton, writing, singing, and performing blues and gospel music were his passions, his calling, and his profession. It came above everything else, and it appears that Patton did pretty well financially, between his "touring" from town to town and his work as a recording artist. His recorded music appealed mostly to African Americans in the Mississippi Delta. However, his live performances appealed to both blacks and whites.

Paramount Records promotional photo of Charley Patton

The Unmasking

Clearly the use of "The Masked Marvel" name on Charley Patton's second blues record was a promotional ploy to aid in the marketing of the disc by Paramount. The success of the contest caused the record to be a big hit for the company, likely selling nearly three times that of a typical hit race record.

Paramount knew it had a remarkable artist in Patton and, given the prolific number of quality songs he had written and recorded for them, studio executives thought it wise to disguise the identity of some Patton tracks so consumers (and competitors) would not see how dependent the label was on a single diverse, popular blues artist of that time.

But was there more to The Masked Marvel than just a slick marketing campaign? Is there evidence to support that Charley Patton himself might have been a participant in its planning? He was an outsider, never allowing himself to get pinned down in any one place or by any one woman. Not being tied to the land provided him the freedom to move around the country on a whim, a highly unusual and liberating lifestyle for a young man of color in the 1920s. He could be whomever he chose to be and could reinvent himself at every town he came across in his travels. According to biographer Dr. David Evans, in this way, "He remained to the end, The Masked Marvel."

However, according to three preeminent blues historians, Tefteller, MacMahon, and van der Tuuk, Charley Patton was not involved in the concept, planning, or naming of The Masked Marvel. Tefteller states, "All he [Patton] would have cared about is how many records am I going to sell, so you're going to pay me to make some more records. If this is going to help you [Paramount] sell more records, and then hey, do what you want."

MacMahon explained, "Patton lived approximately 750 miles away from Grafton, Wisconsin. And would not have had access to a telephone. Patton would not have heard about this marketing idea until it happened. And there is no record of Patton ever touring around the Delta as The Masked Marvel." The Rock And Roll Detective could not find a single public or private document in which Charley Patton referred to himself as The Masked Marvel. MacMahon clearly believes the alter ego release was an "invention of Paramount." Recalling that this was only Patton's second blues record released, the young artist would have been trying to make a name for himself. "It is highly unlikely Patton would have wanted his record being put out as a gimmick with his real name obscured," reasons MacMahon. Once Patton had recorded these records in Indiana, he likely would have had no further communication with the label until they asked him to record again many months later.

Van der Tuuk, who has scoured and studied the original business documents of Paramount Records, echoes the same sentiments, that Patton did not have a hand in The Masked Marvel alter ego. He stated, "The Masked Marvel was just a way of attracting customers. I know Art Laibly, who was sales manager and recording director [at Paramount] came up with the pseudonyms." He points out that after 10,000 Masked Marvel records had been sold of "Screamin' and Hollerin' the Blues," when they went to print up more copies, "... and the contest was over, there was no further need to hide the real name

Charley Patton, 1930 Paramount promotional calendar

anymore. The company wanted to sell more copies of 'Screamin' and it seemed obvious at that point to reveal the name [Charley Patton] on the new labels they printed up."

In the year 1929, around the time Art Laibly came up with the pseudonym Masked Marvel, there were hundreds of other references to The Masked Marvel in U.S. popular culture. These included a traveling wrestler appearing under this name, a billiards champion, a comic strip named "The Masked Marvel Appears," and even a burlesque/vaudeville artist appearing at the Blackstone Burlesque & Photoplay. That ad stated, "The Masked Marvel Burlesque's New Dancer... Who is She?" The stripper's ad was not too dissimilar to the Paramount ad, asking "Who is The Masked Marvel?" Van der Tuuk believes it is quite likely, "because that comic strip appeared nationwide in newspapers and seeing the touring lady burlesque dancer, may have hinted at Laibly to do a contest."

This use of The Masked Marvel alter ego was not the only tactic employed by Paramount on behalf of their up-and-coming recording star. They knew that he could sing and write both blues songs and religious or gospel-oriented songs. As a result, Patton was given another pseudonym on the second release to aid Paramount in the marketing of his non-blues, religious title, "Prayer of Death Parts 1 and 2." The alias created on that song was "Elder J.J. Hadley." And in November 1929, Paramount licensed another Patton gospel song ("Lord I'm Discouraged" backed with "I'm Going Home") to Herwin Records under the pseudonym "Charley Peters." Paramount clearly employed a clever marketing strategy; one which turned a single recording artist, Charley Patton, into four different artists (Charley Patton, Elder J.J. Hadley, The Masked Marvel, and Charley Peters), all at the same time and without cannibalizing sales by the same artist.

As Patton was coming into the recording process, the rural recording boom that began years earlier was starting to wane. Combining that with the stock market crash of October 1929, record companies such as Paramount had to get more creative and push any trick they could to move records. Besides the novelty of in-home records and the Great Depression, the record industry faced stiff competition in other forms of entertainment. As MacMahon pointed out, "By the '30s, if you had a few cents, the choice was essentially between a record and going to the moving pictures, and the pictures won out." This was also the end of the silent film era and the exciting beginning of early talking pictures. Given the price of movies, and the limited spending money of poor people, one could go to three different movies for the same price as one 78-rpm record. Therefore, contests, beautiful graphic advertisements, creating pseudonyms to prevent market cannibalization, and other tricks were all used to push records at the time Patton's recording career began.

Some historians have given the explanation that different alter ego names were used for an artist who recorded both blues and gospel due to moral and religious reasons. In Patton's case, he was actually torn between the life of a pious religious preacher and a nomadic existence traveling around as a heavy drinking blues singer who married multiple wives. The case has been argued that religious households that did not permit drinking, cursing, and carousing would never purchase a gospel record made by a rowdy blues singer, no matter how good it was. Thus, the claim was made that record companies would assign different names for an artist's blues and gospel numbers to fool the more pious customers into buying the record. However, original source documents can often clear up erroneous theories, and are not subject to foggy recollections. The Rock And Roll Detective found such evidence in an old Paramount advertisement for an October 1930 Charley Patton gospel record called "Jesus Is A Dying Bed Maker" b/w "I Shall Not Be Moved" (Paramount No. 12986). The ad features a drawing of Charlie Patton seated in a chair playing guitar with his name featured in big block letters. The ad states, "Famous as a Blues singer and just as popular as a Gospel singer—Be sure to Order." Therefore, the opposite was true here, since Paramount bragged about its star being popular in both

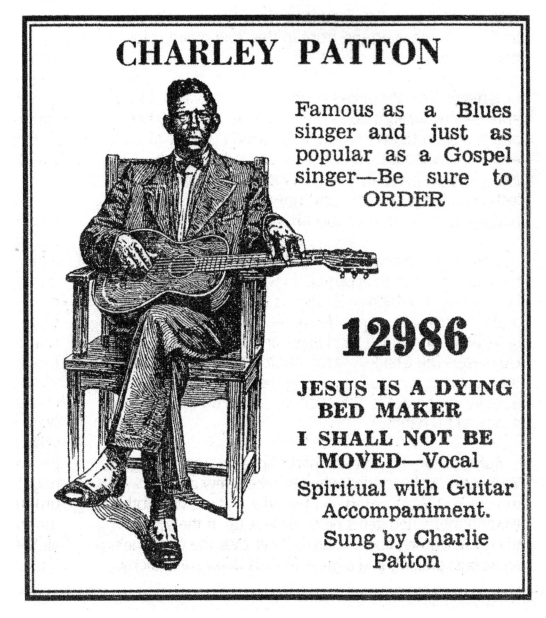

musical genres demonstrates that they were unafraid of offending the pious religious market.

Patton did appear to have a double identity when he played distinct live shows for black and white audiences. Some of his biggest shows were for white audiences, at house parties, picnics, dances, and weddings. He had the ability to play for both races separately and provide each group a "different" Patton experience as he moved between the two. The set lists for each audience usually had different song choices. His niece confirmed, "They [blacks and whites] tried to make him be two folks and play so much for this one and so much for that one." Versatility was a Patton trademark in his playing and it proved to be quite profitable.

Perhaps the two songs chosen by Paramount to be released under The Masked Marvel name lend clues to their selection for an alter ego release. The songs do provide some insight into Patton's personality, interests, and concerns. "Mississippi Boweavil Blues" reveals the story of the black insect that bored into cotton buds, preventing them from blossoming. This was devastating to Delta plantations and did not discriminate between black and white farmers, affecting both equally. Interestingly, Patton likely related to the bug that freely traveled the Delta and was always on the move.

"Screamin' and Hollerin' the Blues" was quite autobiographical and described Patton's life themes of travel, his mother's disapproval of his blues lifestyle, a search for "home," his revolving door relationship with women, and his struggle moving between a blues existence versus a more pious life. The autobiographical nature of the songs may have made this an appropriate release for Paramount to put out under "The Masked Marvel" moniker to provide a layer of mystery and anonymity.

"Masked Marvel" Charley Patton also had to possess several alter egos in order to woo and marry more than a half dozen women (some at the same time) in his short life. Official marriage records from multiple counties in Mississippi document the different wives Patton juggled around the Mississippi Delta, and this number did not take into account any of the casual affairs he was also said to have had on the side. Clearly, The Masked Marvel was neither tethered to the land nor to any one woman! One had to be skilled with juggling different identities to keep everything straight with so many paramours.

Did Patton participate in The Masked Marvel moniker concept? There is no documented evidence to suggest that he did. And none of Patton's contemporaries ever saw him appear live under the moniker. Paramount undoubtedly designed The Masked Marvel campaign for the aforementioned marketing reasons. Clearly The Masked Marvel campaign was hugely successful, benefiting both Paramount and Patton.

What Is Charley Patton's Lasting Legacy?

Some observers have argued that Charley Patton may fairly be described as the first rock and roller, and his performance style certainly reflected this description. As a skilled performer, Patton elicited a number of tricks on his guitar: popping the strings, playing it through his legs and behind his head or back, playing with his teeth, tossing it in the air, and using his fingers to tap out rhythms on the guitar's body. Many of these stunts conjure up the repertoire of rock guitarist Jimi Hendrix decades later.

Patton's tombstone states, "The Voice of The Delta—The foremost performer of early Mississippi blues whose songs became cornerstones of American Music." Many blues musicians have held Patton in high esteem including Willie Brown, Son House, Robert Johnson, Muddy Waters, B.B. King, Big Joe Williams, Pop Staples, Honey Boy Edwards, and Taj Mahal, to name a few. In the world of rock and roll, we can hear Patton's influences in the music of Jack White, Bob Dylan, ZZ Top, Led Zeppelin, Stevie Ray Vaughn, Eric Clapton and Cream, and The Rolling Stones.

Rocker Jack White, who could fairly be called a disciple of Patton's, said, "If a musician listens to Charley Patton and doesn't hear anything at all, I don't think they should call themselves musicians, because they're obviously just looking for fun and kicks and a good time out of it." In fact, classic rock owes much of its success to pre-war blues records. Think about Robert Johnson's "Love in Vain" covered by The Rolling Stones; "House of the Rising Sun" by the Animals, which evolved from Texas Alexander's "Rising Son Blues"; and Led Zeppelin's cover of Memphis Minnie's song "When The Levee Breaks." Commenting on the legacy of Charley Patton, Bob Dylan added, "If I made records for my own pleasure, I'd only record Charley Patton songs." However, despite all of the international fame Patton enjoys today, curiously, it took thirty years after his death before his recordings would earn him praise as a blues great. Why did Charley Patton remain mostly anonymous, while some of his protégés earned greater fame?

One theory set forth by early '60s white blues enthusiasts is that Charley Patton was not very popular in the '20s and early '30s, and that he was merely an obscure Mississippi blues man that recorded but didn't sell very well. Tefteller debunks this myth. "The reality," he said, "is he was a pretty darn big-selling blues singer at the time, even when the stock market crashed." Tefteller has examined the sales numbers of depression era race records and found that "… the sales numbers for the Patton records, are pretty darn high, considering how few people were able to afford records, in comparison to a lot of the other blues records coming out at the same time." Sixties blues collectors viewed Patton's super scarce 78-rpm discs as a reason to claim he had poor sales. However, the reality is that during World War II, the government asked Americans to donate their old records to recycle for the war effort. Many of the pre-war blues records were melted down during this time period. If Patton's hit records sold 5,000-10,000 and many were donated to the war effort, there would only be a handful of each title left in existence. This also explains why a single Charley Patton 78-rpm record sells for thousands of dollars today. Thus, there must have been other reasons for Patton's decades-long anonymity.

Certainly, one reason rests with his choice of recording label. Paramount Records was famous for cheap, inferior audio quality recordings. Even with today's technical advances in digital mastering, Patton's songs were not well recorded, making them more difficult to listen to and appreciate. Moreover, Patton's blues competitors on other labels had wider distribution for their record releases.

Bad timing was another factor in Patton's career. His first records were released as the stock market crashed in 1929. By 1933, roughly half of America's banks had failed, and approximately thirty percent of the workforce was unemployed. Partly due to the crash, Paramount went out of business in 1933, closing its doors for good. Adding insult to injury, laid-off Paramount employees, upset with losing their jobs, took many of the metal master recordings from the catalog vault and sent them flying like Frisbees into the Milwaukee River. Significantly, long before the factory closed, Patton's final Paramount releases went unadvertised in the *Chicago Defender* as a cost-cutting measure. With no publicity or advertising, and declining distribution, many of Patton's greatest recordings went unheard at the time of their release; Paramount's lost distribution prevented the Mississippi Delta from even seeing any of these later releases. Additionally, because of the limits of money and technology in those days, there is really only one surviving photograph of Charley Patton to recall his visage.

Despite all of these factors, the quality of Patton's work has elevated his status as "King of the Delta Blues," a moniker that Paramount Records rightly bestowed upon him, printed right on his original promotional photograph. Blues historian Robert Sacré described Charley Patton as a "griot." Griot is an expression for a West African historian. He described Patton as a person "… who serves the role of historian, musician and songwriter for his people." He believed that Patton's use of the blues and his lyrics helped deliver an accurate oral history of black music from slavery to blues, from country to urban music. This is high praise indeed.

Patton's body of recorded work eventually saw the light of day in deluxe, box-set form. The most significant set of his entire career is called *Screamin' and Hollerin' the Blues: The Worlds of Charley Patton*, a 7-CD masterpiece. Fortunately, Patton's recorded legacy has survived and is now available for more people to study and enjoy.

Patton died of heart failure on April 28, 1934 at 43 years of age. In a bit of final Masked Marvel irony, Charley Patton's death certificate lists the occupation of the deceased as

"farmer," not singer-songwriter, recording artist, or blues and gospel singer. Even at the end of his life, Patton's true identity as a musician had been masked!

It is fitting that present-day blues musician Taj Mahal has the last word on Charley Patton's legacy. Mahal eloquently presented the case for Patton's lasting importance to America's musical heritage. "Charley is a force of nature! He had an incredible voice. It's really hard to know how far reaching the influence of Charley Patton is. I mean, he influenced the first generation of Delta [blues] guys. You know, those guys like Muddy Waters, B.B. King, and John Lee Hooker.... But his big thumbprint is on Howlin' Wolf. Wolf brought it [Patton's style] to a new generation and carried it forward."

Who Won The Masked Marvel Contest?

You are probably wondering if anyone ever correctly guessed the true identity of The Masked Marvel in Paramount's successful marketing scheme. Fans would not find out who The Masked Marvel was until November 1929. Surviving documentation from Paramount Records provides evidence that at least one person sent in the correct entry regarding the true identity of The Masked Marvel. The winning entry read "'Screamin' and Hollerin' the Blues' is by Charley Patton. He is The Masked Marvel." It isn't surprising that the winner, Harvey Parker, listed his address as Harvey Parker, Dockery Farms 3, Mississippi—the very place where Henry Speir had located his new discovery, Charlie Patton. Parker had obviously heard Patton sing live on the farm and in nearby juke joints. According to Tefteller, Mr. Parker may have not only received a new record from Paramount, but he may also have won a copy of the promotional photograph of Charley Patton—King of the Delta Blues, for correctly guessing the true identity of The Masked Marvel.

Certainly, the voice of The Masked Marvel was, in equal measure, revealing, unmistakable, and memorable.

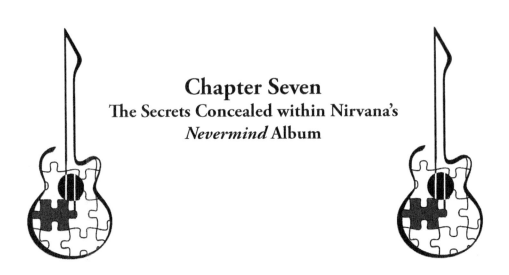

Chapter Seven
The Secrets Concealed within Nirvana's
Nevermind Album

More than twenty-five years after its initial release, Nirvana's *Nevermind* continues to capture the passion, angst, and imagination of a generation. Its release as the band's major label breakthrough was significant. *Nevermind* changed the landscape of radio, music-television, and the music industry, leading the '90s into a new sound labeled "grunge" or "alternative rock"—a sound and movement that would dominate the decade while relegating '80s pop and big hair metal bands to the used record bins.

Over the years, much has been written about the importance of *Nevermind*, yet the album itself has also remained somewhat of an enigma, filled with mystery and myths. Numerous questions have arisen specific to this album. *Why was the album essentially recorded twice? What was the story behind the album's original discarded title? How did the hidden track happen? What was the Punk Song? How did The Beatles, long since disbanded, influence Nevermind?* The Rock And Roll Detective took a look back at the secrets concealed within the grooves of *Nevermind*, an archeological dig that revealed a number of intriguing revelations behind the making of this classic rock album.

Nevermind Was Basically Recorded Twice For Two Different Record Labels

It is well known that the album *Nevermind* by Nirvana began its recording sessions on their major label debut for the David Geffen Company (DGC) at Sound City studios in Van Nuys, California in April 1991. However, one year earlier, Nirvana was under contract to a small indie label called Sub Pop Records that sent the group to Butch Vig's Smart Studios in Madison, Wisconsin to record. During their stay in Madison in April 1990, the group recorded eight songs.

Producer Butch Vig and Engineer Doug Olson
at Smart Studios during the Nirvana sessions.

While the Madison recording sessions can be considered the audio birth of *Nevermind*, they differed by at least one major artistic factor, specifically that the drummer for the Madison sessions was Chad Channing. Channing had played with the band from 1988 to 1990 and recorded with the group on their debut album, *Bleach*. However, by the time Nirvana had signed a major label deal with DGC to record in Van Nuys, they had fired Channing and brought in drummer Dave Grohl. Grohl had been playing and touring with a punk band called Scream. When they disbanded, a mutual friend put Grohl in touch with Kurt Cobain and Krist Novoselic who were looking for a replacement for the newly-departed Channing. Coincidentally, this story of a drummer being fired and replaced by the "right" drummer before the band achieved massive worldwide popularity closely mirrored the story of drummer Pete Best being replaced in The Beatles by Ringo Starr on the eve of recording their major label album debut.

Five of the eight songs recorded in Madison were destined to be featured on the *Nevermind* album, including "In Bloom," "Lithium," "Imodium" (which morphed into the song "Breed"), "Pay To Play" (which morphed into the song "Stay Away"), and "Polly." The three orphan songs, "Dive," "Sappy," and "Here She Comes Now," would find their way onto future releases. "Sappy" was attempted again in the later Van Nuys sessions and made it as far as Butch Vig's first mixes before being rejected for the finished album.

What happened to the early gestation of *Nevermind* after its Madison completion? The plan at the time was for this session to become the album follow-up to their debut album, *Bleach*. The Madison session was only scheduled for a week to complete the entire album because Sub Pop planned to send the band on the road for an eight-week United States tour. Bass player Novoselic confirmed, "Everything was geared to put out this second Nirvana record. We were going to record maybe a few more songs in Seattle. This was going to be on Sub Pop." The Smart Sessions' early version of *Nevermind* was not completed; however, it would soon serve an entirely different purpose.

In the intervening weeks after the Madison sessions, creative differences continued between Kurt Cobain and drummer Chad Channing, resulting in Channing leaving the group. A compounding issue was the band's growing belief that they had outgrown Sub Pop and wanted to move up to a major label. Subsistence compensation and a lack of major promotion by Sub Pop were starting to wear thin with Cobain who felt the band could reach a higher level within the music industry. With Channing's departure, Cobain and Novoselic decided to withhold the release of the Madison sessions on Sub Pop. Given the change in circumstances, the duo created a number of cassette "demos" of the Smart Sessions and began to shop themselves to major labels using the early *Nevermind* prototype. Novoselic gave one cassette to a music friend in Seattle with the instructions, "Don't tell Sub Pop I gave this to you. This is what we're sending out to try to get a deal." Perseverance paid off when the band signed a major label deal with DGC, found a new drummer in Dave Grohl, and began to record the "second" *Nevermind* one year later. The Madison recordings became known as the "Smart Demo Sessions."

Dave Grohl Was Not the Only Drummer Featured On the *Nevermind* Album

If you scan the inside liner notes to the *Nevermind* CD, the band is listed as Kurt Cobain: Vocals/Guitars; Dave Grohl: Drums/Vocals; and Krist Novoselic: Bass/Vocals. That's it. However, Grohl was not the only drummer on this epic album. The other drummer, who never received credit on the record, was the aforementioned Chad Channing. Channing had recorded some minimal cymbal crashes on the song "Polly" during the Smart Demo Sessions one year earlier before losing the drum stool to Grohl. "They put me in this smaller room [at Smart] that normally has guitars and stuff like that," recalled Channing. "I sat there with my ride cymbal, and there were these certain parts where I was just going to hit it." He figured, "Well, I'll just accent these things, because they talked about having something really sparse on it."

Producer Butch Vig confirmed to the Rock And Roll Detective that it was Channing's Smart Studios recording of "Polly" that made it onto the finished major label 1991 version of the *Nevermind* album as the sixth song. The track survived the Madison session without any overdubs, edits, or changes. "It's funny, I never realized that 'Polly,' that version, was from the Madison sessions that made it on *Nevermind*," said Channing. "I mean, it was, I don't know, almost ten years down the road before someone mentioned that to me... I listened to it, and I said, 'Okay, that make sense.'" Channing did reportedly receive an unspecified payment for his drumming on "Polly" from the multi-platinum selling release of *Nevermind*.

Nevermind Was Not the Original Title of the Album

When the Madison sessions took place, the tentative title for this would-be album was *Sheep*. Sheep was a recurring theme that cropped up in Cobain's diaries and journals, a sarcastic label for people who mindlessly followed the crowd and could not think independently. Just as he created multiple humorous biographies of the band throughout its early career, so did Cobain draw future ideas for album covers and print advertisements promoting these albums. One such Cobain promotional poster featured a diagram of the human body in the shape of the chalk outline seen on the sidewalks of a crime scene. The person's head had no face, and in place of facial outlines we saw a question mark. A comic balloon from the person's mouth read, "Mandatory breeding laws?" Above the man was the band's name "Nirvana" in large font; and at the bottom of the poster we see the album title *Sheep*. Underneath the album title, we see the words, "At a store near you." Crossed out, but still readable and clearly referencing the album title are the words, "Because you want to, not because everyone else is."

Novoselic has stated that the early album title stemmed from the band's cynical view of the world and its disgust for the public's seemingly "sheep-like" support for the current U.S. war, Operation Desert Storm. Eventually growing tired of the sheep idea, Cobain came up with the title, *Nevermind*. This came to represent Cobain's attitude towards life at the time and it was an improper grammatical use. Later, Cobain drew an album cover in 1991 that looks very close to the finished photograph. He had crossed out one album title (*Verse, Chorus, Verse*) and replaced it with the final title of *Nevermind*.

Butch Vig Was Not the First Choice to Produce *Nevermind*

On April 30, 1991, as the ink dried on their contract, Nirvana left the ranks of the small indie label Sub Pop and moved into the major-label world of DGC. It was a move that provided the band greater visibility in record stores, on radio, and on MTV. It had the potential to make the band a household name, if they could create a powerful album. The first order of business for the label was to find the group a suitable record producer, one with major label credibility and hits under his belt.

The band began to rehearse for their first recording session with new drummer Dave Grohl. Cobain had already written a new song and recorded it on a cheap boom box cassette machine. While preparing for their sessions, Geffen Records suggested a few big name producers. None, however, were named Butch Vig, who had produced their Smart sessions. One of the first names mentioned was R.E.M producer Scott Litt. Also on the list was Neil Young's producer, David Briggs, as well as Don Dixon (The Smithereens and R.E.M.). Each producer was brought in to listen to songs and hang out with the band.

Kurt Cobain had given the producer choices very serious consideration. He knew this album was a make-or-break proposition for Nirvana. In Cobain's private journals, he created a hand-written list of producers in his spiral notebook for research and consideration. The list included Bill Price (Guns & Roses, The Clash, The Sex Pistols, and Pete Townshend), Gil Norton (Pixies), Alan Moulder (My Bloody Valentine), George Drakoulias (Black Crowes), John Hanlon (*Ragged Glory*—Neil Young & Crazy Horse), Dave Jerden (Jane's Addiction, Talking Heads, and Alice in Chains), Ed Stasium (Living Colour), Ron Saint Germain (Bad Brains, Sonic Youth), and Scott Litt. In reading down this list, one can imagine Cobain sitting cross-legged on the floor of his apartment, sifting through his favorite record albums.

When the band brought up Vig's name and mentioned how well the Smart Demo sessions had gone, the record label had reservations about choosing a relatively unknown producer from the Midwest. Geffen was un-schooled at this point regarding the groups Vig had produced, such as Killdozer and the Smashing Pumpkins. But Nirvana began to lobby its label for Butch Vig. At that point, the conversation turned back to Vig and the idea of a joint production between Dixon and Vig. Meanwhile, Vig was back in Madison producing the album *Gish* for the then-obscure Chicago indie group the Smashing Pumpkins.

The young producer from Madison believed, "the band kind of held out for me, because I think I still had a sensibility for where they were coming from; from more of the punk ethic. And they were afraid of going with someone who might make them too slick or just not understand what they were about."

Novoselic confirmed Vig's feeling and agreed that the band held out for him. He recalled, "We'd worked with him before and he was so encouraging. He drove the band, but in a positive way." Novoselic acknowledged that Nirvana was nervous about being on a major label and having to use a mainstream producer. "We really liked Butch [Vig] because we were really comfortable working with him," said Novoselic. Eventually, Geffen agreed and the young band was sent out to California to meet up with Indie producer Butch Vig.

What About That Song That Got Left off the Album? Or did it?

When Nirvana began recording *Nevermind* at Sound City Studios in May 1991, it became Butch Vig's first major label production. He had already produced nearly 50 indie rock records (at Smart Studios in Madison, Wisconsin) before Nirvana came into his life and changed it forever. As he entered his first West Coast studio, he turned up all of the volume control knobs to "stun" level as he began to produce *Nevermind*.

Early on, Vig and the band attempted to track the song "Lithium" live in the studio. However, after the first three attempts, the band could not achieve the desired feel and sound. At this point, the session began to devolve from a relaxed atmosphere to one of tension within the group. To ease the stress, Nirvana decided to morph from "Lithium" into a jam session, churning and thrashing on one of their rehearsal grooves. Whenever recordings or rehearsals broke down, the band jammed on anything that came to mind in order to work out their frustrations and get back into the groove. "We would always break into stuff like the 'Lithium jam,'" said Novoselic. "So that day we just started busting into that. It was really about trying to find a groove. We were trying to make this wall of noise and turn it into something."

Unfortunately, this particular jam session had the opposite effect of reducing stress because Cobain became even more frustrated and enraged. Fortunately, for posterity, Vig kept the tapes rolling from the last "Lithium" take through the lengthy jam session. At the 6:20-mark, a volcanic musical explosion is heard erupting in the studio as Cobain angrily smashes his guitar to the floor and screams in a rage.

"Kurt got so into it that day that he smashed his guitar," recalled Novoselic. "There was nobody there—no audience or anything. Kurt was in a trance or something. He just flipped out and broke his guitar." The session for the day ended, since Kurt no longer had a guitar. The group later decided the aborted jam session should end up as a "sonically buried" surprise track at the end of the *Nevermind* CD. The song, however, would remain invisible for a time, and it was not listed on the album's liner notes. The track would become known as "Endless Nameless." This "song" (if one can call it that) with screams and guitar abuse was truly a punk rock deconstruction—a hard rock "song" that replaced craft, lyrics, melodies, verses, and chorus with a cacophony of noise.

"Endless Nameless" was so well hidden it was originally and accidentally left off the master tape that went to the pressing plants! Howie Weinberg mastered the album on August 2, 1991, and discussed with The Rock and Roll Detective how "Endless Nameless" got left off the original pressings of the album. "In the beginning, it was kind of a verbal [discussion] thing to put that track at the end. Maybe I misconstrued their instructions, so you can call it my fault if you want." Weinberg continued, "Maybe I didn't write it down…. So when they pressed the first 20,000 or so CDs, albums and cassettes, it wasn't on there." This fluke created an instant collectible for early buyers of *Nevermind*. However,

Kurt Cobain

once Nirvana listened to the finished CD and discovered the song was missing, Weinberg got a "heavy" phone call from Kurt. "Where the hell is the extra song?" he shouted down the line. "Oh fuck," Weinberg replied to Kurt. "Don't worry; I'll fix it right away. No problem." Cobain replied, "Fix it!"

Weinberg immediately went into his studio and added the entirety of "Endless Nameless" to the master tape with a ten minute gap of silence after the last song,

"Something in the Way." According to Weinberg, "It was a cool way to put a song on an album that maybe did not fit on it. It was like a separate album on its own." Weinberg further explained his misdemeanor: "In the end, it was my fault, but it was part of the whole scenario."

In the aftermath, when Hal Leonard Publishing prepared the written scores for people wanting to purchase and learn the guitar and piano parts for *Nevermind*, they too left off the hidden track in their book. Ironically, the publisher forgot to place a note at the front of the music score books stating, "'Endless Nameless' is not an appropriate song for guitar or piano scoring." That is for sure, if you have listened to the song! The publisher told the Rock And Roll Detective, "The note just got accidentally left off." The invisible song survives today, and is yet one more secret uncovered in the making of Nirvana's legendary masterpiece, *Nevermind*.

What Was the "Punk Song?"

The "Punk Song" began its life with a number of disjointed themes found in Cobain's journals. However, it began to really take shape during the Sound City sessions. It was clearly an attack, in part, on typical male macho stereotypes that Cobain had had to put up with in high school. However, the song also touches upon feminism, paranoia, and even being an alien from outer space.

During the sessions, Cobain suggested to the producer that they put some kind of "vocal thing" on the recording before launching into the most steel-cutting, ear-splitting, punk rock guitar speed-riffs ever made. (Note: While interviewing Butch Vig, this author put a rough mix digital audio tape (DAT) of this song on his stereo system. Vig turned it up to "stun" volume, and blew up both of the author's speakers!). Vig turned to bass player, Krist Novoselic, and suggested he go in and sing something "really lame." Novoselic was game and said, "How about this?" He then began to sing an off-key mangling of an old hippy folk anthem called "Get Together." Dripping with derision and sarcasm, rejecting the hippy ethic that had gone sour in the '80s and '90s, everyone in the studio loved it! Novoselic's sarcastic rendering of the Youngblood's hit song, encouraging everyone to get together in peace and love and to love each other, is striking juxtaposed with Cobain's desperate vocal cord-ripping rendition of losing his ideals ("Gotta find a way"). The message was perhaps one born of a disenchanted generation of latch-key kids annihilating the Baby Boomer generation's lost ideals of free love amidst a sky-high divorce rate that had impacted both Cobain and Novoselic.

Shortly after recording the "Punk Song," Cobain came into the studio and asked Vig to change the song title on his tracking sheets. The new title read… "Territorial Pissings."

Artist NIRVANA

Label GEFFEN

Producer BUTCH VIG

Engineer JEFF SHEFFAN

Sound City

15456 Cabrito Road
Van Nuys, California 91406
787-3722   873-2842

M. REEL 4

☒ 24 Trk   Tape 456
☐ 16 Trk   Speed 30 IPS +5 @ 250
☐ 8 Trk   Tones MRI
☐ Dolby   ☒ Non-Dolby

TITLE						
	BASS	BASS	KICK	SNR Top	SNR Bottom	HAT
PUNK SONG Territorial PISSINGS	1	2	3	4	5	6
	Toms Lo ←	→ Hi	O.H.S L ←	→ R	Room L	R
	7	8	9	10	11	12
CODE	original GTR 57	original GTR 421	Snr Voc	GTR fuzz D.I. one	GTR fuzz two	GTR fuzz D.I. Three Gtr
	13	14	15	16	17	18
		Chris intro vox VOX one Kurt				
	19	20	21	22	23	24

"Territorial Pissings" Control Room Production Sheet Written By Butch Vig.

How Did The Beatles Influence Kurt Cobain and *Nevermind?*

Although journalists have built up Kurt Cobain's punk ethos over the years, they often overlook the pop-rock influences that Cobain grew to love in his younger years. In one of his high school journals, Cobain listed in numerical order, from one to twenty-nine, his favorite artists and their works. Number two on his list is The Beatles. He had crossed out *Meet The Beatles*, the group's first U.S. Capitol release, and replaced it with *Something New*. (Note: This album was a cobbled together "extra" LP prepared by Capitol in 1964 to "capitalize" on the release of the film *A Hard Day's Night*. Capitol did not want to be left out in the cold by United Artists, the label which released the official soundtrack album at the time.)

The journal would not be Cobain's only Beatles' reference. From an early age, Cobain listened to his uncle's record collection that was filled with Beatles albums. At age 14, his uncle gave young Kurt a used guitar and some Beatles records. Before Cobain wrote one of his early compositions called "About A Girl," he reportedly sat down and listened to *Meet The Beatles* for three hours, over and over and over, and then wrote the song. If you listen closely to the notes played by Cobain during the chorus of that song, you can hear chord changes that would have fit in nicely with The Beatles.

When Nirvana went into the Sound City sessions for *Nevermind*, the early influence of Lennon and McCartney served Cobain well. "Kurt loved The Beatles," recalled Butch Vig. "He loved John Lennon. So I know that he felt self-conscious, coming from a punk background and having these kind of gorgeously crafted rock songs. Even though his songs might have been kind of noisy, they still had really beautiful melodies and melodic structure." And like The Beatles' best work, the songs written for *Nevermind* were simple and catchy, yet elegant.

Butch Vig was also heavily influenced by the great music recorded by The Beatles; and he was equally influenced by their masterful producer, Sir George Martin, and his innovative techniques. During the recording of *Nevermind*, Vig shared this knowledge with Cobain in order to gain his cooperation. "There was a point where I wanted Kurt Cobain to double-track his vocal on a song when we were recording *Nevermind*, and he was reluctant to do so because he thought it sounded too fake," recalled Vig. Vig told Cobain, "'Well, John Lennon double-tracked his vocals.' And as soon as I said that, Kurt said: 'OK.' He pretty much double-tracked all the vocals after that."

Perhaps the best person to sum up The Beatles' influence found in the grooves of *Nevermind* is superstar session drummer Jim Keltner, who recorded and played live with John Lennon, George Harrison, and Ringo Starr. "Kurt really reminded me a lot of John [Lennon] in his writing, singing and guitar playing," said Keltner. "More attitude than technique, but he had incredibly strong rhythm and a great solo sense. Nirvana's *Nevermind* album is as good as anything ever produced in rock 'n' roll. It was talking to me. I'd finally heard a new band speaking to me from the past, present and the future." In his journals Cobain had crafted his own design for the back cover of the *Nevermind* album. He created a "Thanks to" section listing friends and musical influences he wanted to remember. Nestled within the list of old drummers, friends, punk bands, and label personnel was a "thank you" to The Beatles.

Had he lived long enough, Kurt would have been proud to see his band Nirvana reunite, jam, and record a new song with The Beatles' Paul McCartney on lead guitar, entitled "Cut Me Some Slack" in Dave Grohl's documentary, *Sound City*. The song sounds like a mash-up of Nirvana meets "Helter Skelter." And the band asked Butch Vig to produce the reunion track.

What's the Story Behind the Album Cover with the Naked Baby?

The cover of *Nevermind* is perhaps one of the most recognizable, iconic rock album cover designs in popular music history. It features an infant baby floating underwater in a sea of blue and purple, seemingly reaching for a dollar bill attached to a fish hook. If you look at the liner notes for the album, you might feel misled by the credit which reads: "Original Art Direction/Design: Robert Fisher." The album cover design was very much Kurt Cobain's "baby."

During this time, Cobain continued to draw many ideas in his journals. One drawing featured a baby floating underwater, with two hands reaching up from below for the child with the words, "Sell the kids for food." Another drawing featured the cover with a naked floating baby reaching for a fish hook. Next to the cover drawing are the song titles for the album, with interesting identifications next to each one such as "happy," "sad," or "mad."

The original idea for *Nevermind's* cover came about when Cobain and Grohl were watching TV one day. The show was a documentary that described the process of underwater birth. Cobain thought the photo of a birthing mother was a really cool image. He told Grohl, "Let's put that on the album cover." Robert Fisher at Geffen was immediately tasked with locating such a photo. However, the selections available for licensing were deemed too graphic and risqué by the label. Fisher did locate photos of babies floating underwater; however, the photo agency demanded too much money to justify their use.

Since the record label brass would not agree to commercially license and pay for a baby photo for Cobain's cover idea, they decided to hire a photographer to create their own. Certified rescue diver and underwater professional photographer Kirk Weddle was hired to take photos of a naked baby. The chosen baby was four-month-old Spencer Elden. While his mother practiced dunking her son in a tub to test his abilities at the shoot, Weddle was working with a stand-in stunt doll to prepare for the real shot. An outtake shot survives showing another diver holding the stunt doll for Weddle. The photographer explained, "That's a rescue diver holding the doll so I could frame and practice the shoot. You don't want to do that with the kid, because you only get one shot with him. Once we got it lit and framed up, we brought in the baby."

When the shoot was ready to go, Weddle called over Spencer's mom, Renata, to assist with the shot. "The mom was on my left, and blew a puff of air into the child's face," he recalled. "Then we dunked him in and, bang-bang, pulled him out. We did it twice and that was it." For his efforts, young Spencer was paid two hundred dollars, and is likely the youngest person to ever receive an RIAA platinum record award. Twenty-five years later, Elden talked about the experience, "It's strange that I did this for five minutes when I was 4 months old and it became this really iconic image," he said. "It's cool but weird to be part of something so important that I don't even remember." In an about-face, Elden (who has "Nevermind" tattooed on his chest) filed a lawsuit in 2021 against members of Nirvana, claiming the defendants had violated federal child pornography laws, among other things. In January, 2022, Elden's case against Nirvana was dismissed by the judge, who ruled in favor of the band.

With the principle photography completed, it was again Cobain's idea to add the fish hook and dollar which were later added to the pool photo by the label's art department. "When we got back a picture of the baby underwater," recalled Cobain, "we thought it would look nice for [there to be] a fishhook with a dollar bill on it. So the image was

The Nevermind LP Cover Featuring Baby Spencer Elden, signed By Butch Vig.

born." It was born indeed, as the image closely resembled the early drawings conceived in Cobain's private journals.

A second underwater session was requested of Weddle, but this time with the band posing underwater. The photos would be considered for use later to promote the album. Weddle's job was a bit more difficult to get all three band members underwater at the same time. Cobain had to nap for two hours by the pool before they could get started. Weddle observed, "They were intrigued a little bit with the instruments in the water. Then we had to choreograph it all together and get it going. It's hard to get three guys underwater at the same time, looking kind of good. So we did a lot of practice and a lot of trial and error and finally banged it out."

Nirvana underwater.

As the album cover was being prepared, another controversy arose when the record label wanted to edit out Spencer Elden's penis. The label felt that certain "family stores" (such as Wal-Mart or Target) would rather carry a penis-free cover. Cobain stood his ground and refused to budge. In the end, the label backed down and allowed a form of public nudity that artists like Mick Jagger and David Bowie could never accomplish on their album covers.

With the cover art finished, Cobain aptly titled the album *Nevermind*. The word was ideal for the album title as a metaphor for the apathy Cobain viewed in his generation. He commented at the time, "There's no rebellion in rock 'n' roll anymore. I hope underground music can influence the mainstream and shake up the kids." *Nevermind* was the perfect name for the album, a summation of Generation X's cynicism, boredom, anger, and angst at the dawn of the '90s.

Who came Up with the MTV Video Concept for the First Single, "Smells Like Teen Spirit," and what Does "CHAKA" mean?
Dave Grohl has referred to the Smells Like Teen Spirit music video as a "pep rally from hell." But people who first saw the debut music video from *Nevermind* were likely so blown away by the power of the music and imagery that they could not grasp the themes.

Kurt Cobain began imagining the video for "Smells Like Teen Spirit" almost as soon as the song was recorded at Sound City. He wrote in his journals, "Punk is musical freedom. It's saying, doing and playing what you want. Nirvana means freedom from pain and suffering in the external world and that's close to my definition of punk rock!" Just a couple pages later, Cobain began to assemble a list of items needed for his vision of the "Teen Spirit" video: "A Mercedes Benz, an abandoned mall, lots of fake jewelry, a school auditorium (Gym), a cast of hundreds, 1 custodian, students, 6 black cheerleader outfits with Anarchy A's on chest."

The video shoot took place in Culver City, California at GMT studios on August 17, 1991. As with all ideas, Cobain's vision for the video was modestly trimmed down by commercial video director Sam Bayer. Bayer's vision was tamer than the band's, and conflicts arose almost from the start of filming. Gone was the scene in the abandoned mall where Cobain had planned to illustrate the negative impact of materialism and consumerism to (in his words) "… throw thousands of dollars into the air as mall goers scramble like vultures to collect as much as they can get their hands on." Also removed was Cobain's scene of punks going to a jewelry store in the mall to smash-and-grab the jewels in a showing of anarchy.

Cobain did receive his anarchists' high school pep rally. The gym was filled with mosh-pit fighting students, fires raging, cheerleaders with anarchy A's on their chests, a creepy janitor, and all-around chaos flamed by the music of Nirvana's iconic song "Smells Like Teen Spirit." At one point, the viewer sees a shot of Dave Grohl's bass drumhead which contains the cryptic word "CHAKA." Astute pop culture aficionados would soon figure out the drummer's homage was to another brother in anarchy, Daniel Ramos, who had recently gone to jail for graffiti-tagging his moniker "CHAKA" on public places over 50,000 times, causing a half million dollars in damage.

After filming was complete, the creative clash over the final edit of the famous video continued. "I came up with the idea for the 'Smells Like Teen Spirit' video, but the director had different ideas, and what emerged wasn't what I had in mind," recalled Cobain. "I had to go into the editing room in the last days of post-production to salvage whatever I could, like inserting certain scenes which the director had left out, to salvage it and make it tolerable. It was our mistake to go in with a commercial director."

Despite the creative differences between Cobain and the director, the music video became a successful musical marketing and political statement. It was aesthetically and musically a punk rebellion. The visually disturbing images were perfectly married to the carefully crafted arrangement of the song. The video perfectly connected the band and their feelings to Generation X which could immediately, in turn, relate to the band as one of their own. As a result of the video blowing up on MTV, the album and the single did something quite amazing, crossing over from underground college radio stations to Top

40 and Album-Oriented Rock radio to reach millions more listeners. Today, the song is so commonly known that it airs in grocery stores!

Nevermind's Legacy

Perhaps no album of the past thirty-odd years has become more mythologized than *Nevermind.* The power and lyrical relevance of this masterpiece for a generation of angst-ridden latch-key kids served to catapult Kurt Cobain into the unwanted position as the "voice of his generation." Novoselic recently recalled Cobain's ability to paint pictures within the music. "The way that the lyrics blend with the vocal and aesthetic of the song, it just creates a world of its own."

Clearly the pop/punk sensibilities of producer Butch Vig served to make the music both alternative and accessible at the same time. It is difficult to imagine another album that was so raw and hardcore, but which still gained as much commercial appeal as Vig's production of *Nevermind.* The addition of Dave Grohl's powerful drumming to the group at this crucial juncture, combined with the fluid, powerful bass playing of Krist Novoselic, made punk's version of *Meet The Beatles* an instant classic.

When you jump-start an album release with a single and music video like "Smells Like Teen Spirit," it is hard to miss the significance of this album announcing the beginning of the alternative music scene to the world. It was a scene that came from Seattle, Chicago, and New York—one which would invade radio, TV, films, and culture for a decade. Big hair, heavy-metal music, and robotic pop songs withered on the vine almost instantly after *Nevermind* hit the airways, knocked to the mat by a sound that was more authentic, culture-shifting, and urgent. According to Vig, "Timing in art is so important because it's a reflection of the culture, and you can't predict it." By November 1991, *Nevermind* was

in the Top 40, and the band was selling out bigger and bigger concert venues. In January 1992, *Nevermind* toppled the King of Pop, knocking Michael Jackson's *Dangerous* album out of the No. 1 spot on the Billboard Album Chart.

Nirvana was probably the last great pre-internet band. Many have called Kurt Cobain the last rock and roll superstar. For alt-rock fans, the mysteries and the mythology surrounding *Nevermind* are almost as important to the album's history as the music itself. The folklore helped to spread the name of the group and its music further than mere radio and MTV airplay. Nirvana became a household name throughout the world. Just as fans of The Beatles scoured their album covers for clues about Paul McCartney's alleged death—particularly on *Sgt. Pepper, The Beatles* ("White Album"), and *Abbey Road*—so would this generation endlessly wonder about the secrets buried within the very deep grooves of Nirvana's *Nevermind*.

Chapter Eight
Deal With The Devil:
Did The Beach Boys Steal A Song From Charles Manson?

In American folk mythology, the "crossroads" are the setting where the devil can be summoned in order to negotiate a supernatural deal. There is a classic early 20th century legend concerning blues artist Robert Johnson meeting the evil spirit at the crossroads to broker a deal—trading his soul for enhanced instrumental skills, only to be poisoned to death after attaining success. In the case of Beach Boys drummer Dennis Wilson, who unwittingly picked up two young female hitchhikers at a highway crossroads, little did he know that he would be bartering his own pact with the devil. Suddenly, via this simple act of kindness, Dennis Wilson and The Beach Boys, "America's band," had unwittingly intersected with a real-life demon named Charles Manson.

The hitchhikers turned out to be members of Charles Manson's cult and would introduce Manson to Wilson. Over the years, many have heard the story of Dennis Wilson befriending Charles Manson. Given Manson's notoriety from the "Helter Skelter" murders, and Wilson's premature death, the media spin has sensationalized the story, claiming that a song written by Charles Manson and shared with Beach Boy Dennis Wilson was in fact "stolen" by The Beach Boys, and that this alleged theft likely *caused* Manson to become a murderer! If one looks at the headlines this is what you would be led to believe…

"Beach Boys *stole* music from Charlie Manson"
"Watch Charles Manson Discuss Beach Boys *Song Theft*"
"How a *Stolen Beach Boys Song* Helped Lead to Charles Manson's *Murderous Path*"
"Dennis Wilson *Caused* Charlie Manson"

Is this reporting fair and accurate, or yet another case of fake or exaggerated news reporting? Are these outrageous headlines merely click-bait to sell online advertisements? The Rock And Roll Detective wanted to discover the true back story of this Faustian musical bargain.

The media has correctly stated that Manson wrote a song called "Cease to Exist." Dennis Wilson, impressed with Manson's ability to write music, paid for Manson to record some demos with Wilson's partner, Gregg Jakobson. Subsequently, the allegation is that Wilson changed the title and lyrics, and added a Beach Boys-styled vocal and musical arrangement to this Manson composition. The Beach Boys then released the song under the title "Never Learn Not To Love." The media, without digging into the facts or the law, concluded that Wilson stole the song, altered it, and failed to credit or compensate Manson. This, in turn, created the theory blaming Wilson and The Beach Boys for The Manson Family's subsequent murders based upon a revenge motive for cheating him and not giving him a record deal. Other media reports blamed Wilson's friends, Gregg Jakobson, producer Terry Melcher, and even The Beatles!

These news reports do not even begin to scratch the surface of the untold story of Wilson's bargain with this earthly prince of darkness. The Rock And Roll Detective looked back in time fifty-plus years to locate eyewitnesses and sift through the facts and fiction of a case that has never been truly investigated or solved… until now. The goal was to discover answers to the questions behind Wilson's "deal with the devil." Did Dennis Wilson and The Beach Boys *steal* Charles Manson's song? Did The Beach Boys intentionally strip Manson's name off the credits of their song "Never Learn Not To Love"? Are there any documents or eyewitnesses that could lead to the truth behind this disturbing bargain? And did the "stolen" song lead Charles Manson down a dark path resulting in the Tate/LaBianca murders? Alternatively, is it possible that Wilson legally owned the copyright to "Never Learn Not To Love"? This would perhaps be the most challenging rock and roll archeology dig to date, given the reluctance and discomfort of The Beach Boys and their inner circle to discuss anything related to this dark Manson-cloud that continues to hang over a group that only wanted to sing about surfing, hot rods, and California girls.

"Catch A Wave"

Dennis Wilson was the only member of The Beach Boys who truly looked the part of a "beach boy." It was Dennis who suggested to producer/brother Brian Wilson that the group sing about surfing and cars. When asked in an interview if he was the best surfer in the Beach Boys, Dennis smiled and replied, "The *only* surfer." Once Dennis got his first car, he recalled, "Then you discover cars have back seats [a nod to discovering girls]." It was indeed Dennis Wilson's lifestyle that provided legitimacy to the band's early surf-rock music.

When he was asked to join the group by his brothers, it was Brian Wilson who had to show Dennis how to play drums. Dennis then used his personality and physicality as an athlete to create his own simple, but powerful, style of drumming. With a rough voice and limited vocal range, Dennis found his home playing the drums and could intuitively find the groove in every song. He was described as adventurous, inquisitive, and a risk-taker by those who knew him well.

As Dennis Wilson and The Beach Boys progressed into young recording stars and reached great success in the 1960s, Dennis went through boundless personal and emotional growth. He threw himself into everything at breakneck speed, including the hedonistic delights of drugs, alcohol, and the pursuit of women. To balance his extracurricular pleasures, Dennis looked for greater meaning to his newly-found fame in a search for spirituality focusing on Transcendental Meditation (TM). In fact, it was Dennis who arranged for The Beach Boys to have their first meeting with Maharishi Mahesh Yogi in Paris in December 1967. Speaking on the benefits of TM, Dennis revealed, "It's a very personal, fulfilling thing. It stimulates the mind and body and gives you a greater appreciation of life. It puts you in communication with something infinitely greater and more important than self."

In October 1966, "Good Vibrations" was released by The Beach Boys, instantly becoming an anthem for the Baby Boomer generation. Composer Brian Wilson had stopped touring in order to concentrate on writing and producing more hits for his band. At this point in time, heavy pressures began to take its toll on Brian, and he began to deteriorate from a combination of mental health issues, work overload, and heavy drug use.

Meanwhile, as The Beach Boys gained wealth and fame, Dennis Wilson began to question his relationship to material things. His cousin, Beach Boys lead singer Mike Love, recalled, "To his credit, Dennis was generous to a fault. He really didn't give a damn about cars or clothes or anything of material value, and was glad to give away what he had." But Dennis also had a weakness for the fairer sex. Mike stated, "The other thing about Dennis, and this is the negative, was that his appetite for sex was insatiable. For Dennis, too much was never enough." Cousin Mike felt that this combination of altruism, new age spirituality, and a weakness for sex and drugs proved to be a dangerous mixture, especially given the evil spirit Dennis would soon meet at the crossroads.

The Beach Boys, From left: Al Jardine, Dennis Wilson, Mike Love,
Carl Wilson, Bruce Johnston. (Absent: Brian Wilson)

"People Say I'm No Good"

So where did this "Devil of the Sixties" come from? According to the late Charles Manson, "Jails, courtrooms, and prisons had been my life since I was twelve years old. By the time I was sixteen, I had lost all fear of anything the administration of the prison system could dish out." Born in 1934, Manson was the product of his sixteen-year-old mother, Kathleen, and a drifter named William Manson. For a time, Charles lived with his mother and her many suitors, constantly moving around. As his mother's problems led her to jail, Manson's education progressed from boys' schools to juvenile centers to a lifetime in and out of jail. Manson spent roughly seventeen total years in lockup until his release from Terminal Island prison in San Pedro, California at the age of thirty-four in the late 1960s.

While serving time in prison in the early 1960s, Manson chose music to take his mind off of the slow, repetitive days of prison life. He recalled, "Music is always an enjoyable time-killer in prisons. Whether you are playing or listening, it takes your mind out of the joint." Manson decided to focus on music two years into his multi-year sentence, and his principle guitar teacher in prison was, at the time, even more notorious than Charlie. He revealed, "One of those who taught me a few things was a nationally known gunman of the thirties, Alvin (Creepy) Karpis... a member of the notorious Ma Barker gang." Karpis was serving time for fourteen gangster hits. "He taught me a few chords and I had the opportunity to teach him a few things," said Manson.

Manson practiced guitar nearly every day and gradually began to improve. He used his music to impress people and would write his own songs based upon his life experiences and would occasionally cover the songs of others. As Manson progressed with his music, he also began to receive a special type of "schooling" from his fellow inmates exposing him to a variety of belief systems, including the occult, hypnotism, born-again Christianity, Dale Carnegie, and Scientology. He blended these beliefs together in a way that gave him power over other people, and this enabled him to manipulate others for his own ends, a tool that he would employ with deadly consequences in the second half of the 1960s.

Paul Watkins, a musician who would later join the Manson Family cult, observed first-hand Manson's pied piper approach, molded in prison. He described Manson's modus operandi: "From these studies he extracted certain phrases such as 'cease to exist,' and 'come to now.' Utilizing these, together with other precepts gained through reading, music, friendships and his own observations of human nature, Charlie evolved an eclectic 'theology' of his own which seemed to harmonize beautifully with the budding spiritual notions of a new generation of flower children."

In 1966, Manson was transferred from the McNeil Island Corrections Center in Washington State to Terminal Island prison in California. One day, as Manson was strolling around the prison yard playing his guitar and singing, he met fellow prisoner Phil Kaufman. Kaufman had been a movie extra in the Hollywood film industry making decent money. However, he decided to visit Mexico on weekends to buy pot to sell to his friends back in L.A., and he was eventually arrested and sent to Terminal Island. He recalled, "There was this guy playing guitar in the yard one day at Terminal Island jail. And it was Charlie [Manson], singing his ass off. He had an old guitar with all kinds of writing on it, all kinds of songs." Kaufman, who had connections in the L.A. music world, was impressed with Manson and began to advocate for him even before Manson got out of prison. Eventually, Kaufman referred Manson to Gary Stromberg at Universal for a recording test and a possible record deal.

"Good Vibrations"

By the late 1960s, The Beach Boys' popularity began to wane as a result of several factors. Brian Wilson suffered from mental health issues and drug use, withdrawing into his bedroom. Musical styles were progressing away from safe pop songs to more serious musical themes, and The Beatles had eclipsed The Beach Boys with the psychedelic sounds of *Sgt. Pepper's Lonely Hearts Club Band*. Racial rioting in inner cities, combined with Vietnam anti-war protests, made songs about surfing, girls, hot rods, and good vibrations seem almost irrelevant. The other Beach Boys began to step up to fill the songwriting gap left by Brian Wilson, and even drummer Dennis Wilson decided the time was ripe to get involved in songwriting.

In early 1968, Dennis separated from his wife Carol before ultimately getting divorced. He leased a bachelor pad at 14400 Sunset Boulevard that had once been a hunting lodge belonging to Will Rodgers. He began to spend time with songwriter/talent scout/session booker/engineer Gregg Jakobson, and with hot record producer Terry Melcher, who was cranking out hits for The Byrds and Paul Revere and the Raiders. They formed a bachelors' version of the Three Musketeers in L.A., dubbing themselves the "Golden Penetrators."

In April, Wilson and the Beach Boys headed out on tour with their guru, Maharishi Mahesh Yogi. Unfortunately, the tour was a disaster. No rock crowd was ready to listen to the giggling advice of the Maharishi when they were partying hard and looking for a rock concert. The tour ultimately collapsed from bad word of mouth and a lack of ticket sales. "It was devastating, a fucking nightmare," according to the band's manager, Nick Grillo.

With the tour collapsing, Dennis had some days off and returned to his life as a swinging bachelor on Sunset Boulevard. He decided to go up into the mountains to take LSD with a friend. No matter what inner spiritual awakening he may have enjoyed from that acid trip, it would soon pale in comparison to the "trip" he was about to make to the crossroads and his meeting with dark destiny.

"Home Is Where You're Happy"

Charles Manson was released from prison in March 1967, having completed a ten-year sentence. He actually asked the guards if he could stay in prison. "That is true," said Manson. "I asked if I could stay. I had dreams and plans, but as I was being processed for release, I knew the dreams would never be realized and the plans were nothing more than wishful thinking." It is too bad the guards couldn't reconsider! Manson's former parole officer described the newly freed ex-con this way, "Charlie was what he needed to be at any given time. He was clearly an anti-social personality. He was superficial, he was glib, and he was very adaptable."

The adaptable Mr. Manson moved to Haight Ashbury in San Francisco and began to fit in almost immediately with the "lost children of the sixties" who had (in the words of Timothy Leary) "turned on, tuned in, and dropped out." It was during the "Summer of Love" when this new guru began to ply his mix of Scientology, sales techniques, Bible-babble, and music to attract the first of many young female followers. Charlie, the Pied Piper of prison, manipulated people to get what he wanted in the way of food, sex, money, and help getting an entrée into the music business.

Manson recalled his early days of freedom, "My guitar, my voice, my songwriting and my homeless state put me right at home. I was just one of thousands who called wherever they were at the moment, home.… There was a communication through music." This "communication" was all part of a plan (along with LSD and other drugs) to program these lost children to do his bidding.

According to Manson Family lieutenant Paul Watkins, "Charlie's trip was to program us all to submit, to give up our egos… generally the girls were easier to program than the guys into a form of submission…. It was this 'Cease to Exist' programming that enabled Manson to build a loyal following who would do whatever he wished…. We'd sing Charlie's songs, which reinforced his words, 'Cease to Exist' and 'Your Home is Where You're Happy.'" Family member Tex Watson recalls, "I think the acid was the key, not just to the women, but to all of us; it combined with Charlie's diabolically forceful personality and his joint-nurtured insight to turn rebellious American kids into pliant slaves." With his plan set in motion, Manson acquired an old school bus and eventually made his way with a gaggle of his new Family members down to Los Angeles in hopes of getting a recording deal.

In the fall of 1967, Manson and his Family took up a new home in L.A. where he decided it was time to pursue his musical career. Manson followed up with Phil Kaufman's friend and producer Gary Stromberg in December. Stromberg was working at Universal Studios in North Hollywood at the time. He arranged for a three-hour demo session for Manson to play his guitar and sing, accompanied by a significant number of his girls. Stromberg gave a fly-on-the-wall description of the scene: "So they all take acid and go into the studio. The girls all take off their clothes. They're dancing around in the dark… and I'm the producer (laughing). Charlie is improvising the whole time. He is just making shit up."

According to Stromberg, Manson was unable to follow the directions of recording engineers and they could barely understand what he was talking about. At one point in the session, Manson told Stromberg, "I ain't used to a lot of people [referring to the engineers]." Stromberg replied, "And a lot of people ain't used to you." The session was a bust. Manson could not get used to microphones and people positioning him for proper sound. A promised second session never materialized. Manson later offered a creative excuse for this failed first try at a recording career. "When I went to Hollywood, they offered me these positions and I told them no. They wanted to pick who's gonna play in my band."

When the school bus became too small to hold Manson's growing harem of mostly female followers, he decided the family needed yet another home to be happy, one that would provide seclusion as well as proximity to the city of LA. Eventually, Manson and company found the Spahn Ranch above Chatsworth, California in the Simi Hills. Though it was secluded, it was close enough to L.A. to advance Manson's goal of networking into the music industry. The ranch was owned by George Spahn, a man in his eighties who rented out horses and buildings for Hollywood TV and films.

As 1968 dawned for Manson, he knew he needed a better plan to pursue his dreams of a record deal. He needed to snag a rock star to lobby his case to the record labels—

someone with clout who was already signed to deals. It was time for Charlie to find a rock and roll patron to facilitate his entry into the entertainment industry. He began to use his girls as scouts and bait, sending them out to troll Topanga Canyon and the Sunset Strip to find him a rock star to befriend. It would not take long before an artist and the devil would merge at the crossroads.

"I Can Hear Music"

In the spring of 1968, Dennis Wilson was taking a break from the disastrous Beach Boys tour with the Maharishi. This break was fateful, because it brought the swinging drummer into the sights of a new guru. Wilson recalled, "I went up into the mountains with my houseboy to take an LSD trip. We met two girls hitch-hiking. One of them was pregnant. We gave them a lift." Wilson met up with the girls again. "About a month later, near Malibu, I saw the pregnant girl again," he said. "Only this time she'd had her baby. I was overjoyed for her and it was through her that I met all the other girls. I told them about our [Beach Boys] involvement with the Maharishi and they told me they too had a guru, a guy named Charlie who'd recently come out of jail after 12 years." The young women were two of Manson's followers, Ella Jo Bailey and Patricia Krenwinkel, who had just struck gold for Manson to gain entree into the professional world of rock and roll.

After inviting Manson's girls over to his home in the afternoon, Wilson explained he was headed to a Beach Boys recording session, and he told them to make themselves comfortable. When he returned later that night, he was welcomed into his own home by Charles Manson who, along with a group of girls, had already moved in. In a chance encounter at a highway junction, Wilson had suddenly moved from the Maharishi to Manson. Unwittingly, he had traded in a harmless guru for a murderous messiah and invited him to live in his home. Wilson quickly came under Manson's spell. As a lonely young man soon to be divorced, he could hardly resist the bait that Manson set with a harem of naked and drug-loving girls floating around his house.

Manson's plan fed right into Wilson's "free love, get high, fast living" lifestyle. Paul Watkins observed that Wilson was easy prey for Manson:

> At the time, I viewed Dennis [Wilson] as an all-American middle-class surfer kid who suddenly made it rich and didn't know quite how to handle it. He was a prime target for the [Manson] Family. Charlie Manson self-righteously played the role of Robin Hood, taking from the rich, namely Dennis, to give to the poor, namely Charlie. He really went to work on Dennis, made him feel guilty for possessing so much wealth, and urged him to renounce it in exchange for a simple communal life based on love: Charlie's love.

189

Beach Boys' Mike Love also observed Wilson's descent down the demon's rabbit hole. "While Dennis [Wilson] had been drinking heavily for a number of years, he'd also developed an appetite for drugs, including LSD, and Manson's blending of psychedelics, sexual servants, rock music and new-age rhetoric was too much for Dennis to resist and he joined the Family." Manson's plan was beginning to work. Over the summer of 1968, Dennis Wilson hosted the Family at his home, paid for their food, medical bills, and penicillin shots, and gave them his clothing, use of his car, and even some of his gold records. Wilson was generous to a fault. When Paul Watkins and fellow Family member Clem Grogen totaled Wilson's Ferrari into what Watkins described as "a crushed tin can… twisted mass of glistening metal and broken glass," Wilson shrugged it off.

Manson's vice grip tightened around Wilson in the summer of 1968. Charlie had become his sorcerer. Wilson remarked to a reporter, "Sometimes the Wizard frightens me—Charlie Manson, who is another friend of mine, says he is God and the Devil! He sings, plays and writes poetry and may be another artist for [The Beach Boys' label] Brother Records." Dennis was impressed with Manson's guitar playing and his seemingly easy method of making up lyrics to go with his songs.

Wilson wanted to offer more at the Beach Boys sessions with original songs. He was proficient at creating instrumental rock, but he needed assistance in writing lyrics, and Manson's spontaneous work with lyrics appealed to Wilson. "When I met him [Manson] I found he had great musical ideas," said Wilson. "I accept[ed] his approach and have learned from him." And of course, Wilson's co-ownership of the Beach Boys' new record label was just what Manson was looking for. "The good times with Dennis lasted for well over a year. In that time, he and I worked on several songs together," recalled Manson. According to Manson follower Dianne Lake, "Dennis really took Charlie under his wing. Charlie was teaching Dennis how to play the guitar and I think he admired Charlie." But the guru-guitarist also wanted the same kind of money and lifestyle as the rock stars who would frequent the Wilson household. The devil's bargain was moving toward fruition.

Ironically, Manson seduced Wilson with the mantra that would contain the very same lyrics as the Manson song that Wilson found most intriguing. Paul Watkins recalled, "Charlie was always sending over contingents of girls to keep Dennis fucked, sucked and steeped in the Manson doctrine, telling his followers to lose their ego, tell Charlie they loved him, that he was all-knowing and to surrender to him. Dennis all but capitulated. One night he gave Charlie and me not only most of his wardrobe (five-hundred-dollar suits, shirts, shoes and ties), but all of his gold records…" Watkins believed that if not for Wilson's family and entertainment commitments, he may well have renounced all of his material wealth to formally join the Manson Family.

Manson was also smart enough not to put all his eggs into one basket. He would preach, play guitar, and sing to any rocker who could possibly advance his career. Lake

Charles Manson Playing Guitar While Living At Dennis Wilson's Home.

recalled, "He [Wilson] was proud to show him [Manson] off to his friends. They had a good time together." At the time, the rock royalty of L.A. and London all found their way to Mama Cass Elliot's house to hang out and jam. Aside from The Mamas & The Papas' presence, David Crosby, Stephen Stills, Eric Clapton, and many others would drop by her Laurel Canyon salon. Charles Manson wafted into the rarified company of rock royalty attached to his new patron, Dennis Wilson.

Manson also met Wilson's Golden Penetrator buddies, Gregg Jakobson and Terry Melcher. He was keen to befriend Melcher who had produced a string of hits. If Wilson couldn't punch his meal ticket, at least Manson would have some other rock stars and producers to latch onto. No one saw Manson as a psychotic killer at the time; to them, Charlie was merely a dope-smoking, acid-tripping, kooky jailhouse guru… and an aspiring musician.

On more than one occasion, Manson tried to get The Mamas & The Papas' bandleader John Phillips to give him a chance in the studio, but Phillips demurred. When asked by Manson repeatedly to record, Phillips recalled, "I'd just shudder every time. I'd say, 'no, I think I'll pass.'" But Manson was not deterred by rejection.

On one occasion, Wilson invited Buffalo Springfield singer, songwriter, and guitarist Neil Young over to jam and party. It was there that Young first met and played music with Charles Manson. "After a while, a guy showed up, picked up my guitar, and started playing a lot of songs on it," recalled Young. "His name was Charlie. He was a friend of the girls and now of Dennis. His songs were off-the-cuff things he made up as he went along, and they were never the same twice in a row. Kind of like Dylan, but different because it was hard to glimpse a true message in them, but the songs were fascinating. He was quite good." Not only did Young give Wilson high praise on Manson's ability as a songwriter, he went so far as to ask his Reprise Records boss Mo Ostin to sign Manson to a record deal. Ostin wisely passed. After Young's enthusiastic endorsement, Dennis Wilson realized he had made a significant musical discovery. Manson dug the life of wealthy hippie rock stars, and was determined to attain this lifestyle, and Dennis Wilson was going to be his winning lottery ticket.

"Cease to Exist"

Having concluded that Manson was a rough diamond that could be polished into a bonafide recording gem, Wilson confided his plan to Gregg Jakobson who was also enthusiastic. Wilson hired Jakobson to produce a demo session with Manson in a proper recording studio. "It was Dennis Wilson's idea," recalled Jakobson. "Dennis wanted me to get a feel for Charlie [Manson] and his music. He didn't want to do it at Brian [Wilson's] studio… you know which was at Brian's house. So he wanted me to go to a studio. And it was kind of a demo date."

Gregg Jakobson

The sessions took place on August 8-9, 1968. At the session, Jakobson recalls guitarist Bobby Beausoleil, as well as other Family members, playing a few random instruments to back Charlie and his acoustic guitar. These were likely overdubbed on August 9 after Manson had laid down his guitar and vocal tracks the day before. "I recall some of the songs he did that day," said Jakobson. "Some of the titles were 'Garbage Dump,' 'Mechanical Man,' and 'Cease to Exist.'"

The sessions started off slowly with all of the Family members partying, singing, and talking. Eventually, Jakobson suggested to Manson that the session would proceed faster and get better results if he could just "lose the entourage." "Charlie looked at me," recalled Jakobson, "and he realized it wasn't a bad idea. Manson responded, 'Let's do this and not have the cheerleading section.' So, the entourage headed out someplace else during the session."

Roughly twelve Manson songs were recorded by Jakobson at the recording console. "Charlie had a lot of songs and they were not really written down," said Jakobson. "But he could kind of bring them up from memory and they maybe would even change from different performances of the song." Jakobson likened Manson's musical singing approach to that of a rapper. "He was probably the original rapper, before anyone else had ever rapped. He could just spout that shit out with just a little bit of rhythm and rhyme. He wasn't a good guitar player either. He was just hitting big fat chords." Manson's songs often featured him going back and forth between two chords, with a bit of rhythm, while he sang or rapped his song lyrics.

Manson did find the studio an intimidating place, but Jakobson's skills and bedside manner helped produce some decent recordings on tape for Wilson. Manson recalled the process, "I never really dug recording, you know, all those things pointing at you. Gregg [Jakobson] would say, 'Come down to the studio, and we'll tape some things,' so I went. You get into the studio, you know, and it's hard to sing into microphones. Giant phallic symbols pointing at you. All my latent tendencies… my relationship to music is completely subliminal. It just flows through me."

The following day, Jakobson recorded some overdubs of Family members on top of Manson's songs. Manson's girls provided backing vocals on some tracks, while Steven Grogan played some bass and Bobby Beausoleil added an electric guitar. With the sessions concluded, Jakobson left the studio with a master tape to play for Dennis Wilson.

Not long after the sessions, Jakobson recalled, "I played the demo of Charlie for Dennis. We sat down and listened to Charlie's demo session recording and Dennis liked what he heard, and he especially liked the idea of the song 'Cease to Exist'… the idea of 'never learn not to love,' which is a line in the song, because Dennis was never much of a lyricist really." In fact, that is the reason Wilson had also begun writing songs with Jakobson at the time. Clearly Wilson had an ulterior motive for helping Manson with his career. Because his brother Brian, the hit songwriter, could not contribute much to the band while hiding away in his bedroom, Dennis knew he had to step up and contribute some song ideas for the group's next album. *Might one of Manson's songs work for The Beach Boys and at the same time help Charlie?*

The lyrics to Manson's song "Cease to Exist" clearly illustrated the brainwashing rap he used to attract new members to his growing cult family. His lyrics were geared to giving up one's self and one's money to Charlie. Jakobson recalled, "The song that seemed most viable to Dennis was 'Cease to Exist.' Don't forget, this was the Sixties. You know, don't be the person you think you are. It's just imagination." Manson would later claim that the song was written for Dennis and his band. "You know," said Manson, "'Cease to Exist.' I wrote that for The Beach Boys. They were fighting among themselves, so I wrote that song to bring them together. 'Submission is a gift; give it to your brother.' Dennis has true soul, but his brothers couldn't accept it." But Jakobson never bought Manson's claim. "You know all that shit in the song… Charlie just picked up all that philosophical shit in prison and up in Haight Ashbury. That song was a recruitment song to bring in more girls to Charlie's family."

Regardless, Wilson liked the song and had some ideas for turning it into a track for the next Beach Boys album. Having settled on the creepy composition, Wilson sat down with Manson to discuss purchasing the rights to the song. The only living person to witness this transaction was Gregg Jakobson. He told the Rock And Roll Detective, "Dennis did pay a specific sum of money to Charlie to purchase all of the rights to the song, 'Cease to Exist.' He gave Charlie literally cash money for the song. I mean Dennis could start the day off with $10,000 cash. And by the end of the day it might be gone." The transaction was made at Wilson's house. "So, he gave Charlie three hundred bucks. And don't forget, this was in the Sixties and the Manson Family was broke, so that was a lot of money! To Charlie, that was a nice bit of money for writing one song. You know smoking pot and buying and selling a song." It was clear to Jakobson that the intent of both parties was for Manson to sell *all* of his rights in that song to Wilson, which would allow Wilson to do whatever he wanted with the creative work.

The only problem was the deal was not in writing. Jakobson related, "Dennis paid for me, the sessions and the master tape. But there was no assignment of copyright, no written contract and no documents. The deal was just a handshake. Charlie didn't sign any legal documents for any of this and Dennis didn't either. He [Manson] really wasn't big on that sort of thing." According to Jakobson and contrary to popular mythology, Manson never told Wilson at the time of the transaction, "*Do not change the title or words to my song!*" When asked about the Manson-Wilson transaction, former Beach Boys manager Nick Grillo told the Rock And Roll Detective, "I have no recollection of the details of the deal."

At the time, Manson felt that his musical career was about to take off. He had written a song that might end up on a Beach Boys album. He recalled, "I had dreams and expectations of making it in the music world, which I felt confident would begin materializing in just a few more weeks." Wilson was pleased that he could take Manson's song and begin to rework it into a contribution to the upcoming Beach Boys album sessions. Wilson and Manson even began to discuss writing songs together. Manson claimed later that Wilson told him, "I'll give you my house if you help me write some songs." This statement is hardly believable since Wilson didn't even own the home; he was merely a renter.

Later in August 1968, Dennis Wilson and The Beach Boys went back on the road for some tour dates. Although still friends with Manson and his Family, Wilson grew weary of them living at his home and spending his money. Pressure was also coming from Brother Records' manager, Nick Grillo, who saw Wilson's roommates living large and creating a money pit. "Someone at Brother Records checked Manson's background and discovered his criminal past, and our accountants were raising flags about unexplained expenditures on Dennis' charge card," recalled Mike Love. "By summer's end, Dennis figured he'd lost about $100,000 to his Manson Family roommates, and even for him, that was too much." (Considering inflation, $100,000 in 1968 was equivalent in purchasing power to about $700,000 in today's world.)

The lease on the Sunset Boulevard house was allowed to lapse so that the landlord could evict Manson and his Family while Wilson was out of town. Jakobson was tasked with closing down the house on Sunset and moving whatever had not been swiped by Manson. Jakobson later found a house on the L.A. side of Malibu, past Santa Monica, that he would share with Wilson upon his return.

"Eyes of a Dreamer"

Brother Records Incorporated (BRI) was initially created to guarantee Brian Wilson the creative freedom to make whatever music he desired. The Beach Boys could create their own work at the studio of their choice and license the songs to Capitol Records, instead of being under the microscope of their label's producer and studio. BRI also served as a management company and a creative outlet that permitted The Beach Boys to sign and develop other artists and to work on solo projects. In this way, each member could be a producer, sign artists, and give life to their own individual creative ambitions.

In September, upon Dennis Wilson's return from touring, he began talking up Charlie Manson to his bandmates and the possibility of BRI signing the guitar guru. "Dennis wanted Brother Records to record Manson, bringing him into our offices and hyping his talents," recalled Love. "He [Manson] gave most people the creeps." Dennis set up recording sessions for Manson with engineer Stephen Desper in Brian's home studio. The idea was to cut another demo good enough to convince The Beach Boys to consider signing Manson to their record label.

Wilson advised Manson to prepare for another demo session at the BRI studio. Manson recalled, "The next time was at Dennis' brother's home studio, which was larger than a lot of the commercial studios." The night before the session, Beach Boy engineer

Stephen Desper was called by manager Grillo and told that a friend of Dennis' would be coming down to the studio.

For years, numerous books, articles, and scribes have claimed that Manson recorded songs *with* The Beach Boys' members, including Dennis, Brian, and Carl Wilson either playing or producing on Manson's sessions. The myth of The Beach Boys jamming with Manson has grown exponentially over the years. But it is Fake News! Stephen Desper cleared up this fabled story with the Rock And Roll Detective: "Charlie did *not* record with any Beach Boys! Dennis was not there. Brian was out. Carl had no interest. It was Charles, myself and a few of his girls." The plan, according to Desper, was to listen to what got recorded and see if Dennis' friend was worth a chance on the Brother Records label.

Desper recalled more about Charlie's personality at the sessions than the actual music recorded by him. "From my perspective, here was a single artist playing a single instrument, and I had eight tracks to capture whatever I wanted. There were no overdubs." He observed, "[Charlie] was constantly standing up and being fidgety. Finally, I told him that if he wanted a successful demo recording he was going to need to settle down and listen to me." Eventually, Manson got more comfortable with the environment and put down some decent tracks. Manson had arrived with a Sears quality six-string guitar. Desper, wanting to give Wilson's friend the opportunity to be his best, went into the back room and pulled out a high-quality Martin D-28 acoustic guitar. Manson appreciated using such a great sounding instrument.

"This time we did a pretty fair session," said Manson, dreaming of success on the same level as his rock royalty friends. "But getting some money out of it and getting us on the market was still going to take some time." Brother Records paid for the session time, Desper's work, and the master tape. Nick Grillo told engineer Desper that eight songs were enough and called off further sessions.

Desper sent the master tape up to the BRI office with a note. It said, "Not yet ready to be a recording artist; temperament issues. [Note: At one point, Manson pulled a knife on the engineer.] Hard to deal with." Brian Wilson and his wife were freaked out by Manson and his Family being in their home. One Beach Boy who listened to the demo tapes, but refused to give his name on the record, stated, "We've got several eight-track tapes of Charlie and the girls that Dennis cut, maybe even some 16-track. Just chanting, fucking, sucking, barfing. Maybe we'll put it out in the fall. Call it 'Death Row.'"

Coupled with Charlie's expenditures at Dennis' house, his criminal background, and the session note from Desper, there was enough information for the other Beach Boys and their manager to put Manson's dreams on the back burner. When Manson eventually discovered his potential signing was on hold, he became agitated. He made his frequently confrontational presence known at the BRI offices, which did not help his cause. Desper explained, "I think if Manson had been more patient and not gone to the office to complain and harass the staff, he might have gotten a small deal to record and put out a couple of songs. His own ignorance of the way the music business works was his own undoing, heading on to the very tragic events that followed."

Manson's peaceful persona was beginning to unravel. The once-goofy guru was morphing into a more dangerous, angry, and desperate person. Manson himself admitted, "The simplicity of our previous life, the love and thoughtfulness for each other, was being replaced by the greed for possessions. I consoled myself and condoned my actions by telling myself that all this bad shit would end just as soon as our records got on the market." Soon enough however, Dennis Wilson's song purchase from Manson would make the ex-con even more angry.

"Never Learn Not To Love"

In September 1968, The Beach Boys were back on the worldwide charts with their hit song "Do It Again," but the band was starting to lose steam as Brian Wilson, their principal songwriter and producer, was exhausted and burned out. Dennis was very concerned about his brother Brian's mental state. "I remember him crying. Saying, 'I can't take it anymore.' I think he said he was having a nervous breakdown…. I was terrified for my brother." Brian reflected on his feelings and the atmosphere surrounding the fall 1968 album sessions. "If there was a desperation to my excess, it was fueled in part by how desperately The Beach Boys needed a hit. In my downstairs studio, the guys worked on the band's latest LP, *20/20*." The work continued on despite Brian being AWOL. The album epitomized much more of a group effort in Brian's absence. The sound and songs were considered very "un-Brian."

Brian recalled his brother Dennis supplying "the album's oddest cut, 'Never Learn Not To Love." He eventually learned that the tune owed its origin to the song called "Cease to Exist" that came from Dennis' new wild-eyed, songwriter-friend, Charlie Manson. Gregg Jakobson verified that Manson and Wilson never sat down together to write "Cease to Exist." He stated, "Dennis bought it from Charlie and then changed it into The Beach Boys' song." Engineer Stephen Desper described Manson's song this way, "With 'Cease to Exist,' Manson only had a song with basic chords on the guitar and a melody lead line. It was The Beach Boys who took that basic concept and turned it into a real commercial tune."

On September 11, Dennis Wilson introduced this new song to his bandmates at Brian's home studio. In a strange moment of twisted irony, The Beatles had finished recording the song "Helter Skelter" the day before—a song that would soon play into Manson's transformation into a "guru-some" murderer. Charles Manson was not invited and never sat in on the "Never Learn Not To Love" sessions, according to Desper. "In fact," said Desper, "Dennis Wilson was never in the studio at the same time as Manson."

Beach Boy Al Jardine recalled the song being brought in. "It was just a melody in 'Never Learn Not To Love'… but there was a mantra behind it." At the time of the first session, no one knew about the song's origin. "I did not recognize the song," said Desper. "Dennis just said he was bringing a new song to the studio. He never said where the song came from. It was just the song he was working on at the time."

Dennis Wilson's priority at the session was the sound of his lead vocals and the harmony vocal arrangement of the other Beach Boys. Dennis, who technically produced the session, initially came in alone and sang the lead part, plus all of the harmony parts on a multi-track tape. According to Desper, "He could not write music at that point in his career, so he recorded what he thought would be a good vocal arrangement with the song." Once Dennis got the vocals down, Desper saved his lead vocal. Then each Beach Boy, one by one, recorded and replaced the guide-vocal harmonies that Dennis had created for his new song. Desper confirmed, "Every Beach Boys' voice is on that song, but at different points, there are fewer than all of them. On some vocal parts, I put on the 'Desper lick echo.' We would feed the vocal part through the echo chamber a few times to get the effect." The echo certainly adds to the haunting nature of the song, along with another effect the engineer added on the front end of the track. It was Desper who thought of the idea to record a spooky backward cymbal hit at the start of the song which crescendos into the opening vocals on the stereo master. A haunting flute sound was also added by Desper's then-girlfriend, Kathy Dragon (Note: she was the sister of musician Darrel Dragon, of *Captain and Tennille* fame).

The sessions continued at Brian's studio on September 16, 17, and 18. Gregg Jakobson recalled, "I stuck my head in during the session to hear a mix or a playback of the song." What he noticed most about the song that he had originally recorded with Manson was the way in which Wilson changed the title, lyrics, and subject matter into a more romantic theme from Manson's original cult-like recruitment lyrics. "Dennis was definitely a romantic. And he loved that name, 'Never Learn Not To Love,'" said Jakobson. Aside from the title change, Wilson made a significant alteration to Manson's lyric "cease to exist," changing it to "cease to resist." He also added a line to the chorus, where Dennis sings to the girl in the song to come over to him and get closer in a seductive manner. He ends the lyrical phrase with a satisfied sigh of "ahh." Wilson had artfully turned Manson's bare bones dirge into a romantic, psychedelic song of seduction.

Dennis and the Boys continued working on the *20/20* album into the late fall. Manson had come to L.A. to meet again with Dennis, lobbying for a record deal on Brother Records. According to Paul Watkins, The Beach Boys' organization had put Manson off again with delays and excuses (basically because Dennis could not convince the other band members to sign Charlie). Manson returned to Spahn ranch agitated. He also came back with a new concern for his family. He had seen growing racial violence in the city and believed that African Americans were on the verge of a full scale revolution. He would soon combine these observations with a new, evil mission, one that would be fueled by LSD and the release of The Beatles' *White Album.*

"Helter Skelter"

In 1967, Paul McCartney of The Beatles was reading an interview in *Guitar Player* magazine that inspired him. The Who's Pete Townshend described one of their singles, "I Can See for Miles," as the "loudest, dirtiest song The Who had ever recorded." Never to be outdone, McCartney was motivated to surpass The Who with a louder, rougher song. McCartney ended up writing the song "Helter Skelter" as his answer to The Who. True to form, the song was a louder, dirtier, and more hard-rocking rager than The Who's song. Many writers have credited this Beatles track as a prototype for the hard rock music genre that would follow in the late 1960s and 1970s.

A helter skelter was an amusement park attraction that featured a tall spiral slide winding around a tower. McCartney told biographer Miles that he used "the symbol of a helter skelter [playground slide] as a ride from top to bottom; the rise and fall of the Roman Empire—and this was the fall, the demise."

In early December, The Beach Boys released a new single in the United States entitled "Bluebirds Over The Mountain," with Dennis' song, "Never Learn Not To Love," as the B-side. The song was credited solely to Dennis Wilson as composer and producer (however, subsequently, the singles were credited to "The Beach Boys" as producer). There was no mention of Charles Manson in the credits. Interestingly, Dennis' song would again appear on the forthcoming *20/20* album, stating that "Never Learn Not To Love" was produced by Carl and Dennis Wilson. Clearly there was some confusion at Capitol Records as to who the producer was. Steven Desper explained, "Technically, Dennis brought in the song and he was the producer of the session. When the record came out, for consistency, it might read, 'Produced by The Beach Boys' as a way to say that each of the Beach Boys was actually contributing to the songs."

The 45-rpm single mix of "Never Learn Not To Love" by Capitol had deleted the haunting backward cymbal at the beginning of the song and added a bit of additional echo on the Outro, ultimately creating two different commercial versions of the song. The single had the dubious honor of being the lowest charting 45-rpm record in The Beach Boys' history at the time, reaching only number 61 in America, with virtually no radio airplay.

On November 22, 1968, "Helter Skelter" was part of the double album released by The Beatles worldwide. The album *The Beatles* became quickly known as the "*White Album*," due to its stark white cover. Charles Manson was living out at Spahn Ranch with the Family and had recently made plans for the cult to move further into the desert. Manson

first heard The Beatles' *White Album* in mid-December on a trip into Los Angeles. After that, according to follower Paul Watkins, "things [with Manson] were never the same."

To Manson, the message for a racial Armageddon was all reaffirmed in his mind. Charlie "heard the messages" in The Beatles' lyrics of the *White Album*, as his acid-fueled Family listened to his lectures at the end of 1968 and through the following year. "Helter Skelter," "Piggies," "Blackbird," and "Revolution" were all speaking to Charlie's vision of an apocalyptic uprising. Watkins described Manson's vision of a race war that he had derived from The Beatles. Quoting Manson, Watkins recalled, "'Are you hep to what The Beatles are saying? Dig it, they're telling it like it is. They know what's happening in the city; blackie is getting ready. They put the revolution to music. It's "Helter Skelter." "Helter Skelter" is coming down.'" Watkins described the acid trip lectures of Manson's vision of a race war. Manson had developed a theory that a revolution was coming down fast, one that would pit African Americans versus whites for control of American society. Manson and his gang would hide underground in the desert until the war was over. Then Manson would arise and be the leader of the African American race who would inevitably (in his mind) win the

The Beatles studio used "Helter Skelter"
lyrics handritten by Mal Evans.

revolution. The message seemed to connect with his Family. Watkins confirmed, "By the time the *White Album* was released, with 'Helter Skelter,' both Charlie and The Beatles had been more than validated in our minds."

Manson felt an urgency to get his musical communiqués carrying his apocalyptic predictions out to the world. Family member Tex Watson bought into Manson's rhetoric. "We knew we were part of something bigger than any album ever cut," he said. "Bigger than Dennis Wilson and his average Beach Boys had ever been, bigger even than The Beatles themselves, because this was more than just music. This was Charlie's message to the world, this was Charlie giving his soul to all the free children that were waiting for him, whether they knew it or not."

As 1969 dawned, Manson told his Family that he had to stay closer to the action in L.A. to work on his music, since he believed Wilson and Jakobson's other friend, producer Terry Melcher, might give him a record deal. But, at the same time, Manson's vision of "Helter Skelter" *was* getting darker. He told his Lieutenant, "You know what's gonna happen one of these nights… the blacks from Watts are gonna break into the houses of some rich white piggies in Beverly Hills and start wasting them… you know… and it ain't gonna be very pretty… they'll chop them up and mutilate them and fling blood around, then whitey is gonna retaliate…" Watkins did not realize that Manson was predicting an impending holocaust that *he* would actually initiate. "We had been conditioned to agree," recalled Watkins. The Family was being moved toward murder.

The Beach Boys Album Cover "20/20."

Manson had a need to be recognized for his success as a budding rock star in the eyes of his Family in order to keep his minions believing in, and following him. He needed to maintain control and a belief system. To Charlie, a record deal and rock star money was not too far down the road. Tex Watson realized later that acid was also crucial to solidify Manson's followers. "I think the acid was the key, not just to the women, but to all of us; it combined with Charlie's diabolically forceful personality and his joint-nurtured insight, to turn rebellious American kids into compliant, plantation slaves."

In February 1969, The Beach Boys released the album *20/20* which featured Wilson's song, "Never Learn Not To Love." In April, Dennis Wilson sang the song on TV's *Mike Douglas Show*, and the album peaked at number 68 on the Billboard album charts. Ironically, Wilson's album track had the distinction of indirectly putting Manson on the music charts for the one and only time in his life. Manson did not celebrate this achievement, however; instead his anger boiled over when he heard The Beach Boys' song "Never Learn Not To Love" for the first time.

"Shut Down"

Manson became aware of the release of The Beach Boys' new album in the spring of 1969, containing what he thought would be his song "Cease to Exist." He believed his success as a recording artist was just around the corner. However, when "Never Learn Not To Love" was released on the *20/20* album, there were no credits mentioning Manson. He noticed the song title had been changed along with several of the lyrics and the arrangement. Rather than consider it an honor that he had sold a song that ended up on an international Beach Boys album, and that he could likely continue to collaborate with Wilson in the future, Manson was livid.

When asked by *Rolling Stone* magazine why Manson was not given credit on the label, Dennis Wilson replied, "He [Manson] didn't want that, he wanted money instead." This is clearly a true statement based upon Jakobson's eyewitness account of the transaction. Instead of detailing all of the actual facts of the cash-for-song deal, Wilson blithely intoned, "I gave him about $100,000 worth of stuff." While this was true and Wilson felt morally justified in stating this, the $100,000 was really a gift that Wilson gave or allowed Manson and his Family to have while living with him. However, it was the $300 cash that specifically represented the legal consideration actually spent to "purchase" the song.

Manson was not upset with having his name left off the composing credits; however, he flew into a rage stemming from the fact that Wilson had changed the lyrics to his song. It was *his* message, one that suggested the surrender of ego to Manson, that gave him his recruiting power. Wilson had stripped that away and turned the tune into a more optimistic, romantic song. "My words!" exclaimed Manson. "I lived and died by my words all my life. I keep my word. My word is my bond. I live on my word."

Manson shared his anger and the perceived slight with his Family and anyone else who would listen. Gregg Jakobson (who had recorded Manson's original version of "Cease to Exist") got an earful. He told the Rock And Roll Detective, "Charlie was all about getting whatever the message was—to get it out there. And Charlie really was angry with Dennis for changing the song… let's put it that way. That really pissed Charlie off. He didn't like it, changing his message." According to Tex Watson, "The Beach Boys had managed to turn the central theme of Charlie's message into a corny sex lyric." To Manson, it was as if Wilson had taken away a piece of his soul. Unwittingly, Wilson had messed with the soul of an evil spirit. "When I come up with a song and they [The Beach Boys] change the words," said Manson spitting out venom, "I say, 'don't change the words.' If you change the words, my shadows are running fast man." Manson's words delivered a chilling warning.

"Never Learn Not to Love"

Cease to resist, come on say you love me
Give up your world, come on and be with me
I'm your kind, I'm your kind, and I see

Come on come on, ooo I love you pretty girl
My life is yours, and you can have my world
I'm your kind, I'm your kind, and I see

Never had a lesson I ever learned
I know I could never learn not to love you
Come in now closer
Come in closer closer closer ahhhh

Submission is a gift, give it to your lover
Love and understanding is for one another
I'm your kind, I'm your kind, and I see

Never had a lesson I ever learned
I know I could never learn not to love you
Come in now closer
Come in closer come in closer ahhhh

Ahhh-ahhh-ahhh-ahhh-ahhhhhh
Ahhh-ahhh-ahhh-ahhh-ahhhhhh

Beach Boys Lyrics To "Never Learn Not To Love" signed by Mike Love.

In Dennis Wilson's mind, he had paid for the song and could do what he wanted with it. Jakobson recalled, "He [Wilson] owned it. Therefore, he was absolutely going to make the song more like a Beach Boys tune." Apparently, Manson had forgotten that day in 1968 when he had agreed (though not in writing) to sell his song to Wilson. The Rock And Roll Detective asked Jakobson, the only living witness to the transaction, a key question no one had previously asked, "Did Charles Manson ever put any restrictions on the sale of the song to Wilson at the time of the transaction?" Jakobson replied, "No. He didn't put down any restrictions at that time. The moment he accepted the $300 from Dennis for the song, I realized he did not understand what he was giving away. He was not schooled enough to even put down any restrictions, such as changing the title or lyrics. That story came later after the song was released."

Manson's rage intensified. He stormed over to Brother Records to complain to the band's manager, Nick Grillo. Only his anger was no longer focused on the changed title and lyrics. Manson recalled, "When I went into Dennis Wilson's Beach Boys' [office], I said, 'You owe me money for music. Where's my money?'" Grillo told Manson (according to Manson), "Oh, you don't have any money coming." Manson replied, "What do you mean I don't have any money coming? You'll pay me. Gimme what I got coming…. And they won't give me my dues." Grillo allegedly told Manson, "Sue me." Manson said, "I won't sue you; I'll bomb your car man, I [will] blow your house up." Clearly, peaceful guru Charlie Manson had been supplanted by a murderous, crazed, and out-of-control man. Grillo turned the tables on Manson. "You haven't a contract or any kind of agreement. We owe you nothing. And because of your attitude, nothing is what you get." According to Manson, Grillo made an implied threat that he would call the mafia to take care of him if he didn't leave the office. When questioned about the deal, Grillo again had amnesia, telling the Rock And Roll Detective, "I have no recollection of the details of the deal. Whatever transpired was a long time ago, and I don't want to misinform you."

Manson had been shut down by The Beach Boys and big business, but he had not given up on his goal. After he left Brother Records in a rage, Manson decided it was time to focus his energy on producer Terry Melcher and attempting to get the famous producer to listen to his music in hopes of securing a record deal to spread the Family gospel of Charlie's philosophy and the coming revolution.

"So You Want to Be A Rock and Roll Star"

Manson and his Family continued to prepare for Charlie's race war, while simultaneously rehearsing his music in hopes of interesting Terry Melcher in producing and signing him to a record label. Melcher, the son of movie star Doris Day, was hired as a staff producer for Columbia Records at the age of only 22. He was renowned for supporting the careers of the Byrds, Ry Cooder, and Paul Revere and the Raiders. Melcher produced mega-hits by the Byrds, including "Mr. Tambourine Man," "Turn, Turn, Turn," and "So You Want To Be A Rock 'n' Roll Star." He had hung out with Manson from time to time since 1968, through his friendship with Jakobson and Wilson.

Jakobson tried to bring Melcher and Manson together in the spring of 1969. Jakobson was fascinated with capturing on film the Manson Family lifestyle out at Spahn Ranch. He wanted Melcher's involvement as both a music producer and a financier of the film. "God, I wish we had filmed Manson and his group," recalled Jakobson. "I wish we had had a couple hours of film out there at Spahn. We sure would have had some valuable footage. And that is why I brought Terry [Melcher] into it. Because I didn't want Terry to record Charlie [Manson] per se as a musician, but I definitely told Terry, 'We gotta document this guy.'" Jakobson also wanted Melcher's connections and financial backing. Manson merely wanted a recording deal with a big cash advance.

Jakobson related that, in the meantime, he continued recording Manson "fairly extensively in the spring of 1969." He recalled a session at Wilder Brothers Studio, "Sometime later I started recording Charlie at a little studio here called Wilder Studio. And the owner George Wilder was leery of Charlie because he knew Charlie was an ex-con and because Charlie, to a straight[-laced] person, is sort of a wild-looking-guy—his eyes, his hair, his movements and everything." Wilder told Jakobson, "Listen, this guy is an ex-con. I don't know what he's going to do. He might flip out or beat me up or something." Little did Wilder know that Manson was about to "flip out" and orchestrate a series of horrific murders.

After skipping one proposed meeting with Manson, Melcher finally made a couple of visits out to Spahn ranch in June to listen to some live music. Manson recalled, "I was still after Dennis, Jakobson and Melcher to come through with something good for us. At Jakobson's insistence, Melcher and a guy finally came out to Spahn's." Manson and Family had all been busy rehearsing for days before Melcher's arrival to make the best possible impression. However, Melcher was *not* impressed. He gave Manson the usual producer noncommittal-polite-turndown of *I'm not sure how to position your music.* However, in front of the entire Family, he handed Manson $50 cash. In the psychotic, drug-addled mind of Manson and his followers, they believed Melcher "liked" his music and was giving him some cash in "advance" of a pending recording contract. At least that is what Manson portrayed to his Family. However, as Melcher later testified under oath at the Manson murder trial, "I think it was $50. Well, they all seemed to be hungry." It had merely been a gift. (Note: An actual record advance would've been a much larger sum of money, provided at the time of signing a recording contract.) Melcher also told the court he never formally recorded Manson because he wasn't impressed, and because Manson did not want to join the musician's union which was technically required in order to record at a professional recording studio. However, David Gold recalled to this author that Melcher did supervise a demo session with Manson in approximately July 1969 at Gold Star Studio only one month before the Tate/LaBianca murders. He still has a 7 ½ ips tape copy from the session. Gold recalled, "It is over fifty years ago since he [Manson] was at Gold Star. I remember talking with him in the hall like it was yesterday. George Fernandez was the engineer. And yes Terry [Melcher] was the client."

When Manson subsequently learned that he was not going to be signed to a major label by Melcher he grew very angry again. Referring to his disdain for Melcher, Manson said, "He [Melcher] did wrong. He lied. Will you make a contract? What does the contract mean to you? Will you make a contract? You keep your word or you lose your life." Of course, no contract ever existed, except in the mind of Manson.

Manson badmouthed Melcher to his followers, including Susan Atkins, who recalled, "We knew Terry [Melcher] very well. The reason Charlie picked that house [as the location of the Tate murders, the house that Melcher had recently vacated,] was to instill fear into Terry Melcher because Terry had given us his word on a few things and never came through with them." Melcher shared, "Manson said I was a fraud because he said I lied about a record contract. As a singer, Manson was third rate." According to Melcher, he and Manson would not meet again face-to-face until the Tate/La Bianca murder trial.

According to Paul Watkins, who had left the Family before the August 1969 murder spree, "I didn't learn until later that he [Manson] had gone to 10050 Cielo Drive [the scene of the Tate murders]." Manson had learned that Melcher had moved prior to the Tate murders. Watkins added, "On August 9, he [Manson] sent four people there to pay a visit: Tex Watson, Susan Atkins, Patricia Krenwinkel and a new girl named Linda Kasabian."

"Piggies"
In a case of macabre irony, the Sharon Tate murders committed by Manson's Family occurred exactly one year after Gregg Jakobson recorded Charles Manson singing "Cease to Exist," which Dennis Wilson would later turn into his own version. Manson's followers murdered eight-month pregnant actress Sharon Tate and her friends on August 9, 1969. The next night, they killed Leno and Rosemary LaBianca at their home a few miles away. The resulting news of these slaughters sent L.A. celebrities into frozen fear. The murders were bloody and horrific, exactly as Manson had prophesized when he attributed these heinous acts to African Americans starting a race war. The words "Pig," "Death to Pigs," and "Helter Skelter" had been written with victims' blood at the homes, a clear reference to two songs ("Piggies" and "Helter Skelter") on The Beatles' *White Album*. When the story broke, Dennis Wilson, The Beach Boys, Gregg Jakobson, and Terry Melcher had no idea that crazy Charlie and his Family were responsible for these horrific murders.

While the police began their investigation, with no real suspects or motive, Manson needed money to complete his Family's move out into the desert and for supplies. "I

PIGGIES

1. HAVE YOU SEEN THE LITTLE PIGGIES, CRAWLING
   IN THE DIRT? AND FOR ALL THE LITTLE PIGGIES
   LIFE IS GETTING WORSE — ALWAYS HAVING DIRT
   TO PLAY AROUND IN.

2. HAVE YOU SEEN THE BIGGER PIGGIES IN THEIR
   STARCHED WHITE SHIRTS? YOU WILL FIND THE
   BIGGER PIGGIES STIRRING UP THE DIRT, ALWAYS HAVE
   CLEAN **SHIRTS** TO PLAY AROUND IN —

BRIDGE
   IN THEIR STYES WITH ALL THEIR BACKING
   THEY DON'T CARE WHAT GOES ON AROUND
   IN THEIR EYES THERE'S SOMETHING LACKING
   WHAT THEY NEED'S A DAMN GOOD WHACKING

3. EVERYWHERE THERE'S LOTS OF PIGGIES — LIVING
   PIGGY LIVES — YOU CAN SEE THEM OUT FOR
   DINNER WITH THEIR PIGGY WIVES — CLUTCHING
   FORKS AND KNIVES TO EAT THEIR ~~PORK CHOPS~~.
                                  BACON

4. EVERYWHERE THERE'S LOTS OF PIGGIES — PLAYING
   PIGGY PRANKS YOU WILL SEE THEM ON THEIR
   TROTTERS AT THE PIGGY BANKS — GIVING
   PIGGY THANKS TO THEE, PIG BROTHER.

The Beatles' studio used lyrics for "Piggies" handwritten by Mal Evans.

told Charlie, I told him, that's a great idea Charlie," said Jakobson, who was fed up with Manson's antics and frequent begging. "A little Death Valley… that's a great place for you. In other words, Charlie, you don't belong in society." Manson had started coming around

Jakobson's house looking for money from him and Wilson. "That was one of the first times Charlie looked visibly upset and seemed visibly shaken. He was like a wild man," recalled Jakobson.

During Dennis Wilson's Beach Boys tour in Canada, Manson came by again looking for Dennis. When Jakobson informed Manson that Dennis was on tour, Charlie handed him a 44-caliber bullet and threatened, "Tell Dennis, there are more where this came from." According to Manson follower Stephanie Schram, who accompanied Charlie on a subsequent visit to Wilson's home, "Well, I guess he [Manson] did a record a long time ago and he wanted to see if there were any royalties left on it or something; but he [Wilson] didn't give him any." Much to Manson's chagrin, when he was subsequently turned down by Wilson, he used the same bullet threat again, telling Dennis Wilson he knew where his son lived. This was too much to take for the normally peaceful drummer. Wilson slugged Manson and knocked him, bloodied, to the ground. He had no idea he was dealing with a psychotic murderer. "I never kept the bullet. No, no," said Jakobson. "That was a fear thing. Talk about the antithesis of the Sixties."

It took four months for the police to figure out who to charge for the Tate/LaBianca murders. On December 8, 1969, Charles Manson, along with Tex Watson, Susan Atkins, Patricia Krenwinkel (one of Wilson's hitchhiker pickups), and Linda Kasabian were indicted for the murders of Sharon Tate and her friends. The grand jury also indicted those five, plus Leslie Van Houten, for the LaBianca murders. The arrests sent shockwaves through the L.A. entertainment community. Shortly after Manson's arrest, the L.A. Musician's Union quickly disassociated themselves from the so-called musician. In checking its records, the union found that Charles Manson was never a member and therefore, "that Manson was definitely not a musician."

Charles Manson would tell the District Attorney (DA), Vincent Bugliosi, that it was The Beatles' fault for the murders that occurred. He was quoted by the DA as saying, "'It's not my conspiracy. It is not my music. I hear what it relates. It says 'Rise!' It says 'Kill.' Why blame it on me? I didn't write the music. I am not the person who projected it into your social consciousness…. It's The Beatles, the music they're putting out…. It's subliminal." Of course, the idea of blaming his actions on music that he had clearly misinterpreted (after too much acid) was complete madness.

The fallout from the shocking murders hit especially hard on those who had tried to help Manson with his musical career—Stromberg, Wilson, Jakobson, and Melcher. Gary Stromberg thought about the tapes he had made of Manson in 1967 and wondered if they still existed and could somehow connect him. Terry Melcher was terrified, knowing that the Tate murders had taken place at the Cielo Drive residence that he had recently vacated. The police showed up at his new home, rang his doorbell, and asked the shocked producer, "Do you know anyone who would want to kill you?

Most likely Dennis Wilson was the one person most affected by his association with this devil incarnate. According to DA Vincent Bugliosi, "Wilson was terrified when Manson was arrested for the murders. He refused to testify. He was just terrified." Wilson told Bugliosi that the Manson demos recorded at Brian Wilson's house had been destroyed. Stephen Desper revealed to the Rock And Roll Detective that he believes the Manson tapes are still in the Beach Boys' vault, collecting dust.

Even Manson himself had to admit that his irrational behavior and drug use had pushed him over a cliff. Although he denied directing his Family members to commit the murders, he admitted, "I still don't believe any of the violence would have erupted if we had controlled the drugs instead of letting them control us." This statement seems incredibly disingenuous coming from the man who performed systematic LSD brainwashing on his Family, wherein he preached about the violence of a race war coming down fast and ordered his family to kill innocent victims.

"Lie—The Love and Terror Cult"

When Manson and his cohorts were arrested for the Tate/LaBianca murders, Manson wanted to continue to spread his gospel. Perhaps it was also a ploy to paint himself as a pacifist, as part of his self-defense. Manson's musical message was, in his mind, a great way to characterize himself as the misunderstood guru of peace and love.

While awaiting trial in 1970, Manson turned to his ex-con buddy Phil Kaufman, who had gotten him his first recording audition in 1967. "When they were first arrested, I didn't believe that they were the participants in the grisly murders," recalled Kaufman in his memoir, *Legend of the Road Mangler*. He knew Manson was a "loose cannon," but explained, "Charlie called me and asked me to put this album out, this *Lie* album as we called it. They were just quarter inch tapes, of rough mixes. And we put this album out." Kaufman told the Rock And Roll Detective that he did not add any overdubs to the tapes that Jakobson had already recorded. "No, just a mix down and clean up," he confirmed.

In fact, the majority of tracks on the album, *Lie: The Love And Terror Cult*, were from the tapes that Dennis Wilson paid for and were recorded by Gregg Jakobson in August 1968. The recording of "Cease to Exist," the song Manson had sold to Wilson, appeared on the *Lie* album.

The music was "… indicative more of Charlie's music at the time he was nonviolent and more manipulative," said Kaufman. Clearly Manson was hoping to potentially influence a future jury pool and public opinion for sympathy, singing songs about "Home Is Where You're Happy," "Eyes Of A Dreamer," "Garbage Dump," and "Cease to Exist." In the liner notes, Manson is quoted as saying, "I can sing for them and I have some music that says what I like to say, if I ever had anything to say…. If you love everything, you don't have to think." The album was released on March 8, 1970, about three months before the start of his trial. "He thought it would offset the yellow journalism. You know, it's gentle music. It's not slash, maim, and kill," said Kaufman.

The album sleeve ripped off the cover of a national magazine exposé on Manson. Kaufman explained the rationale, "The *Lie* album, we took the cover of Manson on a *Life* magazine and just dropped the 'F' and made it 'Lie' because they [Manson and Family] were saying that everything they were charged with was a lie." The original pressing was only about 300 copies, according to Kaufman, but no one in L.A. would distribute it.

Even the radicals in Berkeley turned the record down. "Nobody would touch it with a 10-foot pole," joked Kaufman. Ultimately, it was released on British label Awareness Records.

Kaufman never recouped his $3,000 investment in the making of the album, but later in the summer of 1970, he got a prison call from Manson granting him the publishing rights to the songs released. "Charlie called me and said you have the rights to all my music and he put it in writing," according to Kaufman. "They [the Manson Family] had a lawyer named Ron Hughes, who had authenticated my owning all of Charles Manson's music. Another dubious honor. It is, as they say, 'bad juju.'" However, there appears to be no record at the U.S. Copyright Office of either Manson or Kaufman registering the tracks that Dennis Wilson had paid for Charlie to record. The alleged assignment of copyright from Manson to Kaufman also does not appear to be registered with the U.S. Copyright Office either. As for attorney Hughes, the Rock And Roll Detective could not interview him because he is dead. "Eventually," Kaufman believes, "they [Manson's Family] killed Ron Hughes too."

Later in 1970, Kaufman signed a deal in New York with the label ESP-Disk to arrange for the *Lie* album's first legitimate national distribution. Due to negative publicity from the details revealed at trial, and Manson's notoriety as the scariest man since Hitler, the album did not sell well. Today, copies of the original album are considered a morbid collectors' item in the record marketplace. Not only did Manson not earn a gold record for his sophomoric, acid-poetry music, but he also could not change the public perception of his horrific crimes.

"20/20"

The terror and guilt experienced by Dennis Wilson was overwhelming. It was Wilson who had invited Manson and Family into his own home and into L.A.'s rock royalty circle. It was Wilson who had been so generous to Manson's Family while living with him. It was also Wilson who had paid for Manson to record demos at studios around town, including his brother's own home studio! And, it was Wilson who had done a deal with the devil to buy a song that he had turned into a Beach Boys track on their latest album, a track that would forever link Dennis and The Beach Boys with the most notorious murders of the sixties. Beach Boy Bruce Johnston bemoaned the indelible black mark this association left on the group. "It is just a horrific footnote in the career of this band. It should never have been."

It was apropos that the album containing the song Dennis Wilson had bought from Charles Manson was titled *20/20*. As the saying goes, "Hindsight is 20-20." The saying is, of course, a nonsensical way to express the concept that it is easy to see what the right course of action *was*, once the dust has settled. It is easy to declare that Dennis Wilson should not have invited Charlie Manson (a stranger) into his home, his life, or his professional career. However, no one saw through Manson and his evil intent at the time.

The benefit of 20-20 hindsight would have instructed Dennis Wilson not to sponsor Charles Manson into the entertainment world in his attempt to get him a record deal. And it would have prevented Wilson from entering into a devil's bargain for a creepy composition, a song that would forever remind Wilson and the world of his connection to the cult Family. In the end Manson's musical ambitions were nothing but a pathetic footnote to a life of crime. However, to Wilson, the simple purchase of a song cost him a much higher price than the $300 he gave Manson for "Cease to Exist"—even more than Wilson's money, cars, and personal property Manson squandered. Wilson paid with his own soul.

To this day, Dennis Wilson and The Beach Boys' reputation has been sullied. They have been blamed for allegedly "stealing" a song from Charles Manson, recording it as their own, keeping the royalties, and stripping Manson's name from the composing credits. Worse yet, Wilson has been blamed for leading Manson down a murderous path, allegedly because Manson felt cheated on the song deal and never got a recording contract. Of course, upon reflection, Wilson should have put his purchase and Manson's assignment of copyright in writing by an attorney to avoid any confusion or blame over credits and royalties. In hindsight, Wilson really didn't need "Cease to Exist" to forge his career as a songwriter because he and Jakobson would go on to write beautiful songs together in the future.

Although one cannot alter history, the Rock And Roll Detective wanted to determine, once and for all, who indeed were the *Heroes and Villains* from the deal Wilson forged with Manson. No one has ever uncovered the true ownership of this song, nor has anyone closely analyzed the blame that befell Wilson, The Beach Boys, and others for Manson's heinous crimes… until now.

"Don't Do Anything Illegal"

Before one can evaluate whether or not Wilson "stole" the song "Cease to Exist" from Charles Manson, it is important to understand the facts and applicable law relevant to the transaction. After meeting Manson, Dennis Wilson believed that the wannabe musician had some potential. He paid for Gregg Jakobson to produce a collection of Manson's songs, funding the cost of Jakobson, studio time, and the master tape.

Wilson liked Manson's song "Cease to Exist," and offered to purchase all of the rights to the song for $300 cash. The parties agreed in front of one eyewitness, Greg Jakobson, but never memorialized the deal in writing. Jakobson has confirmed that Manson clearly intended to transfer all rights in the copyright to Wilson in exchange for the cash, and Wilson believed he was receiving all intellectual property rights to the song as if he had written it himself.

We know that Wilson took the song, presented it as his own to The Beach Boys, changed the title, the lyrics, the arrangement, and added a bridge. After The Beach Boys recorded the song, they released it as a single B-side and on the album *20/20*, calling it "Never Learn Not To Love," with Dennis Wilson credited as the sole composer. Wilson registered the composition of both words and music with the U.S. Copyright Office on October 18, 1968 as his own composition. In his lifetime, Manson never registered "Cease to Exist" with the U.S. Copyright Office. Upon the release of "Never Learn Not To Love," Manson was angered that Wilson had changed the lyrics and the title to his song, and because it was now on a Beach Boys album, demanded additional compensation in the form of royalties. The Beach Boys refused Manson and he never brought any legal claims in his lifetime. The question is, which law(s) apply to this transaction, and what can one conclude about the ownership and use of the copyrights in the songs "Cease to Exist" and "Never Learn Not To Love"?

The U.S. Copyright Act of 1909 provides guidance on this question. The Act requires that, for a song copyright to be sold, it must be accomplished with "… *an instrument in writing signed by the proprietor of the copyright* [i.e., Manson]…" As we know, that did not happen in this case. The statute fails to address the sale of a song *without* a written agreement. When statutes fail to cover specific situations, judges look at other factors such as relevant case law and may even *create* judicial solutions that are equitable and reflect the parties' true intentions. In this case, it was clear to the parties and the sole witness that Manson was happy to receive $300 for the song, and that he intended to sell it lock, stock, and barrel to Wilson who had his own ideas on creating a derivative version of this song.

According to copyright scholar Carol Ellingson, "The author of an original copyrighted work may choose to exploit his work by transferring rights to produce and distribute a new 'derivative work' based on the author's original work." The 1909 Act allows the new derivative work (in this case, "Never Learn Not To Love") under a *valid transfer*. However, since a "valid transfer" did not take place in writing between Manson and Wilson, did Wilson have the right to make his own derivative work?

According to the authoritative legal text on intellectual property, *Nimmer on Copyright*, courts developed a reasonable solution in which a valid transfer of rights comprising copyright could take place *without* a written agreement. Nimmer notes, "If the transfer is not in the required form of a *written* assignment of copyright, then a transfer of anything less is considered a license." A license is a use or permission. In the absence of a written agreement, judges have created the concept of an *implied* license. An implied license is an *unwritten* permission, allowing the licensee (Dennis Wilson), to do something that would normally require the written permission of the licensor (Charles Manson).

Legal academic Afori Orti, an expert in the field of implied licenses, explained:

> The implied license doctrine is used to approve different acts done with respect to a copy of the song by its purchaser such as modification of the lyrics, title, structure, melody, and arrangement. It is a mechanism for injecting reasonable uses into the parties' relationship by implication. It has been held that [an implied] license to record a musical work implies a further license to distribute and sell such records, and to make copies of a work, and in the absence of a written reservation by the seller [Manson], that ownership of such copies of the derivative work vest in the purchaser/licensee [Wilson].

The Rock And Roll Detective reviewed the facts of this case with a veteran copyright attorney of the law firm Boardman and Clark, and U.S. District Court Judge James Peterson. If your eyes are glossing over by all of this legal mumbo jumbo, it will all soon become clear.

Judge Peterson, who reviewed applicable law in this case, concluded, "Based upon the facts of the Manson/Wilson transaction, a court would likely find that an implied license existed which would give Wilson all the rights he needed to exploit and copyright *his* version of the song." A copyright license does not have to be in writing and can be verbal. The Boardman attorney examined the facts of the transaction and stated, "It is quite clear that Manson was ready to part ways with the song and all aspects of it for $300, despite the parties' lack of knowledge about the need for a written agreement. From an implied licensing perspective, which does not require writing, the conversation seems to be Manson saying to Wilson, 'Do whatever you want with this song.'"

Peterson agrees with the copyright attorney's legal position. "I think a court would be inclined to find, by looking at the actions and intentions of the parties, that there was an implied license even if the transfer of ownership failed [for lack of a written document] as a matter of law, so that he [Wilson] could do what he wanted with the song. He could record his own version and he would be able to prepare a derivative work ['Never Learn Not To Love'] from it," said Peterson. "Given that it was talked about by the parties [Manson and Wilson] as a transfer of ownership [sale] that is a pretty comprehensive grant of rights to Wilson."

Interestingly, both the copyright attorney and Judge Peterson informed the Rock And Roll Detective that Manson, the original author of the song, would *also* retain some rights to do what *he* wanted with his song, "Cease to Exist"! Thus, the law would allow Manson to register the copyright, publish, and sell his song "Cease to Exist"; and Wilson could do the same with "Never Learn Not To Love." It was therefore okay for Manson to tell Phil Kaufman to commercially release "Cease to Exist" on the *Lie* album. (Note: Given that Wilson paid for the Manson demo session and owns the master tape, Manson technically should have paid Wilson a nominal fee for permission and use of Wilson's master tape containing the song "Cease to Exist.")

Should Dennis Wilson have credited Charles Manson as a co-composer of "Never Learn Not To Love" and shared The Beach Boys' royalties with him? Judge Peterson said the answer is "No." He explained, "Because we start with a comprehensive grant of rights under the implied license, he'd [Wilson] be able to do whatever he want[ed] in terms of the derivative work. And then I don't think Manson would have any claim for credit or profits or any right to the derivative work." Manson never pursued a claim against Wilson (or his heirs) in his lifetime. As a result, a court today would likely find, by Manson's inaction, that Wilson did indeed possess the comprehensive rights he thought he had purchased in the original transaction.

Therefore, we can now and forever correct the long-held, libelous disinformation campaign, led in part by Manson, as well as lazy biographers and fake news journalists. Dennis Wilson did *not* steal a song from Charlie Manson, strip off Manson's credits, and/

or steal the royalties. Rather, he legally purchased a comprehensive set of rights to the song via an implied license and legally created his own derivative version. Wilson was entitled to change the title, lyrics, and arrangement; create a new bridge; copyright the song as his own composition and creation; and collect all of the royalties flowing from "Never Learn Not To Love." In reality, two different songs now legally exist: "Cease to Exist" and "Never Learn Not To Love."

"Heroes and Villains"

Is it reasonable or justified for history to blame Dennis Wilson, The Beach Boys, or anyone else for leading Charles Manson down a "murderous path" simply because his musical aspirations failed to work out? Is it good journalism to state that "Dennis Wilson *caused* Charlie Manson?" Similarly, should history blame Terry Melcher for not signing Manson to a label and producing his record? And should The Beatles accept any blame since Manson was taking what he believed were cues from their lyrics on the *White Album*, allegedly encouraging him to start a revolutionary race war? The Rock And Roll Detective sifted through the available evidence.

The primary motives for the Tate/LaBianca murders came from the psychopathic mind of Charles Manson. He later blamed letting LSD get control of his family, and he pointed to The Beatles' lyrics. According to Manson right-hand man, Paul Watkins, Charlie was obsessed with The Beatles and thought they were directing secret messages to him in their songs. Both Watkins and Gregg Jakobson observed how Charlie changed in 1969 from a wacky guru to a materialistic, agitated, and crazed madman. Jakobson noted, "Charlie changed in Spring, '69. He was collecting guns, vehicles, ropes and stuff to live underground in the desert. He thought The Beatles' *secret message* was ordering him to kill, and that 'Helter Skelter' and the other songs were about the uprising in which blacks would murder a third of the world's population." There was even a report of phone calls from Manson to The Beatles' Apple Corps office in London, trying to get past press officer Derek Taylor, to discuss his crazy theory with the band.

Obviously, Manson's twisted interpretations of Beatles lyrics cannot be blamed on The Beatles. There are plenty of interviews with John Lennon, Paul McCartney, and George Harrison in which they discuss the meanings of their songs "Helter Skelter," "Piggies," "Revolution," and "Blackbird." None of them had anything to do with Manson, murder, or a race war. There is no record that The Beatles ever spoke to Manson, nor did they support any of the horrific murders he masterminded. There is simply no credible evidence with which to blame The Beatles for Manson's twisted murderous interpretation of their lyrics. The late George Harrison put an exclamation mark on the attempt to connect The Beatles to Manson's reign of terror, "It was mentioned as if we were sending him messages. It's just sick. It just shows that everyone is on their own trip, but they can attribute *their*

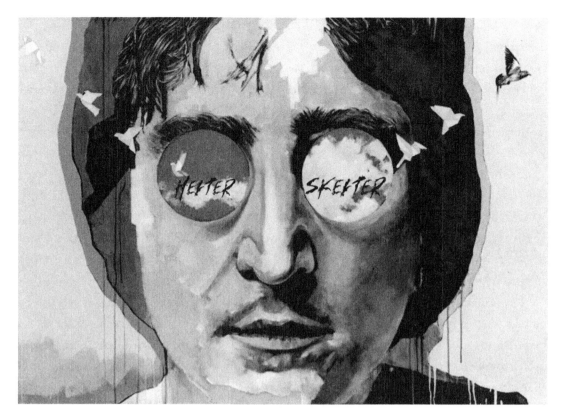

actions to someone else." The late John Lennon added his perspective, "I'm a peace-loving man," said the songwriter. "If I were a praying man, I'd pray to be delivered from people like Charles Manson who claim to know better than I do what my songs are supposed to mean…"

There is, however, a clear record of documentation of Manson's racist views and how to deal with minorities from his *Rolling Stone* interview given around the time of his trial. "Have you heard of the Muslims? Have you heard of the Black Panthers? Englishmen, do you remember cutting off the heads of praying Muslims with the cross sewn onto your battledress? You and all Western Man killed and mutilated them [blacks] and now they are reincarnated and they are going to repay you," said Manson.

Tex Watson confirmed this racist Manson profile. He admitted, "Manson made it clear that he thought blacks were inferior to whites and [were] only created to serve them… and it didn't take long to figure out that the black/white terrorism and Helter Skelter meant pretty much the same thing: violent revolution."

For those who dig deeply into the Manson murders, one finds that Manson initially put his race war uprising into play after his Family's participation in the murder of an associate named Gary Hinman, in order to cover up the murder and blame it on African Americans. Tex Watson revealed Manson's true, but twisted, motives for the Hinman and Tate/La Bianca murders. "There were three basic motives behind the murders that took place… Charlie had articulated to us that afternoon: 'To do what blackie didn't have the energy or the smarts to do—ignite Helter Skelter and bring Charlie's Kingdom.'" He continued, "There was also a need for more cash to finance our preparations for Armageddon… and also to pay $600 bail for [Family member] Mary Brunner, arrested for using a stolen Sears credit card… and there was a third less important purpose; to clear [Family member] Bobby Beausoleil of the Hinman slaying by committing a *similar* crime [the Tate/La Bianca murders] while he was in jail."

At the end of his life, Charles Manson tried to clarify the motives for murder in his final rambling "confession" to a *Rolling Stone* writer. "Helter Skelter wasn't a lie," he said. "It was just Bugliosi's perspective. Sure, it was going on. But it was just part of the part. The reasons was [*sic*] all kinds of different things that were happening in Tex's mind and all of our minds together, and there's lots of collective ideas." Manson concluded, "It was an episode. A psychotic episode and you want to blame me for that?"

DA Vincent Bugliosi also felt there was an alternative motive to Manson's murders, perhaps one of revenge against Wilson and Melcher for not making him into a rock star. Both Jakobson and Melcher denied that they had let Manson down in his goal to be a professional musician. From late spring of 1969 into the summer, Melcher had visited Manson twice at Spahn Ranch to listen to his songs. Under oath at the Manson trial, Melcher stated that he could not properly record him in a studio since Manson was not in the musicians' union. Although Melcher did not agree to sign Manson to a record deal at that time, he was aware his friend Jakobson wanted to film Manson and his family in the desert and record Charlie's music for a possible film documentary.

Jakobson's sworn testimony at the Manson murder trial confirms his intent:

Q: (Bugliosi) Did you ever want to make a documentary film, on him?
A. (Jakobson) Yes.
Q: Did you discuss your interest in Manson with Terry Melcher?
A: Yes.
Q: Did you want Melcher to somehow be involved in this project?
A: I did.
Q: In what fashion?
A: As a producer, financier. I wanted Terry Melcher to meet Charlie and make this film of him. If we could see the man, his music would emerge, so I wanted some backing for the film.

What about Dennis Wilson? Manson was unhappy that Wilson had changed the words to one of his songs. He also felt that he was owed additional compensation for the song that he had sold outright. Wilson had let Manson and his followers live at his home, use his credit cards, go to the doctor, order expensive food and liquor, take his clothes

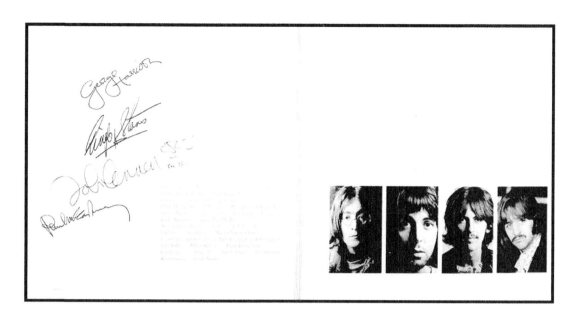

and gold records, and even crash his car. Wilson arranged and paid for the spring 1968 demo session, and at brother Brian's home with Stephen Desper. Wilson even talked up Manson to his circle of rock royalty friends. Thanks to Wilson, Manson had sold a song that was on a Beach Boys album and that made the pop charts. If Manson's motive in killing innocent victims was because Wilson betrayed him, why wouldn't Manson have just killed Wilson instead of total strangers? Bugliosi's theory just doesn't add up. In fact, Wilson was still talking to, and in contact with, Manson at the time of the murders.

The only thing Dennis Wilson was guilty of was bad judgment for befriending an evil spirit. Manson recalled the optimism with his music career as well as the coming madness at that crucial time before the murders. "When our records hit the market, we'll build our own town. Think about it: no rent to pay, no laws to obey, and no cops on our asses. Hey, we'll be one step ahead of anything that goes on in this world…. Blackie's tired of being the doormat for the rich man's pad. Real madness is going to explode soon—everything is going to be Helter Skelter. But that won't affect us…. *I wanted to start the war* and straighten out the world afterwards." This sure doesn't sound like someone who wanted to get revenge on three musicians who were still trying to help his career.

The evidence of a revenge motive against Melcher, Wilson, and/or Jakobson simply is not supported by the facts. Far from having a "dead-end" music career caused by these three men, it appears that Manson's career was progressing better than it ever had to that point. But as Stephen Desper told the Rock And Roll Detective, if Charlie had just been more patient, "he might have been a recording artist instead of a murderer."

Based upon Paul Watkins' diary of events, the idea of murder and the race riot uprising of "Helter Skelter" was contemplated and pushed onto the Family members via LSD, playing the *White Album*, and Charlie's psycho-pathetic ramblings in December 1968.

At this point, Manson had not obtained a copy of the Beach Boys' album with the song he had sold to Dennis, and he was still meeting in L.A. that month with Wilson and Jakobson to advance his music career.

Clearly Charles Manson was the *villain*. The fact that Wilson, Jakobson, and Melcher all attempted to assist a wannabe musician clearly qualifies The Beach Boys' drummer and his entertainment friends as *heroes*.

"Sail on Sailor"

The murders encouraged by Manson and committed by his followers crushed Dennis Wilson. Far from feeling good about all the help he had tried to give Manson, Wilson felt deep guilt, shame, and terror about his association with this antichrist who could corrupt lost children to ultimately murder innocent people. This episode in his life clearly left Wilson a changed man. Aside from his guilt over the murders and bringing this psycho messiah into his circle and into his brother's home, Wilson was haunted by Manson the rest of his life. Some attribute Wilson's self-destructive spiral after this point (which included drug and alcohol addiction, broken marriages, virtual homelessness, and termination from The Beach Boys) to his fears and guilty feelings for introducing the "Wizard" to L.A.'s entertainment scene.

Wilson was a talented, powerhouse percussionist and budding songwriter when Manson came into his life. Wilson loved life and traveled it at the speed of sound, rarely stopping to rest. After Manson, he kept himself in motion, but he was clearly troubled by the terrible experience. "There was always that melancholy and painfulness in him," says long-time friend and photographer-videographer, Ed Roach. "As long as he kept his excitement going on—whether it was jumping in the ocean or jumping onstage or jumping into being the life of the party, then he never really had to deal with it."

The dangers of hitchhiking… Wilson's generous, yet naïve spirit led him to the dangerous crossroads. Meeting the hitchhiking Manson girls turned into an inescapable devil's bargain that secured him a creepy song. But in the process, Dennis lost his soul because he suffered intense guilt by association with Manson. The juxtaposition of America's clean cut, fun, fun, fun Beach Boys intersecting with Charles Manson, the soul scalper on the dark side of the highway, clearly was a cautionary tale, one that continues to haunt The Beach Boys decades later.

Family insider Paul Watkins, who managed to escape the Manson cult before any of the murders took place, does not blame Wilson, The Beach Boys, or other musicians who failed to sign Charlie to a record deal. He places the blame squarely on Manson and his theory about our society:

Charlie did more than give hitchhikers and hippies a bad name. He manifested and expressed not only the mechanism of his own twisted psyche, but the latent evils existing in our own society. You cannot divorce Manson from the culture that spawned him.

Manson murderer Tex Watson similarly does not give credence to the legendary pop culture motives advanced by the District Attorney. He opined:

I feel Manson was possessed by demons and I think I was possessed by the same spirit that Charlie was possessed by… we were all in one devil and we did what the devil said to do.

The last time Dennis Wilson spoke of Charles Manson to his brother Brian Wilson, he said, "What a sick fuck Manson was, and what a lucky SOB I am." Mike Love added, "For my cousin [Dennis]… our group member to be involved with that and to have the guilt associated with that, I mean, had to be a tough burden for him to carry for the rest of his life."

At the end of his life, Dennis Wilson was deeply troubled. Although he had given much away to Manson in terms of money and his soul, Wilson went looking for happy reminders of a happy life in his final days. He loved to sail. His sailboat "The Harmony" was the only place where he felt truly free. Sadly, before his death, The Harmony was repossessed. The Beach Boy and surfer died in the water, where his favorite boat had been moored, the only place he had ever felt true solace. He was diving to recover lost relics that had been thrown off the Harmony, trying to recover a piece of a happier life, when he drowned on December 28, 1983. "Sail on Sailor."

When Manson learned that Dennis Wilson had died, as he sat in jail, the demon guru, channeling the devil's deal at the crossroads, opined just what you would have expected. "Dennis Wilson's brotherhood took my songs and changed the words. His own devils grabbed his legs and pulled and held him under water." Clearly, Wilson never stole any songs from Manson. Wilson's only mistake was trying to help this psycho. Manson never took personal responsibility for his horrific crimes or those of his sick cult Family. Blaming Wilson, The Beach Boys, The Beatles, or Wilson's associates was merely a ruse to hide Manson's racist and evil actions. Wilson's bargain with this earthly devil should never have cast a dark light on the good intentions of The Beach Boys' drummer or his associates.

As for the guru-some cult leader, Charles Manson, a man who caused so much fear, terror, and heartache in the world, he died in prison on November 19, 2017. Now, the song that he legally sold to Dennis Wilson takes on a new meaning: "Cease to Exist."

Interviews

The author wishes to thank all of the people who gave of their valuable time to provide interviews:

The late Scotty Moore

The late Jerry Dennon

The late Jack Ely

Jann Wenner

Glyn Johns

Al Kooper

Candy Leonard

Jeff Walker

Joey Ex-CIA agent

U.S. Marine Corps Lieutenant Colonel Oliver North

Roger Steffens

Keidi Obi Awadu

Butch Vig

Jim Keltner

John Tefteller

Bernard MacMahon

Alex van der Tuuk

Phil Kaufman

Gregg Jakobson

David Gold

Nick Grillo

Stephen Desper

U.S. District Court Judge James Peterson

The late Derek Taylor

Dinah Gretsch

Klaus Voormann

Anonymous

Alex Orbison

David Leland

Endnotes

Chapter One
Did The CIA *Kill* Bob Marley?

"Agee, Philip/ASEC- Administration – Security/CIA – Central Intelligence Agency," Unclassified Cables, Margaret P Grafeld, Declassified/ Released, US Department of State EO Systematic, May 4, 2006, and https://wikileaks.org/plusd/cables/1976KINGSTO3978_b.html

Agee, Phillip, *Inside The Company: CIA Diary*, (New York City: Farrar Straus & Giroux, 1975)

The Alex Constantine Report – Mind Control Crusader, https://alexconstantinereport.wordpress.com/

Autopsy: The Last Hours of Bob Marley, featuring Dr. Michael Hunter, San Francisco Chief Medical Examiner, Reelz channel, February 25, 2017.

Baer, Robert B., *The Perfect Kill: 21 Laws For Assassins*, (New York City: Plume, An Imprint of Penguin Random House LLC, 2014) TOC, 1, 24, 42, 51,58, 84, 107, 140, 186, 199, 201, 209, 210, 311.

Bailey, Chauncey, "Is the CIA Meddling In Jamaica?" *California Voice*, Oakland, July 17, 1980.

Bernal, Richard L., *The Influence of Small States on Superpowers – Jamaica and US Foreign Policy*, (Lanham, Lexington Books, 2015) 82-83.

Biography, https://www.biography.com/people/oliver-north-9425102

Blum, William, *Killing Hope*, (Monroe: Common Courage Press, 2003) 263-264.

"Bob Marley Interview," Auckland, New Zealand, April, 1979, *Bob Marley: The Lost Tape*, DVD, Bealeave Pictures, Directed by Samantha Fields, 2014.

Bob Marley Interview, by Gil Noble, "Like It Is" WABC-TV, September, 1980, *Bob Marley: The Lost Tape*, DVD, Bealeave Pictures, Directed by Samantha Fields, 2014.

The CIA, *A Study of Assassination*, (Washington: US Government (FOIA Release, July 12, 1995) Training File of Operation "PBSuccess," December 31, 1953) 1-2

Constantine, Alex, "Chanting Down Babylon: The CIA And The Death Of Bob Marley." *High Times*, Issue 318, February, 2002.

Drugs as Weapons Against Us: The CIA's Murderous Targeting of SDS, Panthers, Hendrix, Lennon, Cobain, Tupac and Other Leftists, by Potash, John, (Walterville, OR: Tine Day Publishing, 2015) 256.

Fessenden, Marissa, "Is Cancer Contagious? Could Hugo Chavez Have Been Deliberately Infected?" *Scientific American*, March 18, 2013, 2.

Freeze, Colin, "Police raise curtain on the 'Shower Posse'," *The Globe and Mail*, May 5, 2010, A-11.

Goldman, Vivian. *The Book of Exodus*, (New York City: Three Rivers Press, 2006) 96, 99, 114, 115, 120.

Goldman, Vivian, "Dread, Beat and Blood," *The Guardian*, www.theguardian.com/music/2006/Jul/16/urban.worldmusic, July 16, 2006, pg. 4.

Haines, Gerald K., "The Pike Committee Investigations and the CIA – Looking for a Rogue Elephant" https://www.cia.gov/library/center-for-the-study-of-intelligence/csi-publications/csi-studies/studies/winter98_99/art07.html

Halfnight, Drew, "No remedy for 'Posse'; International drug cartel calling the shots in Toronto's northwest end," *National Post*, May 8, 2010, A-14.

"I Shot The Sherriff," by Bob Marley, copyright © 1973, Tuff Gong Music Ltd. All rights reserved.

"Intelligence Memorandum – Jamaica: In Pursuit of its National Identity," Declassified Top-Secret CIA document, April 28, 1976, (Approved For Release 2003/09/29) 1, 3, 11, 17, 19.

Interview with Bob Marley, *Remastered: Who Shot The Sheriff? A Bob Marley Story*, Documentary, Netflix Series/ Triangle Entertainment Production (2018)

Interview with Bob Marley historian and author, Roger Steffens, by author Jim Berkenstadt, September 6, 2017.

Interview with Colonel Oliver North, by author Jim Berkenstadt, September 12, 2017.

Interview with Jeff Walker (former National Director of Publicity for Island Records), by author Jim Berkenstadt, August 23, 2017

Interview with "Joey" CIA Deputy Chief of Station, US Jamaican Embassy, by author Jim Berkenstadt, September 12, 2017.

Interview with Keidi Obi Awadu, by author Jim Berkenstadt, via email, September 10, 2017.

Interview with Laurie Gunst, *Remastered: Who Shot The Sheriff? A Bob Marley Story*, Documentary, Netflix Series/ Triangle Entertainment Production (2018)

Keith, Sherry and Robert Girling, "Jamaica vs. the Transnationals: Battle Over Bauxite," North American Congress on Latin America, https://NACLA.org, 4, 7-8.

Manley, Michael, "The Caribbean Basin: Its Political Dynamic and Possible Directions in Third World Affairs," (London: Third World Foundation for Social and Economic Studies, 1985) 247.

Manley, Michael, *The Politics of Change – A Jamaican Testament*, (Washington, DC: Howard University Press, 1975) 271.

Marley, Rita with Hettie Jones, *My Life with Bob Marley - No Woman No Cry*, (New York City: Hyperion, 2004) 145, 146, 148, 197.

Meroney, John and Sean Coons, "Talking With The Son of 'The Man Nobody Knew'," *The Atlantic*, October 14, 2011, https://www.theatlantic.com/entertainment/archive/2011/10/talking-with-the-son-of-the-man-nobody-knew/246639/

News Punch, https://newspunch.com/?s=bob+marley

Official Bob Marley Tour History, www.bobmarley.com/tour/history/

"The President's Daily Brief" – *Phillip Agee activity in Jamaica*, Declassified Top-Secret CIA document, September 17, 1976, Sanitized Copy Approved for Release 2015/07/14, 2-3.

"Profile Pike Committee" History Commons, http://www.historycommons.org/entity.jsp?entity=_pike_committee_1

"Rat Race," 1976 copyright ©, Fifty-Six Hope Road Music Ltd., Odnil Music Ltd., Blue Mountain Music Ltd., (PRS). All Rights for North and South American Controlled and Administered by Rykomusic Inc. (ASCAP). All rights for the rest of the world Controlled and Administered by Rykomusic Ltd. (PRS). All rights reserved.

Salewicz, Chris, *Bob Marley: The Untold Story*, (New York City: Farrar, Straus and Giroux, 2011) 234.

Snopes, https://www.snopes.com/

Steffens, Roger. *So Much Things To Say*, (New York City: W.W. Norton & Company, Inc., 2017) 220, 217, 221, 224, 225, 227.228, 230, 231, 237, 248.

Taylor, Don, *Marley and Me*, (Fort Lee: Barricade Books, 1994) 137, 144, 149.

Volkman, Ernest and John Cummings, "Murder as Usual," *Penthouse*, December 1977, 112, 114.

"War," From speech by H.I.M. Haile Selassie I king of Kings, Lord of Lords, California February 1968, 1976 copyright© Fifty-Six Hope Road Music Ltd., Odnil Music Ltd., Blue Mountain Music Ltd., (PRS). All Rights for North and South American Controlled and Administered by Rykomusic Inc. (ASCAP). All rights for the rest of the world Controlled and Administered by Rykomusic Ltd. (PRS). All rights reserved.

Webb, Gary, *Counter Spy Bulletin*, Winter 1976, http://www.narconews.com/darkalliance/

White, Timothy, *Catch A Fire: The Life Of Bob Marley*, (New York City: St. Martin's Griffin, 2000 & 2006) 291, 334, 335, 336, 337, 427, 428, 429.

Who Killed Bob Marley? Interview with Keidi Obi Awadu, *Strange Universe*, produced by Paul Barrosse, Episode 1996, UPN network.

Chapter Two
The FBI vs. "Merchants of Filth"

Blecha, Peter, *Sonic Boom! The History of Northwest Rock: From Louie Louie to Smells Like Teen Spirit*, (Milwaukee: Backbeat Books, 2009) 144.

Faggen, Gil, "Indiana Gov. Puts down 'Pornographic' Wand Tune," *Billboard*, February 1, 1964, 3.

Freedom of Information Act records, FBI Files 145-2961(January, 1964 – October, 1966)

Inflation Calculator, www.saving.org

Interview with Jack Ely, by author Jim Berkenstadt, March 10, 2010.

Interview with Jerry Dennon, by author Jim Berkenstadt, March 15, 2010.

Ken Chase interview, *Louie & The G-Men*, Little Steven Van Zandt, BBC radio, December 6, 2007.

Lindop, Edmund and Sarah DeCapua, *America in the 1950's*, (Minneapolis: Twenty-First Century Books / Lerner Publishing, 2009) 1987.

"'Louie' Publishers Say Tune Not Dirty at All," *Billboard*, February 8, 1964, 4, 57.

The Louie Report, http://www.louielouie.net/lindahl/lindahl-excerpt.mp4

Marsh, Dave, *Louie Louie*, (New York City: Hyperion, 1995) 97-98, 100, 124-125.

"Musical Garbage," *Indianapolis Star*, January 27, 1964, 14, Editorial page.

Peterson, Richard with Jim Ojala, *Louie Louie: Me Gotta Go Now*, (Sherwood, OR: Thalion Press, 2006) 343-345.

Robert Lindahl interviewed by Eric Predoehl, http://www.louielouie.net/lindahl/lindahl-excerpt.mp4

Theoharis, Athan G., with Tony G. Poveda, Susan Rosenfeld, Richard, Powers, *The FBI: A Comprehensive Reference Guide*, (Tucson: Oryx Press, 1999) 5.

"Young Singers Dismiss As Hooey Obscenity Charge in 'Louie Louie,'" *Indianapolis Star*, January 24, 1964, Editorial page.

Chapter Three
The Masked Marauders: Super-Group or Masquerade?

Bates, Daniel, "From UFOs to JFK: Conspiracies," *Daily Mail*, http://www.dailymail.co.uk/sciencetech/article-3196819/From-UFOs-JFK-Conspiracy-theories-romanticised-believers-willing-ignore-factual-errors-boost-argument.html, August 13, 2015.

Berkenstadt, Jim and Belmo *Black Market Beatles: The Story Behind The Lost Recordings*, (Toronto: CG Publishing, 1995)

Bjorner, Olof, "The Bob Dylan Session Pages," http://www.bjorner.com/DSN01679%201969.htm, 2015.

"Bob Dylan Discografic - Nashville Skyline 1969," http://www.n-b-u.de/discografic6_nashville_skyline_1969.htm, 1969.

Christgau, Robert, "Album of the Year," www.robertchristgau.com/xg/rock/album-70.php, January 8, 1970.

Christian, T.M., "The Masked Marauders," *Rolling Stone*, October 18, 1969, Record Reviews.

Gleason, Ralph J., "On The Town," *San Francisco Chronicle*, October 18, 1969.

Hannan, Ross and Corry Arnold, "Cleanliness & Godliness Skiffle Band – Family Tree," https://www.chickenonaunicycle.com/Cleanliness%20and%20Godliness.htm, April 6, 2013.

Harper, Tim, "Is Beatle Paul McCartney Dead?," *Drake Times-Delphic*, September 17, 1969, 1, 3.

Hendrix and Traffic, www.Bootlegzone.com, 2015.

Hopkins, Jerry, "'New' Dylan Album Bootlegged In LA," *Rolling Stone*, September 20, 1969, https://www.rollingstone.com/music/music-news/new-bob-dylan-album-bootlegged-in-l-a-187656/.

Interview with Al Kooper, Producer/Musician, by author Jim Berkenstadt, June 23, 2015.

Interview with Candy Leonard, PHD Sociology, by author Jim Berkenstadt, July 28, 2015.

Interview with Glyn Johns, (Engineer and/or producer of many recordings by The Rolling Stones, The Beatles, Led Zeppelin and more), by author Jim Berkenstadt, July 31, 2015.

Johns, Glyn, *Sound Man: A Life Recording Hits with The Rolling Stones, The Who, Led Zeppelin, The Eagles, Eric Clapton, The Faces*, (New York City: Blue Rider Press, 2014)

Lefsetz, Bob, "Alice Cooper on WTF," *Bob Lefsetz Newsletter*, September 2, 2017, 1.

Marcus, Greil, "The Masked Marauders: The Complete Deity Recordings," *Warner Archives/Rhino*, RHM2 7746 (2001) CD Liner Notes, 1-19.

Marcus, Greil, "Online Exchange with Greil Marcus," http://rockcriticsarchives.com/interviews/greilmarcus/01.html, March 12, 2002 .

"The Masked Marauders," www.allmuisic.com/album/r44197, 2015.

The Masked Marauders, "Cow Pie," 45-rpm, Deity, 0870, (1969).

"Nashville Skyline," Rock's Back Pages, http://www.teachrock.org/resources/article/bob-dylan-nashville-skyline/, 2015.

"Nashville Skyline," Ultimate Classic Rock: http://ultimateclassicrock.com/bob-dylan-nashville-skyline/, 2015Interview with Jann Wenner, Founding Publisher and Editor of *Rolling Stone*, by author Jim Berkenstadt, July 21, 2015.

Roth, Pierre Rene, "Hoax Masked By Rock Record," *The Milwaukee Journal*, December 24, 1969, 19-20.

Rowland, Mark, "The Quiet Wilbury," Musician, No. 137, March, 1990, 33.

Super Session, Bloomfield, Kooper, Stills, Columbia, 508071 2, (1968)

Chapter Four
Who Really Discovered Elvis Presley?

Burke, Ken and Dan Griffin, *The Blue Moon Boys: The Story of Elvis Presley's Band* (Chicago: Chicago Review Press, 2006) 20–31.

Edited by Country Music Hall of Fame and Paul Kingsbury, *The Encyclopedia of Country Music: the Ultimate Guide to Music*, (Cary, N.C.: Oxford University Press, 2004) 519.

"Eye Witness: Elvis Cuts His First Record," Marion Keisker interview, *Q Magazine*, July, 2000, www.biwa.ne.jp/~presley/elnews-Q.htm

Guralnick, Peter, *Careless Love: The Unmaking of Elvis Presley*, (New York City: Little Brown /Back Bay Books, 2000) 1, 13.

Guralnick, Peter, *Sam Phillips: The Man Who Invented Rock 'n' Roll*, (New York City: Little Brown and Company, 2015) 29-30, 53-54, 63, 204-5, 212-213, 218.

Howard, Edwin, "In A Spin," *Memphis Press-Scimitar*, July 28, 1954, http://www.scottymoore.net/article540728.html

"Interview with Marion Keisker," BBC Documentary: *Presley: I Don't Sing Like Nobody*, (Broadcast Footage), August 16, 1987.

"Interview with Marion Keisker," BBC Documentary: *Presley: I Don't Sing Like Nobody*, (Raw Footage), August 16, 1987.

"Interview with Sam Phillips," by Elizabeth Kaye, *Rolling Stone*, RS 467, February 13, 1986, 56.

Interviews with Scotty Moore, by author Jim Berkenstadt, July 27, August 3, 11, 18, 20, 2004.

Jorgensen, Ernst, *Elvis Presley: A Life In Music (The Complete Recording Sessions),* (London: St. Martin's Press, 1998) 9-10.

Jorgensen, Ernst Mikael, *Elvis Presley -A Boy From Tupelo*, (New York City: Follow That Dream Records/FTD Books, 2012) Discs 1-2, Liner Notes, 6-9,12, 17,18, 19.

Keisker, Marion, *Letter from Marion Keisker to Jerry Hopkins*, (Memphis: University of Memphis, Jerry Hopkins Collection.

Lindop, Edmund and Sarah DeCapua, *America in the 1950's*, (Minneapolis: Twenty-First Century Books / Lerner Publishing, 2009) 1987.

Marion Keisker interview http://www.musicianguide.com/featured_biographies/pages/cmx6f6tgi1/-That-s-All-Right--I-Don-t-Sound-Like-Nobody.html

Meade, M.D., "More Than A Supporting Role: Marion Keisker, Gender, Radio History", (Montreal: International Communication Association, May 22, 2008) http://citation.Allacademic.com/meta/pmla_apa_research_citation/2/3/4/5/3/pages234535/p234535-1.php

Memmer, Darrin Lee, *Elvis "The Cat" Presley*, (Memphis: Memmer Publishing, 2018) 27, 35, 36, 39, 43, 70, the Archives at Mississippi Valley Collection, The Jerry Hopkins Collection, MSS 135, The University of Memphis Special Collections.

Moore, Scotty and James Dickerson, *That's Alright, Elvis – The Untold Story of Elvis' First Guitarist and Manager, Scotty Moore*, (New York City: Schirmer Books, 1997) 46-47.

Morrison, Craig, *Go Cat Go!: Rockabilly Music and Its Makers,* (Champaign: University of Illinois Press, 1996) 40.

Peter Guralnick radio interview with Leonard Lopate, *The Leonard Lopate Show*, November 23, 2015, www.wnyc.org

Prown, Pete, and Harvey Newquist, *Legends of Rock Guitar: The Essential Reference of Rock's Greatest Guitarists,* (Milwaukee: Hal Leonard, 1997) 16.

Tim Sebastian BBC *HARDtalk* programme, July 31, 2000, http://news.bbc.co.uk/2/hi/entertainment/853003.stm, www.sunrecords.com/marionkeisker

Touches, Nick, *Country: The Twisted Roots of Rock 'N' Roll* (Boston: DaCapo Press, 1996) 45-46.

Tucker, April, "First to Record Elvis – Marion Keisker," https://soundgirls.org/first-to-record-elvis-marion-keisker/#prettyphoto, (2019) 3,4,6.

Whitburn, Joel, *Top R&B/Hip-Hop Singles: 1942-2004,* (Menomonee Falls: Record Research, 2006)

http://movies.elvispresley.com.au/elvis-employment-history.shtml and http://www.rocandrollgps.com/crown-electric-co-where-elvis-drove-a-truck/

http://www.elvis.com.au/presley/marion-keisker.shtml

http://www.elvisrecordings.com/masters.htm

http://www.memphistravel.com/sun-studio

https://www.wunderground.com/history/airport/KMEM/1954/7/4/DailyHistory.html?req_city=&req_state=&req_statename=&reqdb.zip=&reqdb.magic=&reqdb.wmo=

www.scottymoore.net

Chapter Five
The Secrets Concealed within Nirvana's *Nevermind* Album

Berkenstadt, Jim, *Celebrity Legacies: Kurt Cobain*, Reelz channel network, Season 1, Episode 9, 2014.

Berkenstadt, Jim and Charles Cross, *Nirvana: Nevermind (Classic Rock Albums)*, (New York City: Schirmer Trade Books, 1998) 8,9,10, 63, 52-55, 103-106, 109-10, 122-124, 136 .

Cobain, Kurt, *Journals*, (New York City: Riverhead Books, 2002) 51, 94, 134, 139, 154, 156, 160, 170.

Cross, Charles, *Here We Are Now: The Lasting Impact of Kurt Cobain*, (New York City: It Books/ Harper Collins, 2014).

Cross, Charles, "Requiem for a Dream," *Guitar World*, October, 2001.

Grow, Kory, "Inside Nirvana's 'Nevermind' Pool Party, 25 Years Later," *Rolling Stone*, September 15, 2016, https://www.rollingstone.com/music/pictures/inside-nirvanas-nevermind-pool-party-25-years-later-w439840

Interview with Butch Vig, by author Jim Berkenstadt, Smart Studios, Madison, Wisconsin, June 26, 1994.

Interview with Jim Keltner, by author Jim Berkenstadt, Los Angeles, April 30, 1998.

Nevermind, by Nirvana, CD liner notes, DGC, 1991.

Nevermind: The Butch Vig Mixes, by Nirvana, produced and mixed by Butch Vig, Van Nuys, CA, June, 1991, master tape.

O'Neill, Natalie, "Nirvana Baby Recreates Iconic Album Cover 25 Years Later,," *New York Post*, September 23, 2016, https://nypost.com/2016/09/23/nirvana-baby-recreates-iconic-album-cover-25-years-later/

Ownership of Nirvana – Part One, Nirvana Legacy, January 11, 2013, https://nirvana-legacy.com/2013/01/11/ownership-of-nirvana-part-one/, 6.

Prato, Greg, "Songwriter interviews – Chad Channing," www.songfacts.com/facts/nirvana/polly

Raul, "Why Was 'CHAKA' Tagged On Dave Grohl's Drums in the Nirvana *Smells Like Teen Spirit* Video?," *Feel Numb*, November 3, 2009, http://www.feelnumb.com/2009/11/03/chaka-tagged-on-dave-grohls-drums-in-smells-like-teen-spirit-video/

Renshaw, David, "Nirvana producer explains how George Martin influenced Kurt Cobain on *Nevermind*," *NME*, March 11, 2016, http://www.nme.com/news/music/nirvana-7-1205590

Rock Paper Photo, "Floating Babies, What? The Story Behind Nirvana's *Nevermind* Cover Shoot," Huffington Post/ The Blog, December 6, 2017, https://www.huffingtonpost.com/rock-paper-photo/the-story-behind-the-neve_b_2670500.html

The Smart Session Demos, by Nirvana, produced by Butch Vig, Madison, WI, April, 1990, Smart Studios master tape.

"Town hall Meeting: Butch Vig/ Dave Grohl," *Sirius XM* radio, September 16, 2017.

Chapter Six
A Blues Marvel – Unmasked

Calt, Stephen, Gayle Wardlow, *King of the Delta Blues*. (Newton: Rock Chapel, 1988) 183.

Certificate of Death, Charley (aka "Charlie") Patton, Mississippi State Department of Health, Vital Records, *The Complete Recordings 1929-34.* 2-CD set (Middlesex: Acrobat Records, 2011), 2.

Evans, David, "Charley Patton: The Conscience of The Delta." *Screamin' and Hollerin' the Blues: The Worlds of Charley Patton,* 7-CD Box Set, (Austin: Revenant Records, 2001) 19, 22.

Evans, Dr. David. "Charley Patton Biography." www.paramountshome.org (2015), 10, 14, 15.

Fahey, John. *Charley Patton.* (Studio Vista: *UCLA Folklore* Department, 1964), 1.

Garofalo, Reebee, Steven Waksman, *Rockin' Out: Popular Music in the USA.* (Boston: Allyn & Bacon, 1997), 44-47.

Havers, Richard, "So Just Who Was The Masked Marvel?" www.udiscovermusic.com *Udiscover Music,* (2016), 1.

History of the Chicago Defender, (2020) https://chicagodefender.com/history-of-the-chicago-defender/, 1.

History.com Editors, "October 29, 1929: Stock Market Crashes.," http://www.history.come/this-say-in-history/stock-market-crashes, 1.

Howse, Pat and Jimmy Phillips, "Godfather of Delta Blues – H.C. Speir, An Interview with Gayle Dean Wardlow," *Peavey Monitor* (1995) 1,2.

Interview with Alex van der Tuuk (Blues historian and Paramount Records author and historian) by author Jim Berkenstadt, July 15, 2020.

Interview with Bernard MacMahon (Blues historian and Director of *American Epic*) by author Jim Berkenstadt, June 23, 2020.

Interview with John Tefteller (Pre-war Blues historian) by author Jim Berkenstadt, June 15, 2020.

Koenig, John, "Paramount Findings," *Discoveries,* Issue 185, Dylan quote, (October 2003) 22.

Larson, Zeb. "Blues Music: Marketing Nostalgia Using Race Records in the 1920s & 1930s." www.redefinemag.com, (2014), 1-2.

MacMahon, Bernard, Duke Erickson. *American Epic,* PBS, Lo-Max Ltd., (2017)

Menconie, David, "Blues Genes: 15 of Jack White's Biggest Influences" https://www.rollingstone.com/music/music-lists/blues-genes-15-of-jack-whites-biggest-influences-12012/. *Rolling Stone,* (2014) 1.

Oates, Joyce Carol. "Success and the Pseudonymous Writer: Turning Over A New Leaf." *New York Times,* Section 7, (1987) 12.

Paramount Records advertisement, *Chicago Defender*, (September 7, 1929), 2 https://www.encyclopedia.com/media/encyclopedias-almanacs-transcripts-and-maps/race-music

Sacré, Robert. *Charley Patton – Voice of the Mississippi Delta*. (Jackson: The University Press of Mississippi, 2018) viii.

Slide, Anthony. *The Encyclopedia of Vaudeville,* (Westport: Greenwood Press, 1994) 111.

van der Tuuk, Alex. *Paramount's Rise And Fall*. (Denver: Mainspring Press, 2012), 19, 20, 81, 84, 99, 140, 141,142, 143, 187.

Chapter Seven
A Wilbury Twist: Mischief and Mythology

Anonymous Source, Interview regarding George Harrison Traveling Wilburys' picks, by author Jim Berkenstadt, November 30, 2018.

Beatles, The, *The Beatles Anthology* Book, (San Francisco: Chronicle Books, 2000) 44.

Berkenstadt, Jim, *The Beatle Who Vanished*, (Madison: Rock And Roll Detective® Publishing, 2013) 35.

Berkenstadt, Jim, "The Case of The Mysterious Traveling Wilburys Guitar Picks," (Madison: © *Rock And Roll Detective® BlogSpot*, August 12, 2010) www.rocknrolldetective.blogspot.com, 2.

Berkenstadt, Jim, "The Story Behind The Traveling Wilburys Guitar Picks," © Rock And Roll Detective®, *Pick Collecting Quarterly*, Vol 7 Fall 2010, August 22, 2010) 1.

Bob Dylan: The 30th Anniversary Concert Celebration, Columbia, August 24, 1993.

Bob Dylan, 1966, "Pledging My Time" Lyrics, w & m by Bob Dylan, Copyright © 1966, by Dwarf Music; renewed 1994 by Dwarf Music.

Bob Dylan, 1970, "Minstrel Boy" Lyrics, w & m by Bob Dylan, Copyright © 1970, by Big Sky Music, renewed 1998 by Big Sky Music.

Bob Dylan, 1974, "Idiot Wind" Lyrics, w & m by Bob Dylan, Copyright © 1974, by Ram's Horn Music; renewed 2002 by Ram's Horn Music.

Bob Dylan, 1979, "Gotta Serve Somebody" Lyrics by Bob Dylan dba Special Rider Music, © 1979, Sony Music Entertainment, Inc.

Classic Albums, UK Radio Show, Roger Scott, February 10, 1990.

Classic CD's – Traveling Wilburys Vol. 1, Radio Show, Host: Roger Scott, Radio 1, (February 10, 1990).

Cole, Paul, "ELO Legend Jeff Lynne: I Would Not Have Liked Being in the Beatles," *The Birmingham Mail*, March 13, 2014, https://www.birminghammail.co.uk/news/midlands-news/pop-legend-jeff-lynne-would-6807759

A Conversation with George Harrison, [George Harrison – *All Things Must Pass*], Promotional Use Only, Capitol, DPRO 7087 6 15960 2 4, Interviewed by Chris Carter, (February 15, 2001) Liner Notes, pg. 2, 7.

Dhani Harrison, *Instagram* Post to Jeff Lynne, August 6, 2019.

Electronic Sound, Apple. Zapple Records, Zapple 02, (1969), Liner Notes, 1.

Epstein, Daniel, *The Ballad of Bob Dylan*, (New York City: Harper, 2011)

Fleming, Colin, "Remembering Bob Dylan's Infamous 'Judas' Show," *Rolling Stone*, May 17, 2016, https://www.rollingstone.com/music/music-news/remembering-bob-dylans-infamous-judas-show-203760/

Garbarini, Vic, "Do You Want To Know A Secret?" Interview with George Harrison, *Guitar World*, January 2003, 126.

George Harrison Live in Japan, Warner Bros. Records/ Dark Horse Records, 7599-26964-2, Liner Notes, December 3, 1991.

George Harrison TV Interview, *Countdown TV*, 1990.

Green, Andy, "Fifty Years Ago Today: Bob Dylan Released His Debut Album," http://www.cnn.com/2012/03/19/showbiz/music/bob-dylan-album-50-rs March 19, 2012.

Gretsch Guitar company history, https://www.gretschguitars.com/support/history

Harrison, George (director), *Whatever Wilbury Wilbury*, Promotional Film, © 1988 T. Wilbury and Sons, Ltd., (shown at the 1988 Warner Bros. Records convention in New Orleans)

Hart, Ron, "Traveling Wilburys Vol. 1 at 30: Inside the Supergroup to End all Supergroups," *Billboard*, October 18, 2018 https://www.billboard.com/articles/columns/rock/8480621/traveling-wilburys-vol-1-album-jim-keltner

Heylin, Clinton, *Bob Dylan: The Recording Sessions*, (New York City: St. Martin's Griffin, 1995) 171-174.

Hurwitz, Matt, "Jeff Lynne and Tom Petty Interview," Santa Monica, May 10, 2007.

Idle, Eric, *Always Look on The Bright Side of Life – A Sortabiography*, (New York City: Crown Archetype, October, 2018) 114.

Interview with Alex Orbison, by author Jim Berkenstadt, February 1, 2018.

Interview with Dinah Gretsch, by author Jim Berkenstadt, March 23, 2016.

Interview with Director, David Leland, by author Jim Berkenstadt, October 2, 2019.

Interview with George Harrison, *Countdown*, TV, Netherlands, 1990.

Interview with George Harrison, TV, *AM UK*, November 4 &7, 1988.

Interview with George Harrison, Jeff Lynne, Tom Petty, by Laura Gross, *MTV*, December 10, 1988.

Interview with George Harrison, Jeff Lynne, Tom Petty, Roy Orbison, The Traveling Wilburys, by Rona Elliott, *NBC Today Show*, October 2, 1988.

Interview with Jim Keltner, by author Jim Berkenstadt, March, 2016.

Interview with Klaus Voormann, by author Jim Berkenstadt, January 20, 2016.

Interview with Tom Petty and Jeff Lynne, *Traveling Wilburys Official YouTube channel*, May 20, 2016.

Jinman, Richard, "Bob Dylan: The myths of the singer-songwriter's electric debut at the Newport Folk Festival," *The Independent*, July 25, 2015, https://www.independent. co.uk/arts-entertainment/music/features/bob-dylan-the-myths-of-the-singer-songwriters-electric-debut-at-the-newport-folk-festival-10415946.html

Keller, Joel, "Jeff Lynne Looks Back On Traveling Wilburys & the 30th Anniversary of 'Volume 1': 'It was a Marvelous time'," *Billboard* online, October 19, 2018.

Lifton, Dave, "The Time George Harrison Was Attacked and Nearly Killed in his Own Home," *Ultimate Classic Rock,* December 30, 2014, https://ultimateclassicrock.com/ george-harrison-attacked/

Miles, Barry, *Paul McCartney: Many Years From Now*, (New York City: Henry Holt & Company, 1997) 49-51.

Nobody's Child Romanian Angel Appeal, Warner Bros. Records, 9 26280-2, Liner Notes, by Olivia Harrison, 1990.

Orbison, Roy Jr., & Wesley & Alex, with Slate Jeff, *The Authorized Roy Orbison*, (Nashville: Center Street Publishing, 2017) 36.

Ostin, Mo, "Traveling Wilburys Boxed Set booklet" & "The True History of the Traveling Wilburys" by Wilbury Record Company, a subdivision of the Trans Wilbury Corporation of Bulgaria/ T. Wilbury® Limited, exclusively licensed to Rhino Entertainment Company (2007) Liner Notes, 3.

Palin, Michael, *Halfway to Hollywood: Diaries 1980*-1988, (New York City: St. Martin's Press, 2009) 265, 579.

Ragogna, Mike, "Someone's Mojo is Working: A Conversation with Tom Petty," *Huffington Post*, December 6, 2007, https://huffpost.com/entry/strongsomeones-emmojoem-i_b_610756

Rockline Radio, US Radio Show, Bob Coburn, February 10, 1988.

Rosenbaum, Ron, "Bob Dylan Interview," *Playboy*, March, 1978.

Rowland, Mark, "The Quiet Wilbury," Musician, March, 1990, Issue No. 137, 34-36.

Roy Orbison on Lefty Frizzell, *Toppermost*, https://www.toppermost.co.uk/lefty-frizzell/, May 13, 2019.

Sounes, Howard, *Down The Highway: The Life of Bob Dylan,* (New York City: Grove Press, 2001)

The Traveling Wilburys, 1988, "Dirty World" Lyrics by The Traveling Wilburys, w & m Robert Dylan dba Special Rider Music, George Harrison, Ganga Publishing/ Zero Productions, Tom Petty, Gone Gator, Roy Orbison, Roy Orbison Music Company & Barbara Orbison Music, Jeff Lynne, © 1988.

Traveling Wilburys Collection, by Traveling Wilburys, Rhino Records/ Wilbury Records, 8122-79982-4, June 3, 2016.

The Traveling Wilburys Press Release, © 1988 Wilburys Records Inc., 1-2.

"Traveling Wilburys Volume 1" History by Hugh Jampton, E. F. Norti-Bitz Reader in Applied Jacket, Faculty of Sleeve Notes, University of Krakatoa (East of Java) aka Michael Palin, Wilbury Record Company, a subdivision of the Trans Wilbury Corporation of Bulgaria, Ganga Distributors, B.V. 9 25796-2 (1988) Liner Notes, 5.

Tucker, Ken, "Traveling Wilburys Vol 3," *Entertainment Weekly*, review, November 2, 1990, https://ew.com/article/1990/11/02/traveling-wilburys-vol-3/

TV Interview with Jeff Lynne, Tom Petty and Roy Orbison, *Stage Pass*, 1988.

Unterberger, Richie, *Bob Dylan pseudonyms*, www.expectingrain.com/dok/who/b/blindboygrunt.html, (2016)

Vrabel, Jeff, "Tom Petty had no Schtick, other than making songs you'll sing forever," *The Loop*, October 3, 2017, https://www.golfdigest.com/story/tom-petty-had-no-schtick-other-than-making-songs-youll-sing-forever

"What George Martin Taught Us," *BBC Programme* Articles, https://www.bbc.uk/programmes/articles/2bD2dPzCLFgG2Dkrb4DqgXH/what-george-martin-taught-us

"What is your Wilbury Name?" www.traveliingwilburys.com/namegenerator

Wilburys, Traveling, *Traveling Wilburys*, (Guilford, Surrey: Genesis Publications Ltd, © T. Wilbury Ltd, 2009) 1, 21, 25, 26, 75, 134-5.

Willman, Chris, "Wilburys The Fame of the Names," *LA Times*, October 29, 1988, https://www.latimes.com/archives/la-xpm-1988-10-29-ca-263-story.html

Winter Warnerland, Various Artists, Warner Bros. Records, PRO-A-3328, 2LP, 1988.

www.BeatlesBible.com

"You Haven't Really Heard American Music Before…" *Melody Maker* (February 19, 1966) reprinted, *The History of Rock Uncut*, Time Inc. February 1, 2016, 40.

Zollo, Paul, *Conversations with Tom Petty*, (London: Omnibus Press, Kindle Edition, 2005) 2365, 2374, 2383, 2393, 2473, 2491

Zollo, Paul, *Conversations with Tom Petty*, (London: Omnibus Press, paperback, 2005) 119

Chapter Eight
Deal with The Devil: Did The Beach Boys Steal A Song From Charles Manson?

1909 Copyright Act, Sec. 6, 42

Altham, Keith, "*Dennis Wilson Interview*," *Rave* magazine, May, 1969.

Badman, Keith, *The Beach Boys*, (San Francisco: Backbeat Books, 2004) 216, 233.

Cohen, Scott, "The Dennis Wilson Interview," *Circus* magazine, October 26, 1976.

Cohen, Scott, "Surfer Boy, The Dennis Wilson Interview," *Circus* magazine, Oct 26, 1976, 36, 37.

Davis, Ivor & Jerry LeBlanc, *Five To Die,* (Ventura: Thor Publishing, 1970) 24, 66.

Doe, Andrew, www.esquarterly.com/bellagio/gigs68.html, (Note: The session dates for Manson at Brian Wilson's studio come from tape box notations relayed to Doe, by an employee at Brother Records archives who asked to remain anonymous. There are no union contracts for these songs listed in the American Federation of Musician's archives, since the sessions took place privately at Brian Wilson's home studio.)

Ellingson, Carole A. *The Copyright Exception for Derivative Works and the Scope of Utilization*, (Bloomington: Indiana Law Journal: Vol. 56: Issue 1, Article 1. The Copyright Act of March 4, 1909, chapter 320, 35 Stat. 1075, 1980)

Emmons, Nuel, *Manson: In His Own Words,* (New York City: Grove Press, 1986) 21, 70, 71, 72, 77, 83, 140, 141, 143, 147, 150, 167, 172-3, 176, 175, 184.

Felton, David & David Dalton, "Charles Manson – The incredible story of the most dangerous man alive," *Rolling Stone*, June 25, 1970, 26, 34, 36, 38, 39.

Felton, David & David Dalton, "The Most Dangerous Man in the World, Book Three," *Rolling Stone*, June 25, 1970, 36.

Fromme, Lynette ("Squeaky") *Reflexion*, (Cobb, CA: The Peasenhall Press, 2018)

Gaines, Steven, *Heroes & Villains – The True Story of the Beach Boys,* (New York City: Da Capo, 1986) 190, 197, 216.

"The Gary Stromberg Conversations," *Compared To What* podcast, Episode 8, January, 2014.

Gorightly, Adam, "The Shadow Over Santa Susana," *UK Mail Online,* https://www. mail-archive.com/ctrl@listserv.aol.com/msg73060.html

Gowen, Gwen & Alexa Valiente, "Beach Boys' Mike Love recalls meeting Charles Manson through bandmate Dennis Wilson for the 1st time," ABC News, May 15, 2017, https://abcnews.go.com/US/beach-boys-mike-love-recalls-meeting-charles-manson/story?id=46023397

Griffiths, David, "*Interview with Dennis Wilson,*" *Record Mirror,* December 21, 1968.

Guinn, Jeff, *Manson – The Life and Times of Charles Manson,* (New York City: Simon & Schuster, 2013) 146, 149, 158, 159, 190-191.

Hedegaard, Erik, "Charles Manson Today: The Final Confessions of a Psychopath," *Rolling Stone,* December 5, 2013, https://www.rollingstone.com/culture/culture-news/charles-manson-today-the-final-confessions-of-a-psychopath-58782/

Interview with Attorney Chris Hussin, Boardman and Clark, by author Jim Berkenstadt, June 27, 2018.

Interview with Charles Manson, *20/20 Truth and Lies: The Family Manson,* ABC-TV, (2017)

Interview with Charles Manson, *Cease To Exist* documentary, Saguaro Pictures, directed by Ryan Okseberg, (2007)

Interview with Charles Manson, *Charles Manson Journey Into Evil* documentary, ABC-TV, Diane Sawyer, (1993)

Interview with David S. Gold, by author Jim Berkenstadt, July 26, 2018.

Interview with Dennis Wilson, *Cease To Exist* documentary, Saguaro Pictures, directed by Ryan Okseberg, (2007)

Interview with Derek Taylor, by author Jim Berkenstadt, February, 1996.

Interview with Gregg Jakobson, by author Jim Berkenstadt, May 12, 2015.

Interview with Gregg Jakobson, (No #2), by author Jim Berkenstadt, June 8, 2018.

Interview with Gregg Jakobson, by Deputy District Attorney Vincent Bugliosi, Los Angeles, CA, February 20, 1970.

Interview with Nick Grillo, by author Jim Berkenstadt, May 12, 2018.

Interview with Phil Kaufman, by author Jim Berkenstadt, July 21, 2018, via Facebook Messenger.

Interview with Roger Smith, *Cease To Exist* documentary, Saguaro Pictures, directed by Ryan Okseberg, (2007)

Interview with Stephen Desper, Beach Boys engineer, SmileySmile Message Board, May 10, 14, 16, 2002, www.smileysmile.net

Interview with Stephen Desper, by author Jim Berkenstadt, May 30, 2018.

Interview with US District Court Judge James Peterson, by author Jim Berkenstadt, July 3, 2018.

Jahn, Mike, "Tales of the Ancient Rocker – Hustling Charles Manson," *The New York Times* Special Features, August 23, 1970.

Kaufman, Phil, *Legend of the Road Mangler,* (Ashland, OR: Blackstone Audio, Inc. 2015) audio book, disc one, track 16, 17.

Love, Mike & James S. Hirsch, *Good Vibrations: My Life as a Beach Boy*, (New York City: Blue Rider Press, 2016) 208.

Manson, Charles, *The Love and Terror Cult*, Awareness Records, 08903-0156, March 6, 1970, produced by Gregg Jakobson (all tracks except "Sick City") on August 8-9, 1968, Re-Produced, re-mixed and mastered by Phil Kaufman.

McKeen, William, *Everybody Had An Ocean: Music and Mayhem in 1960s Los Angeles*, (Chicago: Chicago Review Press Incorporated, 2017) 314.

Melville B. Nimmer & David Nimmer, *Nimmer on Copyright* 2 Sec. 119.1 (rev. ed. 2018)

Miles, Barry, *Paul McCartney: Many Years From Now*, (New York City: Henry Holt & Company, 1997) 487-488, 489-90.

Moynihan, Michael, "Interview with Charles Manson," *Seconds* magazine, Issue #32, 1995.

Nolan, Tom, "Beach Boys: A California Saga, Part II Tales of Hawthorne," *Rolling Stone*, November 11, 1971, 52.

Nolasco, Stephanie, "Manson's Youngest Follower Tells All," *Fox News*, October 31, 2017, http://www.foxnews.com/entertainment/2017/10/31/mansons-youngest-follower-tells-all-claims-dennis-wilson-tried-to-mold-cult-leader-into-rock-star.html

Orit, Afori, *Implied License: An Emerging new Standard in Copyright Law*, (Santa Clara: 25 Santa Clara High Technology Law Journal 285, 2008). Atkins v. Fischer, 331 F.3d 988, 991-92 (D.C. Cir. 2003); Effects Assoc., Inc. v. Cohen, 908 F. 2d 555, 558 (9th Cir. 1990), *Patry on Copyright*, Sec 5:131 (2008)

People v. Charles Manson, Sworn Testimony of Gregg Jakobson, November 16, 1970.

Savage, Mark, "Charles Manson's Music Was A Macabre Sidenote," *BBC Music News*, 20 November, 2017, https://www.bbc.com/news/entertainment-arts-42051100

Sharp, Ken, "Al Jardine Interview," *Goldmine* magazine, July 28, 2000.

Statement of Stephanie Schram, Gary Hinman Investigation, by Deputy George A. Palmer, Homicide Bureau, and Deputy William Gleason, Auto Theft, LA County Sherriff's Department, Case File 039-02378-1076-016, December 4, 1969.

Stebbins, Jon, *The Real Beach Boy: Dennis Wilson,* (Toronto: ECW Press, 2000) 22,23,25,26,28.

Sworn Statement of Susan Atkins, Court Ordered by Judge Keene and interviewed by Attorney Paul Caruso for the purpose of determining a plea deal in the Manson murder case, December 1, 1969.

Testimony of Terry Melcher, People v. Charles Watson, August 23, 1971.

Truslow, Ned, "Bad Vibrations: Dennis Wilson & The Manson Family," *Ned Rock*, (George Harrison quote), (©2001), www.nedrock.org

Uncredited, "Interview with Charles "Tex" Watson," *Ellensburg Daily Record*, 1978.

Uncredited, "Interview with John Lennon," Associated Press, November 5, 1970.

Watkins, Paul & Guillermo Soledad, *My Life With Charles Manson,* (New York City: Bantam Books, 1979) Chapters 4, 7, 9, 14, Epilogue.

Watson, Tex, Hoekstra & Chaplain Ray, *Will You Die For Me*, (New York City: Crossroad Publications, 1978) 38,42,43,51, 65.

Wilson, Brian with Todd, Gold, *Wouldn't It Be Nice,* (New York City, Harper Collins, 1991) 180-181, 183, 184.

Wilson, Mike, "A Beach Boy Remembers – Manson's Madness," *People* magazine, September 12, 2016, 64, 66.

www.discogs.com/charles-manson-LIE-The-Love-And-Terror-Cult/release/1506934

Young, Neil, *Waging Heavy Peace: A Hippie Dream*, (New York: Penguin, 2013) 97.

Photo Permissions and Credits

Every effort has been made to acknowledge all those whose photographs and illustrations have been used in this volume. If there have been any omissions in this respect, we apologize and will be pleased to make the appropriate acknowledgement in any future editions.

Front Cover

Paintings: Bob Dylan, Bob Marley, John Lennon and Kurt Cobain. Copyright © 2022 Zina Golmiyyah, Zina.Art, https://www.facebook.com/zinamusicart

Chapter One – Who Really Discovered Elvis Presley?

Page 4:   Memphis Recording Service / Sun Records, Memphis, TN. – Photographer unknown. Wiki Creative Commons.

Page 7:   Elvis Presley's first recording – "My Happiness" 78-rpm (Record Store Day facsimile) – Courtesy of Author.

Page 19:   Promo display of Blue Moon Boys record – photo courtesy of Author, public domain.

Page 20:   A-side of 78-rpm record, "That's Alright" – photo courtesy of Author.

Page 21:   B-side of "Blue Moon of Kentucky" – photo courtesy of Author.

Page 22:   Scotty Moore – Elvis Presley's first management contract (facsimile) – Courtesy of Author.

Chapter 5 – A Wilbury Twist: Mischief and Mythology

Chapter 6 – A Blues Marvel – Unmasked

Chapter 7 – The Secrets Concealed Within Nirvana's *Nevermind* Album

Chapter 8 – Deal with the Devil: Did The Beach Boys Steal a Song from Charles Manson?

Selected Bibliography

Agee, Phillip, *Inside The Company: CIA Diary*, New York, Farrar Straus & Giroux, 1974

Badman, Keith, *The Beach Boys*, San Francisco, Backbeat Books, 2004

Baer, Robert B., *The Perfect Kill: 21 Laws For Assassins*, New York, Penguin Random House, 2014

Berkenstadt, Jim, *The Beatle Who Vanished*, Madison, Rock And Roll Detective, LLC Publishing, 2013

Berkenstadt, Jim, *Black Market Beatles: The Story Behind The Lost Recordings*, Toronto, CG Publishing, 1995

Berkenstadt, Jim and Cross, Charles, *Nirvana: Nevermind (Classic Rock Albums)*, New York, Schirmer Trade Books, Simon & Schuster, 1998

Bernal, Richard L., *The Influence of Small States on Superpowers – Jamaica and US Foreign Policy*, Lanham, Maryland, Lexington Books, 2015

Calt, Stephen and Wardlow, Gayle, *King of the Delta Blues*, Newton, NJ, Rock Chapel Press, 1988

CIA, *A Study of Assassinations*, USA, FOIA, 1953/ 1995

Cobain, Kurt, *Journals*, New York, Riverhead Books, 2002

Cross, Charles, *Here We Are Now: The Lasting Impact of Kurt Cobain*, New York, It Books / Harper Collins, 2014

Davis, Ivor and LeBlanc, Jerry, *Five To Die*, Ventura, CA, Thor publishing, 1970

Emmons, Nuel, *Manson in his Own Words*, New York, Grove Press, 1986

Epstein, Daniel Mark, *The Ballad of Bob Dylan*, New York, Harper Collins, 2011

Fahey, John, *Charlie Patton*, Los Angeles, Studio Vista, UCLA, 1964

Gaines, Steven, *Heroes & Villains – The True Story of the Beach Boys*, New York, Da Capo, 1986

Goldman, Vivian, *The Book of Exodus*, New York, Three Rivers Press, 2006

Guinn, Jeff, *Manson – The Life and Times of Charles Manson*, New York, Simon & Schuster, 2013

Guralnick, Peter, *Careless Love: The Unmaking of Elvis Presley*, New York, Little Brown, 2000

Guralnick, Peter, *Sam Phillips: The Man Who Invented Rock 'n' Roll*, New York, Little Brown, 2015

Idle, Eric, *Always Look On The Bright Side of Life – A Sortabiography*, New York, Crown Archetype, 2018

Johns, Glyn, *Sound Man: A Life Recording Hits with The Rolling Stones, The Who, Led Zeppelin, The Eagles, Eric Clapton, The Faces…*, New York, Blue Rider Press, 2014

Kaufman, Phil, *Legend of the Road Mangler*, Ashland, OR, Blackstone Audio, 2015

Lindop, Edmund and DeCapua, *America in the 1950's*, Minneapolis, MN, Twenty-First Century Books, 2009

Manley, Michael, *The Politics of Change – A Jamaican Testament*, Washington, DC, Howard University Press, 1975

Marley, Rita, *My Life with Bob Marley – No Woman No Cry*, New York, Hyperion, 2004

McKeen, William, *Everybody Had An Ocean: Music and Mayhem in 1960s Los Angeles*, Chicago, Chicago Review Press, 2017

Miles, Barry, *Paul McCartney: Many Years From Now*, New York, Henry Holt, 1997

Moore, Scotty, *That's Alright, Elvis –The Untold Story of Elvis' First Guitarist and Manager*, New York, Schirmer Books, 1997

Orbison, Roy Jr., Wesley, & Alex, *The Authorized Roy Orbison*, Nashville, Center Street Publishing, 2017

Palin, Michael, *Halfway to Hollywood: Diaries 1980-1988*, New York, St. Martin's Press, 2009

Peterson, Dick, *Louie Louie: Me Gotta Go Now*, Sherwood, Oregon, Thalion Press, 2006

Sacré, Robert, *Charley Patton – Voice of the Mississippi Delta*, Jackson: The University Press of Mississippi, 2018

Stebbins, Jon, *The Real Beach Boy: Dennis Wilson*, Toronto, ECW Press, 2000

Steffens, Roger, *So Much Things To Say*, New York, W.W. Norton & Company, 2017

Touches, Nick, *Country: The Twisted Roots of Rock 'N' Roll*, Boston, MA, Da Capo Press, 1996

Traveling Wilburys, *The Traveling Wilburys*, Guilford, Surrey, Genesis Publications Ltd., 2009

Tuuk, Alexander Vander, *Paramount's Rise And Fall*, Denver, Mainspring Press, 2012

Watson, Tex and Hoekstra, Chaplain Ray, *Will You Die For Me*, New York, Crossroad Publications, 1978

Wilson, Brian and Gold, Todd, *Wouldn't It Be Nice*, New York, Harper Collins, 1991

Zollo, Paul, *Conversations with Tom Petty*, London, Omnibus Press, 2005

About The Author

Jim Berkenstadt is the Rock And Roll Detective®. A true musical Sherlock Holmes, Berkenstadt uncovers the lost history and mysteries hidden within decades of popular music. He currently serves as Co-Executive Producer and Script Consultant on the Ecosse Studios feature film based upon his Best-Selling book, *The Beatle Who Vanished*. An international authority on Rock and Roll, he served as historical consultant to Martin Scorsese's HBO Emmy winning film, *George Harrison: Living in the Material World*, and as historical consultant to The Beatles' Company Apple Corps, and the Estate of George Harrison.

In addition to *The Beatle Who Vanished*, Berkenstadt has authored *Black Market Beatles* and *Classic Rock Albums: Nirvana—Nevermind*. All three books have been inducted into The Rock and Roll Hall of Fame Library and Archives. He also appears as an expert on the Reelz Channel TV series' *Celebrity Legacies* and *Celebrity Damage Control*.

Contact Information

The Author Jim Berkenstadt can be contacted here:
www.musicmysterybook.com
www.thebeatlewhovanished.com
www.rockandrolldetective.com
Email: jim@rockandrolldetective.com

Index

Printed in Great Britain
by Amazon

48410432R00152